'A wise and beautifully written book. For Gaita, the bottom line in ethical matters is the preciousness of each individual human being, a preciousness that is not underwritten by reason but exemplified in ever-fragile works of love. *A Common Humanity* is not a work of abstract moral philosophy, but a series of ethical meditations drawn from the midst of things. It is the fascinating discussion of those things that lends Gaita's book its particular strength, whether Australian debates on native title and the stolen generations, or European debates on the Holocaust. It is a wonderful example of how philosophy can still speak without any condescension to the educated reader.'

Simon Critchley, *Professor of Philosophy, University of Essex*

'A wonderful piece of writing. Raimond Gaita's defence of a conception of goodness beyond virtue and of evil beyond vice finds a new clarity and force in these interlinked essays on racism and genocide, shame and remorse, justice and the love of truth, as those issues have arisen in contemporary Australian political debates. The disciplined individuality of Gaita's voice shows how a humanly serious practice of philosophy might make a decisive contribution to our public culture.'

Stephen Mulhall, *New College Oxford*

'A book for anyone who is prepared to think seriously. It is also moving in a way that is rare in philosophy.'

Antony Duff, *University of Stirling*

'Passionate, subtle and profound.'

Christopher Cordner, *University of Melbourne*

'Gaita is obviously not a partisan of any established viewpoint, but an original thinker, someone who marks out his own turf.'

Michael Phillips, *Meanjin*

'has a great deal to say to each of us.'

Veronica Brady, *Courier Mail*

'Fascinating and often disturbing. Whether one agrees with Gaita's philosophy or not, it is essential for the "spider's web of fine distinctions", as he calls them, to be brought like this to centre stage.'

Delia Falconer, *The Age*

A Common Humanity

Thinking About Love and Truth and Justice

Raimond Gaita

Routledge
Taylor & Francis Group

LONDON AND NEW YORK

First published in 1998
By The Text Publishing Company, Australia

Second edition first published 2000
by Routledge
2 Park Square, Milton Park, Abingdon, Oxon, OX14 4RN

Simultaneously published in the USA and Canada
by Routledge
270 Madison Ave, New York, NY 10016

This paperback edition first
published 2002

Reprinted 2006 (twice)

Transferred to Digital Printing 2008

Routledge is an imprint of the Taylor & Francis Group, an informa business

© 2000, 2002 Raimond Gaita

Printed and bound in Great Britain
By TJI Digital, Padstow, Cornwall

British Library Cataloguing in Publication Data
A catalogue record for this book is available from the British Library

Library of Congress Cataloging in Publication Data
A catalog record for this book has been requested

ISBN10: 0-415-24113-8 (Hbk)
ISBN10: 0-415-24114-6 (Pbk)

ISBN13: 978-0-415-24113-7 (Hbk)
ISBN13: 978-0-415-24114-4 (Pbk)

For Yael, my wife

Contents

Acknowledgments

When Robert Manne edited The Australian Literary Journal *Quadrant*, I wrote a column for it. Much of the first half of *A Common Humanity* contains material, considerably reworked, that first appeared there. I am very grateful to Rob for having given me the opportunity to write so often on matters that concerned me.

Much more important, however, have been the many years of our close friendship during which we discussed again and again most of the issues I grapple with in this book. Our con-versations over those thirty-odd years have nourished my thinking. Rob's humane intelligence, humbling for its freshness and depth over an astonishing range of issues and politically more concrete than mine, has, I hope, taken my thought a little closer to political reality than my philosophical and moral temperament naturally incline it to go.

I have indeed been fortunate in my friends, in ways more important than intellectually, but it is my intellectual gratitude that

I record here. To Marina Barabas with whom I share a love of Plato and whose passionate and unsettling combination of worldliness and unworldliness often provoked me in ways good for thinking; to Christopher Cordner for his subtle and humane philosophical sensibility; to Denis Grundy, whose profound idealism and under-standing of the collegiate nature of university life (amongst many other things) is, I hope, reflected in these pages; to Bernard Holiday for his rare combination of philosophical and political depth; to Susan Moore for her fine, spiritual sense of teaching as a vocation; to Barry Oakley who for at least thirty years has insisted to me that philosophy matters outside the academy and that I should try to write as though I believed it; to Tamas Pataki whose Enlightenment temper and defence of psychoanalysis has, I trust, made my anti-reductionism more subtle; to Peter Steele for his humane, ironic love of the world and appreciation of how many sorts it takes to make all sorts; and to Konrad Winkler who, many years ago, helped me to see the wood for the trees on matters to do with the Australian Aborigines when irritation with political correctness distorted my vision.

R. F. Holland taught me to see past the stereotypes about Plato to the wonderful depth in him. Peter Winch taught me the same about Wittgenstein. Both taught me much more besides. Cora Diamond's seminal article, 'Eating Meat and Eating People', first made me think seriously about the philosophical importance of the concept of a human being and she first alerted me to the passages from George Orwell which I discuss in this book.

Michael Heyward, who published the Australian edition, made excellent editorial suggestions which are retained in this one. Their penetration and sensitivity to the overall spirit of the book and to whatever is distinctive in my voice filled me with admiration and improved the book considerably. I thank him warmly for it. I also thank him and Tony Bruce, Senior Philosophy Editor at Routledge, for their preparedness to take to a non-specialist, educated reader a book whose discussion ranges from the injustices suffered by the Australian Aborigines to Wittgenstein's remarks on sensation.

Jane Adamson, Richard Freedman and David Parker kindly gave me their permission to use material from my contribution to their collection, *Renegotiating Ethics in Literature, Philosophy and Theory* (Cambridge University Press, Cambridge, 1998).

Preface

'Why do you want to read philosophy?' I asked the student I was interviewing. 'Because I want to know whether there is a God', he replied. When I asked him why he wanted to know that he looked astonished that I could ask such a question and replied with some force. 'Nothing is more important. Everything depends on it'. What would he say, I asked, to someone who said that nothing was more important than living a decent life, that everything depended on *that*? For a while he was silent. Then, with bemused condescension he responded, 'You must be talking about morality and all that stuff'.

I am sure that his sense of morality is not unusual. Nor is it unusual to fail to see much connection between religion and morality. Even so, it is curious, not least because he was in fact a morally serious young man. This estrangement from morality of morally serious people—young and old—is a mark of the times, I think, as is the hunger for meaning that shows itself in quests for religion and (more often and more vaguely) 'spirituality'. Tempting though it is to see this phenomenon as the result of confusing morality and corrupt forms of it, one should not succumb to the temptation too quickly. Moralizing (in the pejorative sense) goes deep in what we call morality and is, I think, one of the reasons why many keep their distance from it. So deep does it run that there is good reason to suspect we would understand good and evil, virtue and vice, justice and injustice, obligation and practical necessity better if we did not think of them under the concept of morality.

Gitta Sereny reports many brutish examples of this unsavoury side of morality in *Cries Unheard*, the story of Mary Bell who, at the age of 11, was convicted of the manslaughter of two small boys, Martin Brown and Brian Howe. When children kill children, the horror of it provokes strong and sometimes apparently inconsistent reactions in many of us. We respond fiercely to what we regard as crimes not only against innocents, but also, at the same time, against innocence. More people are inclined to speak of the *evil* of those crimes than they are even of the massacre of thousands of adults. At the same time we draw back from the concept, partly because it was not the innocence of this or that child but the innocence of children that ignited our ferocity, and the killers are children too. Furthermore, we hardly know how to attribute to child-killers concepts which they must possess if they are to have the intentions necessary for their actions to be evil. Mary Bell persistently pleaded that she did not fully understand that death is final. When Sereny asked her, 'Did the fact of their being dead mean anything to you?', Mary replied, 'No, nothing, because I hadn't intended . . . Well—how can I say this now . . . But . . . I didn't *know* I had intended for them to be dead . . . dead for ever. Dead for me then wasn't for ever.'

Cries Unheard is a plea that we try to understand Mary. Few people, I think, would be unmoved by Sereny's portrayal of the horrors of Mary's childhood before and after the killings. I doubt that many could keep their hearts hardened against her. Some might think, 'There but for the Grace of God go I'—a thought that need not be pressed in the direction of determinism which, as every professional philosopher knows, is difficult even to state clearly let alone to assess.

Anyone whose contemplation of Mary's life moved them to think, 'There but for the Grace of God go I', would, however, withhold a certain kind of judgement. It is not judgement of the kind implied only by the insistence on truthful, often severe, descriptions of her deeds, her motives for them and her responses to them. The judgment they would withhold is judgement of the sort implied by what we now call judgementalism—judgement that would *blame* her (bearing in mind all the connotations of that word), that would encourage one to point a finger at her and to turn one's back on her. But a preparedness to see (and in that sense to judge) a situation in a severe moral light while at the same time refusing to blame strikes some people as incoherent. That, I think, is the effect of a moralistic conception of morality.

Nearly everyone is vulnerable to the tendency to believe that severe moral appreciation must run together with blame. But there are voices in our culture that speak of different possibilities. Sophocles' *Oedipus the King* shows how moral severity may take the form of pity. The chorus does not blame Oedipus for the evil he did on account of ignorance for which he was not culpable. It pities the evil-doer he became and that informs the quality of the pity it feels at the terrible spectacle of a man who has lost his kingdom, whose wife/mother has hanged herself, who has blinded himself and is exiled. Its severe pity holds him fast in serious moral response—it holds him *responsible to* the evil-doer he has become— insisting that he face the full meaning of it.

Something similar is true of Sereny's attitude to Mary Bell. Sympathetic to her, profoundly sorry for her, even fond of her, she tries to understand her while not for a moment letting that understanding and her fond sympathy undermine her recognition that Mary committed morally terrible deeds. The features of a life that solicit our pity, that might make us say, 'There but for the grace of God go I', may also permit—sometimes they may require—severe moral description. Debate about this matter—particularly as is applies to criminals who suffered terrible abuse during their childhood—has been hostage to a false sense of what the possibilities are: either we hold on to the possibility of moral judgement of their terrible deeds and then we must blame them; or we refuse to blame and must then relinquish the possibility of moral judgement.

Books like Sereny's and to a lesser extent, I think, Blake Morrison's, *As If*, help to free us from the grip of that false disjunction, but its effect can be detected even in them, occasionally showing itself in a degree of conceptual awkwardness. Sereny, for example, says that she doesn't wish to justify what Mary did. But who would? Could anyone in any circumstances think that the killings could actually be *justified* in any ordinary meaning of that term? What Sereny really means, I think, is firstly, that her efforts to elicit sympathy for Mary, to help us to understand her, are not intended to diminish our horror at what she did, and secondly, that moral terms are necessary to describe the *kind of horror* it is. Mary calls herself a murderer and it is quite clear that her resistance to describing what she did accurately and in detail is not mere squeamishness. She hides from the full acknowledgment of the terrible meaning of her deeds, meaning that would be revealed to her only in a lucid remorse. Sereny knows that and her knowledge of it deepens rather than undermines her attempts to lead us to an appreciation of the awful misery of Mary Bell.

More than any of the moral concepts, the concept of evil is associated in people's minds with this moralizing tendency in morality, the tendency in it to be closed to complexity, to shun and even to demonize wrong-doers. Again, many morally serious people refuse to use the word because they see it as an obstacle to understanding and sympathy. Inga Clendinnen, author of *Reading the Holocaust,* is didactic, almost aggressive, in her rejection of the word to describe some of the most terrible deeds known to humankind. Written by someone with a moral sensibility that is deep and subtle, her book has won many prizes and was voted by *The New York Times* as one of the ten best of 1999. I suspect that her refusal of the word and her reasons for it struck a chord in many of those who nominated her book for its many accolades.

As much as anyone, Hannah Arendt taught us to see even the most terrible criminals as human beings rather than as monsters. Her chief exhibit was not a child like Mary Bell, or like Robert Thompson or Jon Venables who killed James Bulger. It was Adolf Eichmann, one of the most conscientious implementers of the Final Solution. Her book, *Eichmann in Jerusalem* has as its subtitle, '*a report on the banality of evil*'. Explaining why she chose it, Arendt said she was often struck when listening to Eichmann and to the evidence by how ordinary he was. Inattentive readers have taken the 'banality of evil' to mean the banality of the concept of evil—the banal thinking to which anyone committed to its use is condemned. Yet it was Arendt who said in *On Revolution*, a book written at the same time as she wrote *Eichmann in Jerusalem*, that 'the men of the eighteenth century did not understand that there exists goodness beyond virtue and evil beyond vice'.

A marvelous epigram, I think, but what to make of it? Is not compassion often an expression of goodness and is it not a virtue? Is not malevolent cruelty an evil, and is it not also a vice? The answer I develop in this book is that someone who affirms that every human being is infinitely precious (or sacred, as a religious person would say), will look differently at compassion and cruelty to someone who cannot or will not do so. The former might speak of goodness in ways that invite a capital 'G' and of evil in ways that make clear that both are interdependent with that sense of preciousness. On account of that interdependence she will think of good and evil as distinctive amongst the moral concepts, rather than merely extravagant expressions of praise in one case and condemnation in the other.

Judge the evil deed, but not the doer, we sometimes say, and rightly. But some evil-doers are not even slightly remorseful, have characters as foul as their deeds and there appears nothing in them from which remorse might grow. On occasions—perhaps on most occasions—it might seem that way to us only because we have not seen the good in them. I doubt that it *must* be so. The belief that it must be possible for sensitive perception to discover some good in them is, I think, a counterfeit of the affirmation, unsupported by reason, that even such people are owed unconditional respect. It is dangerous to put that affirmation in the form of an empirical assessment of what awaits discovery in every evil-doer for those who have eyes to see. If realism forces us to conclude that it is not always so, we are likely to succumb to the belief that there are, after all, some people who deserve to be shot in the street like mad dogs. Ironically, therefore, it is the concept of evil, interdependent with the affirmation that every human being is infinitely precious, that enables us to keep even the most radical evil-doers amongst us as our fellow human beings.

A Spanish song, often quoted by Simone Weil, says, 'If you want to become invisible, there is no surer way than to become poor'. Weil goes on to say, 'Love sees what is invisible'. Were I pressed to state the central concern of *A Common Humanity* I would say that it is with the ways human beings are sometimes invisible, or only partially visible, to one another, with how that effects and is effected by an understanding of morality. No one, of course, means that poor people are literally invisible to wealthy people or black people to white people. When we spell out what we mean, we often say that some human beings are invisible to the moral faculties of their fellows.

Treat me as a human being, fully as your equal, without condescension—that demand (or plea), whether it is made by women to men or by blacks to whites, is a demand or a plea for justice. Not, however, for justice conceived as equal access to goods and opportunities. It is for justice conceived as equality of respect.

Only when one's humanity is fully visible will one be treated as someone who can intelligibly press claims to equal access to goods and opportunities. Victims of racial or other forms of radical denigration, who are quite literally treated as less than fully human, would be ridiculed if they were to do it. The struggle for social justice, I argue, is the struggle to make our institutions reveal rather than obscure, and then enhance rather than diminish, the full humanity of our fellow citizens.

To speak, as I do, of fully acknowledging another's humanity will, I know, sound like rhetoric to many people who would prefer to speak of recognizing someone fully as a *person*, or even as a rational agent, at least when, in philosophical mode, they try to make perspicuous what really is the bearer of moral status. My endorsement of Weil's remark—that love sees what is invisible— will sound even worse to them. In this preface I can only plead that I mean both and soberly. Later I argue that improbable though it may seem at first, placing the weight that I do on our humanity and on love rather than on, say, the obligated acknowledgment of rights, is more hardheaded than the longing to make secure to reason what reason cannot secure, all the while whistling in the dark.

Even those who are sympathetic to the role I accord to our humanity in the shaping of our moral concepts, may, however, be less sympathetic to the role I accord to love. It was not love, they will say, but sober judicial reasoning based on common and international law that delivered the judgment on native title that I praise in Chapter Four as an example of justice beyond fairness. And it was not love, but a sense of justice that I praise in Judge Landaus' inspired intervention against the political manipulation of the Eichmann trial, when he said that the court owed Eichmann justice for his sake, as a human being. Has it not been clear at least since Kant (the objection continues) that we have obligations to those whom we do not love and often could not love no matter how hard we tried, and that obligation, but not love, can be commanded?

All that is true, and I would not wish to deny it. We should not, however, draw the wrong conclusions from it. We have obligations to those whom we do not and could not love, but that does not mean that we would find it even intelligible that we should have those obligations if we did not also find it intelligible that someone could love them, and more fundamentally, if we did not see them as having the kind of individuality I elaborate in this book and which, I claim, is in part constituted by our attachments, of which the forms of love are the most important.

If discussion in Australia (where this book was first published) is any indication, I did not make sufficiently clear the part I assigned to love in the *formation* of the most important of our moral concepts. Its epistemic role—its role of revealing what I often call (though with embarrassed reservations) the preciousness of individuals—is what struck reviewers. Given that I begin with the dramatic example of the nun who revealed that even people who had lost everything that gives sense to our lives are our equals, that was perhaps not surprising. And there are other, less dramatic, examples that reveal something more familiar, but fundamental nonetheless: the ordinary love of parents for their children, lovers for their beloved. Children often come to love their brothers and sisters when they see them in the light of their parents love. Sometimes people who work in dehumanizing institutions are reminded of the full humanity of those in their care or under their guard when they see them in the light of someone who loves and needs them. Often we see something as precious only when we see it in the light of someone's love.

To underscore this part of my argument I shall quote one of the most important passages in the book:

> Our sense of the preciousness of other people is connected with their power to affect us in ways we cannot fathom and in ways against which we can protect ourselves only at the cost of becoming shallow.

There is nothing reasonable in the fact that another person's absence can make our lives seem empty. The power of human beings to affect one another in ways beyond reason and beyond merit has offended rationalists and moralists since the dawn of thought, but it is partly what yield to us that sense of human individuality that we express when we say that human beings are unique and irreplaceable. Such attachments and the joy and grief which they may cause conditions our sense of the preciousness of human beings. Love is the most important of them.

The love of saints depends on, builds on and transforms that sense of individuality, deepening the language of love which compels us to affirm that even those who suffer affliction so severe that they have irrecoverably lost everything that gives sense to our lives, and the most radical evil-doers, are fully our fellow human beings. On credit, so speak, from this language of love, we have built a more tractable structure of rights and obligations. If the language of love goes dead on us, however, if there are no examples to nourish it, either because they do not exist or because they are no longer visible to us, then talk of inalienable natural rights or of the unconditional respect owed to rational beings will seem lame and improbable to us. Indeed, exactly that is happening.

In a review of *A Common Humanity*, Lloyd Reinhardt, a Sydney philosopher, said that talk of Eichmann's preciousness sounds a bit sickly. I agree with him. In fact unless it comes from the mouth of a saint, for whom Eichmann along with every other human being might be just that, it makes one squirm. Reinhardt suggested that it would be better to speak of respect for the human being as such. Given that I also expressed embarrassment at my frequent use of the word 'precious' (partly because it can so easily sound precious), why did I not just abandon it, especially in contexts where it might make one squirm?

In fact, I often do abandon it in such contexts, but the reason I use it as often as I do is that the individuality that is basic to respect for a human being as such is the kind constituted by attachments, deeper and stronger than sympathy, most of which are forms of love. If we unpack what it means to do justice to Eichmann for his sake, because it is owed to him, then we will uncover that conception of individuality, as it is first constituted by our attachments and then as it is transformed, deepened and made wondrous by the love of saints. If someone had shot him like vermin, in the streets of Buenos Aires, and if his assailant were later to be remorseful, then Eichmann's individuality, as I have been speaking of it, would show itself—would haunt him—in his remorse.

Although I fully acknowledge that it is our religious tradition that has spoken most simply (and perhaps most deeply) about this when it declared that all human beings are sacred, I think that the conception of individuality I have been articulating, even as transformed by a language of love nourished by the love of saints, can stand independently of explicit religious commitment and independently of speculation about supernatural entities. What grew and was nourished in one place, I say, might take root and flourish elsewhere. But there is a question, put to me by the theologian Stanley Hauerwas, whose answer I am not sure of. He asked whether the kind of love shown by the nun could exist in the prolonged absence of the kind of practices that were part of her religious vocation.

Iris Murdoch said that attention to something absolutely pure is the essence of prayer and is a form of love. If she is right, then the answer to Hauerwas' question will depend on whether, with the demise of religion, we can find objects of attention that can sustain that love, or whether they will always fail us. I don't know the answer.

Two events of national and international importance occurred in Australia in the last decade of the twentieth century. Both centred on matters of race. In 1992 the High Court of Australia delivered a judgment, now known as Mabo, which delivered to aborigines native title to lands taken from them at the time when Australia was settled. In 1997 a report was handed to parliament which dealt with the policy, enacted from the late nineteenth century until the 1960s, of taking children of mixed blood from their aboriginal parents and sending them to institutions or to foster homes where they were often treated brutally, victims of racist contempt. The report is called *Bringing Them Home*. Mabo and *Bringing Them Home* are important, partly because evils done to this long suffering and gentle people should be more widely known to an international community increasingly conscious of the need to defend human rights wherever it is possible to do so. But they are also important, well beyond the shores of Australia, because both raise profound and subtle questions about the nature of justice, the relation of justice to law, the relations of both to what we call the national interest, and most troubling of all perhaps, about the nature of genocide. Genocide is the international crime par excellence because it is a crime, not merely against this or that community, but against the community of humankind, a crime 'against the human status', as the French prosecutor at Nuremberg put it.

Racism of a certain kind—not all kinds for racism is a complex phenomenon, but the kind usually connected with skin colour—is best characterized as an incapacity on the part of racists to see that anything could go deep in the inner lives of their victims. For such racists it is literally unintelligible that parenthood or sexuality, for example, could mean to 'them'—the victims of their racial denigration—what it does to 'us', just as it is unintelligible that we could see in a face that looked to us like the Black and White Minstrel Show's caricature of an Afro-American face, all the magnificence and misery of Othello.

Legal justifications of colonial settlement in many parts of the world were often infected by racism of that kind. Sometimes, at least, the law was intended not just to rationalize imperial interests, but also to justify settlement of foreign lands to a reasonable conscience. Terra nullius—the doctrine that the land was, for legal purposes, empty—is an example. Consistent in theory with the recognition of the full humanity of those whose lands were colonized, in practice its application was often the expression of a racist denigration of the 'capacities of some categories of indigenous inhabitants to have any rights or interest in land' (to quote Justice Brennan). That denigration expressed the belief that since nothing could go deep with them, their forcible removal from their lands could not do so (could not count as dispossession as we ordinarily mean it) and therefore could not constitute a grievous wrong against them. More than preceding judgments in other lands—America or Canada, for example—Mabo made clear why the rejection of terra nullius and the property laws infected by the racists assumptions which often governed its application, was nothing less than the recognition of the full humanity of the indigenous peoples who had been dispossessed. Reflection on it reveals why that recognition was an act of justice that could only be parodied by calling it an act of fairness.

Just as many of the settlers could not imagine that the aborigines could have relations of any depth to the land, so many of their descendants could not imagine that they had relations of any depth to their children. The first form of blindness enabled whites to take their lands from them with a relatively clear conscience. The second enabled them to take their children for reasons that were various but which sometimes served the intention of eliminating them as a people. Guided by the 1948 United Nations Convention on the Prevention and Punishment of the Crime of Genocide, *Bringing Them Home* accuses past Australian administrations of genocide.

Because the Holocaust is the most striking of our paradigms of genocide, no other crime is so identified with the twentieth century. Were it not for the Holocaust, other instances of genocide—

Armenia and Rwanda for example—might have been seen to be no different in kind from the crime of mass murder, whose frequency and scale also marked that century, but which is as old as political association. After the Holocaust and especially in the two great trials of Nazi criminals—Nuremberg and the Eichmann trial in Jerusalem in 1961—many people were overwhelmed by a sense that they were confronted with a new crime which humanity needed to bring into the space of common understanding, even if aspects of it would always defeat attempts to do so.

No recent writer that I know of has been more alive to what is new in our political experience than Hannah Arendt, no one so resistant to the melancholy wisdom of Ecclesiastes that there is nothing new under the sun. She laboured to make us aware that the crimes that define the Holocaust and which make it a paradigm of genocide were new to our political philosophies.

Perhaps it is too early to tell, but if one is to judge by the rapidly degenerating understanding of the limits to the concept's application, then I suspect she laboured in vain. Early attempts to define or at least to mark the distinctive features of genocide functioned negatively, distinguishing genocide from other terrible crimes. Pogroms motivated by murderous racial hatred, especially when their victims numbered tens of thousands, were the crimes most likely to be confused with genocide, and in fact were so even by Jews who had to be convinced as late as the Eichmann trial that the Final Solution was not merely the worst of the pogroms. Mass murder as a means to the elimination of political opponents was only a little less likely to be misunderstood for the same crime as genocide. The murder (in the death camps) of the Jehovah's Witnesses and homosexuals, however, was almost universally recognized to be a crime different in kind.

Nowadays state instigated mass murders are routinely called genocide. Even an English Law Lord said that General Pinochet was guilty of genocide. So too is 'ethnic cleansing' as it occurred in the former Yugoslavia even though it was motivated by the desire to clear territory of people deemed to be foreigners, its brutality compounded by hatred. As I write there is a Bill before the Australian Senate which proposes to include amongst those against whom genocide can be committed, groups 'based on gender, sexuality, political affiliation or disability', just those groups whose early exclusion from the concept were critical to an appreciation of its distinctive nature. In many parts of the world the assimilation of indigenous peoples to an occupying culture is called genocide if the intention is the destruction of the indigenous culture.

Does it matter? It does, I'm sure. If we stretch the concept too far then injustice will be done to those who might be tried for a crime which should not attract the obloquy that rightly attaches to genocide because of its horrific paradigms. And— perhaps as importantly—our efforts to understand a critical and novel element of our political experience will be subverted, perhaps beyond redemption. It is sad but true that human kind understands itself partly by the crimes it knows itself to be capable of. We must therefore strive to give them their right names.

Thinking about *Bringing Them Home* can help us do that, I believe. The reason why the children were taken changed over the years covered by the report as did the way they and their parents were treated. Sometimes the policy was genocidal, sometimes it was not. As far as I know no children or parents were killed in the service of a genocidal intention. Understanding why the policy was sometimes but not always genocidal and why it was genocidal though no one was killed will help to determine what is rightly called genocide.

Many people believe that if there is no killing then there is no genocide. A thought experiment shows why I believe they are mistaken. Imagine a people forcibly sterilized in order that they be eliminated as a people. Would that count as genocide? I think most people would answer that it does and that hardly anyone would be morally outraged at the suggestion that it does. This thought-experiment stretches the concept of genocide further than many people had thought possible, but I think it will not stretch it so far as to include assimilation, some instances of which achieved, and were intended to achieve, the destruction of a people as surely as mass murder does.

Accepting that there can be genocide without mass killing does not demean the Holocaust and it will enable us to understand better what it is about the Holocaust that we try to understand by bringing it under the concept of genocide. Never before the Holocaust and never after it has there been such a relentless determination to wipe from the face of the earth a people who were vilified as pollutants of it. That is one respect in which it is unique, unprecedented and not yet repeated. There is, however, another aspect that makes it unique, or perhaps more accurately, there are other aspects that have prompted people to call it that, aspects that have also prompted some of them to say that it is mysterious, destined to defeat all our efforts to understand it. For understandable reasons these features—the ones that make it unprecedented and unrepeated as genocide and the ones that make it something different and worse than genocide—get mixed up. The confusion hinders our understanding of genocide, partly because the features of the Holocaust that make it different and worse than genocide are just those that make many people think that only a crime that includes mass murder could count as the same kind of crime as the Holocaust. It is ironical, but I think it is true, that our paradigm of genocide has hindered our understanding of it.

It is possible to characterize the genocidal aspects of the Holocaust and even to explain why it is such a terrible paradigm of genocide without resorting to good and evil as distinctive moral concepts. If we have use for them anyhow, then we will of course see the genocidal elements of the Holocaust as evil, but if we don't have use for them, then we will not be bereft of what is necessary for a full understanding of genocide. To understand the aspects of the Holocaust that make some people say that it is mysterious, we need a concept of evil as something distinctive amongst our moral concepts, something that concepts of cruelty and savagery do not capture, something that captures the insight that 'there exists evil beyond vice'. The death camps make our need of it more evident than do the killings in the east where a relentless genocidal determination was already apparent.

Considerable resistance has grown over recent years to seeing the Holocaust as unique in any sense that implies that it may elude all our attempts to understand it. Though I show sympathy for the claim that it is mysterious, I neither endorse nor reject it. Instead, I try to create conceptual space for it. Resistance to it is sometimes based on the moral objection that it privileges Jewish suffering and sometimes on the belief that it is obscurantist. There can be little doubt that there are corrupt uses of the Holocaust of a kind that are expressed only a little unjustly in the cynical quip that 'there is no business like Shoah business'. Nor can there be doubt that the difficulties in understanding it have attracted obscurantists. That being said, the preoccupation with the Holocaust in *A Common Humanity* is an expression of my belief that efforts to understand it—which must include efforts to characterize the limits of our understanding—are essential to humanity's efforts to understand itself. Anxiety about Holocaust denial of the kind made notorious by David Irving is, I suspect, often an acknowledgment of this.

As always when Irving is in the public eye, free speech is the topic of passionate argument. Though the cause of the celebrated trial in London was Irving's attempt to prosecute Deborah Lipstadt for saying what was plainly true—that he was a Holocaust denier of a particularly virulent sort—it is Irving's right to free speech that is more usually at issue. Denying it to him is dangerous and should therefore be resisted on prudential grounds, but it is not, I think, an affront to free speech conceived as a positive ideal. That ideal presupposes a constituency of argument in which people defend—'to the death' as Voltaire insisted—the rights of radically opposing opinions to be heard. One reason why they should be heard is that, just conceivably, they might be true. And even when there is no requirement that they be heard, they should be permitted to be expressed because, as we say, 'everyone is entitled to their opinion'. Conceived as a positive ideal, free speech enjoins us to be open to the opinions of others and to try to overcome the common psychological obstacles to such openness—hot-headedness, arrogance, hardening of the intellectual arteries, fear and so on. Succumbing to any one of them could make one impervious to reason. There is, however, another way to be impervious to reason, less common but more interesting to anyone concerned to understand the nature of critical thinking, and it is Irving's way. It is to be a crank.

Most people, I think, believe that to call someone a crank is to descend into mere abuse, and that if something of interest is to be extracted from the abuse, then it is that the person who is called a crank suffers from one or more of the psychological disabilities that make one seriously beyond the reach of reason. In one of the more difficult chapters of this book I offer a different perspective on what it is to be a crank and on the ways we rule things out of consideration more generally. From that perspective we can see that the concept is essential to any account of critical thinking because it is essential to any account of judgment, in whose absence critical thinking is impossible. Summing up, Justice Gray said: 'The picture of Irving which emerges from the evidence of his extra-curricular activities reveals him to be a right-wing pro-Nazi polemicist. In my view the Defendants have established that Irving has a political agenda. It is one which, it is legitimate to infer, disposes him, where he deems it necessary, to manipulate the historical record in order to make it conform with his political beliefs'. He was right, of course, but someone can be as he described Irving and be no more than that, while someone can be like that because he is a crank. The difference is critical to understanding why the refusal to engage Irving in debate can be more than disdain for him or piety towards those whose terrible fate he denies.

A myth—edifying and powerful—stands in the way of our understanding this. It is the myth that a serious thinker—a *true* thinker—will fear to think nothing. She will follow reason wherever it takes her no matter how frightened or morally disgusted she may be at the prospect of embracing the conclusions it delivers to her. If necessary she will accept that the whole of morality is a sham to which, as Thrasymachus taught, the strong have fallen victim because of the cunning of the weak.

Were I seriously tempted to such nihilism by living a philosophical life, I would give up philosophy, fearful of what I was becoming. I strongly suspect that virtually all—perhaps all—of my colleagues would do the same. It is a startling fact, given how pervasive the myth is and for how long this kind of scepticism has haunted philosophy, that I have come across no one who is seriously prepared to profess such nihilistic scepticism in her own name and that none of the great philosophers has done so. It survives by being put impersonally or attributed to someone else. Socrates asked his interlocutors to put aside, for the duration of their discussion, what they had heard, what *could* be said by someone or what could theoretically be argued for, and to answer for themselves. When people are asked whether they believe that morality might be a sham, that our sense of the terrible wrongs people have suffered might answer to no genuine moral concept, then if they are also asked to answer seriously in the first person they invariably say they do not and cannot believe it?

Only at this point of seriousness, I think, can there be fruitful exploration of why they cannot profess such nihilistic scepticism. Then one discovers that one would fear to be a person who seriously professed it and that the fear of it is of a different kind from the fear of thinking painful thoughts. One also discovers that the reason one cannot wish to be the kind of person who would follow reason to a nihilistic conclusion is different from an incapacity to question beliefs that are so deeply inculcated that one finds it psychologically impossible even to contemplate their sceptical examination.

Something similar is true of non moral–examples of 'the unthinkable'. Were I to argue with Irving he would almost certainly wipe the floor with me, but were I then to suspect that he has a case, I would not think that I was finally living the life of reason to an exemplary degree. I would think I was losing something that is necessary to keeps my thoughts in touch with reality and, therefore, something that is necessary to prevent the life of reason from becoming the kind of parody of itself that it sometimes became during the trial in London, and always becomes at meetings of the Flat Earth Society.

Unfortunately the forms of the unthinkable have not excited much interest in philosophy, largely, I think, because it is assumed that appeal to them is merely an extravagant way of saying that someone has denied something flamingly obvious or so well established that it is part of common knowledge. Natural though that assumption is, I believe it is mistaken. Certainly it needs more examination than it has received. Understanding the ways we rule things out of consideration matters to how we conceive of free speech as a positive ideal. More basically, it matters to an understanding of what it is to think well and badly and therefore to an understanding of the difference between radical critique and the ersatz radicalism, the superficial enchantment with transgression, that is exposed the moment one calls upon its advocates seriously to profess their scepticism in the first person.

A Common Humanity celebrates the plurality of voices that constitute what Michael Oakeshott called 'the conversation of mankind'. The phrase comes from the title of Oakeshott's essay 'The voice of poetry in the conversation of mankind'. Like Oakeshott, A Common Humanity celebrates what, in a broad sense, could be called the poetic voice. It celebrates the importance of literary art to the understanding of the human condition.

Every writer needs an address said Isaac Bashevis Singer. That is a fine way of putting the need we have for local roots, even when one aspires to speak universally about what life means to us. The universality of great literature—the universality we express when we say that really great writing speaks to all the peoples of the earth—is quite evidently not the kind of universality we associate with science, which aims at a universal abstract language, stripped of all local association, of all local and historical resonance. In literature, the universality one aspires to is of a kind that is achieved when a story or a poem in a particular natural language, historically rich and dense, shaped by and shaping the life of a people, is translated into other natural languages, historically rich and dense, shaped by and shaping the life of different peoples. That, I think, is what Bashevis Singer meant when he said that every writer must have an address. His was written in Yiddish.

Oakeshott would be sympathetic, I think. I am critical, however, of his conception of conversation, seeing in its elegant urbanity the exclusion of voices—sometimes shrill ones—that need to be heard. Arendt pointed out that tradition can be a threat to voices in the past, denying them the power to shake us. Richard Rorty's understanding of conversation, indebted as it is to Oakeshott, shares this failing which gives it a dilettantish air. Be that as it may: my argument that attention to conversation rather than vision will lead to a better understanding of truth, objectivity and judgment does not lead me, as it does Rorty, to scepticism. One of the deepest of Wittgenstein's lessons is that, because our ordinary ways of speaking about truth and objectivity do not presuppose metaphysical theses of the kind that philosophers like Rorty have been concerned to expose criticism of those theses, leaves things more or less as they are.

Simone Weil said that if we see another person as a perspective on the world, just as we are, then we could not treat that person unjustly. By 'a perspective on the world' she meant more than a centre of consciousness. What she meant can be captured in the idea of responding fully to someone as a conversational partner, someone who can be asked—sometimes required—to rise to the challenge to find her own voice, to speak for herself out of a life she must live as her own and no one else's. During the course of discussing an example whose lessons run through *A Common Humanity*, I remark of a woman that her racist denigration of the Vietnamese is inseparable from the fact that she could not find intelligible that she could converse with them and learn from them about what it means to be married, to love someone or to grieve for them.

Socrates tells a young orator, Polus, shamelessly besotted with the power he imagines that oratory gives him, that he is good at rhetoric but bad at conversation. The distinction is critical to the distinction that so preoccupied Socrates and Plato, between philosophy and rhetoric. More often than not, commentators say that the distinction comes to this: that whereas rhetoric appeals to the emotions, philosophy appeals to reason.

If we take the distinction between philosophy and rhetoric to be at least in part the distinction between legitimate and illegitimate forms of persuasion concerning how one should live and what life can mean, then reflection on Socrates as Plato portrayed him will make things look considerably more complicated. Whatever Plato intended, the character he gave us eludes the classification that is implied in a simple contrast between thought and feeling. That is why he has haunted Western thought for some two and a half thousand years, repelling and attracting in turns, exciting admiration even wonder, and at times something close to contempt.

It is therefore natural to ask whether he thought, and if he did whether Plato also thought, that the abstract arguments for which he is famous (the elenchus) could take one to the kind of understanding that he possessed of why it is better to suffer evil than to do it. The characters to whom he tries to 'demonstrate' this sometimes resentfully acknowledge the conclusions that Socrates drives them to, but they believe they have been tricked. Imagine, however, a different kind of character, someone sincerely convinced by the elenchus that it is better to suffer evil than to do it, and who proclaimed it across Athens. Would we believe that he understood what Socrates understood?

In whatever way we answer that question, surely no reading of the dialogues can fail to be struck by the powerful presence of Socrates and the effect that presence had on even the most querulous and resentful of his interlocutors. And it is hard to believe that Plato—poet and philosopher combined—was unaware of it and of the question it naturally raises for anyone who thinks about the difference between philosophy and rhetoric: how should we characterize the difference between Socrates' presence and the charismatic presence of the orators?

One answer has it that the difference is irrelevant because Socrates' presence is irrelevant to the conceptual character of the understanding he sought to provide by means of the elenchus, by means of 'reason'. Another has it that the orator's charisma is a false semblance of the kind of presence that gives to words and deeds a power to move us when we are rightly moved and learn from them. Philosophy—at least the kind of philosophy concerned with the big Socratic questions—would then be distinguished, in part, from rhetoric, legitimate persuasion distinguished from illegitimate persuasion, by whatever makes for the difference between being rightly and wrongly moved.

It is an important fact that we often learn most deeply when we are moved by what people say or do, in life and in art. Often, though, we are moved when we should not be, or in ways that we should not be, or more than we should be. Sometimes we are moved because we are sentimental, or liable to pathos, or in other ways vulnerable to the 'winged words' of rhetoric, as Adolf Eichmann called them. There are, I think, no standards that reason could firmly establish, even in principle, that could be sufficient to assure that we have been rightly or wrongly moved. When we are moved we trust what moves us and trust that we are rightly moved. We trust wisely, however, only when trust is disciplined. The last two chapters of *A Common Humanity* try to say what disciplining trust comes to and to elaborate its implications for the distinctions between legitimate and illegitimate persuasion. It tries, not so much to argue for a shift in the balance between head and heart in favour of the heart, as to make clear what we mean when we speak of an *understanding* of the heart, when, for example, we say that we have understood something in our head but not in our heart.

If we are to find our feet with people of other cultures, in our own communities or in other nations, we must understand what it is to be lucidly open to learning from one another. Nothing much will be achieved if we have only a thin conception of reason that distinguishes between philosophy and oratory on the grounds that the former appeals to reason whereas the latter appeals to the emotions. Nothing much will be achieved either, if in rebellion against such a thin conception of reason, we surrender uncritically to our vulnerability, to sentimentality, pathos and to failings worse still. A thin conception of reason and uncritical gullibility are two sides of the same counterfeit coin. Reality is found in the conceptual space in which the other becomes visible to us and in which we respond to her with disciplined lucidity.

Iris Murdoch said that understanding the reality of another person is a work of love, justice and pity. She meant, I believe, that love, justice and pity are *forms* of understanding rather than merely conditions which facilitate understanding—conditions like a clear head, a good nights sleep, an alcohol-free brain. Real love is hard in the sense of hardheaded and unsentimental. In ridding oneself of sentimentality, pathos and similar afflictions, one is allowing justice, love and pity to do their cognitive work, their work of disclosing reality. It is the same love, Weil tells us, that sees what is invisible.

Introduction:
Take Your
Time

It matters where one starts when one thinks about value, especially the kind of value we call moral. Often people begin focusing
on commands, rules, proscriptions. Confronted with a command
that one ought not to do such and such, it is natural to ask, 'What
if I do?' Once that question is asked, the search is on for the justification of morality, typically, for whether moral rules serve our
(enlightened) interests—social and personal. If they don't, many
people believe, then morality has no rational justification. If moral
rules do not serve the purposes for which they are devised, they
think, then morality is merely a gratuitous interloper in human
affairs.

Some other ways of thinking about morality do not invite the
same sceptical quest for justification. In them morality does not
appear in the first instance in the guise of a command, nor as
anything that might provoke rebellion in a free or inquiring spirit

or excite the impulse to celebrate transgression. In this book I tell the story of a nun whose behaviour showed a goodness that I found wondrous. Her behaviour can be described simply enough. She responded without a trace of condescension towards people who were incurably mentally ill, who had been so for thirty years and more, and who had been abandoned by friends and relatives, even by their parents. Nothing in the circumstances of their lives was likely to encourage the belief that, despite their affliction, they remained fully our fellow human beings.

The wonder of her behaviour has inspired much of my philosophical work. It was, however, not entirely unfamiliar to me. As a boy, I was fortunate to be brought up by two men of fine character and more than considerable goodness. I tell that story in *Romulus, My Father*, an elegy to my father and to his friend Pantelimon Hora. They befriended a man, Vacek Vilkovikas, who like them was an immigrant labourer on a large construction project in country Victoria. A few years after he arrived in Australia, Vacek lost his mind. He lived for a time in hills near us, between two large boulders which he covered with branches and bits of tin to protect him from the weather. Visibly insane, he talked to himself and sometimes cooked in his urine.

After I had written *Romulus, My Father*, a journalist, Rachel Buchanan, asked me whether Vacek had seemed queer to me when I was a boy. I answered sincerely that he had not. Later, my answer puzzled me. Why had he not? Objectively, after all, he was very strange. The answer that came to me was that my father and Hora behaved towards Vacek without condescension. Had they condescended to him—had it shown in their tone of voice or demeanour, in their body language as we say—the cruel sensitivity children often possess would have made me conclude that Vacek was not entirely 'one of us'. As it was, the contrary was true. Their treatment of Vacek enabled me to see him, his strange behaviour notwithstanding, as living yet another form of human life. Though I learned to be wary of his offerings of food and to make other small adaptations, I accepted that it took 'his sort to make all sorts' (to borrow the fine words of D. H. Lawrence).

Most of us would agree that people like Vacek should be treated as fully our equals, but we believe it, I think, in the way young people believe they are mortal, more in our heads than in our hearts. But Vacek was recognisably leading one kind of human life. He did not bear the marks of the incurably afflicted, nor was he constantly and visibly in torment. It would be hard for anyone to say that the men to whom the nun responded in the hospital were living a life of any kind. They were not suffering an affliction which they could with help and courage overcome. No edifying stories of adversity defeated would come from that place. I could absorb without difficulty, could absorb even without noticing, my father's and Hora's attitude to Vacek. Yet even thus prepared, the nun's behaviour astonished me. Not because it was a superlative example of anything (although of course it was), but because it revealed what a human life could mean. Even such people, who appear to have lost everything that gives sense to our lives, are fully our equals. Her behaviour proved it to me.

That last sentence will provoke scepticism, I know. Here I will simply say that the nun's behaviour gave living meaning to words I had heard often enough, but which I had thought could never refer to anything real—'goodness' of a kind that invites a capital G, 'love', 'beauty' and 'purity'. These words had seemed especially suspect when used together, but I came to realise that, if they are to be used to characterise the nun's behaviour, each needs the other. Simone Weil remarks that 'beautiful' is the word we most naturally use to describe saintly deeds. She is right because it is their goodness rather than, say, their nobility that makes us reach for 'beautiful', and we do it because of their purity. It is this goodness that I believe Hannah Arendt had in mind when she wrote in *On Revolution* that 'the men of the eighteenth century did not know that there exists goodness beyond virtue and evil beyond vice'.

Is there something in our experience that can, so dramatically, teach us what evil is? There is, I believe. It is remorse. Or, more accurately, it is remorse as we have experienced it in a culture in which good and evil have been the names of distinctive moral phenomena, and where both have been connected with a sense of the inalienable preciousness of each human being. There could be, and no doubt there is, remorse for wrongdoing not informed by that sense of the individual. But, for the most part, it has not been that way for us, in the West.

With that qualification, I take remorse to be the pained recognition of the meaning of the wrong one has done—characteristically, of what it means to have wronged someone. It differs from shame in that it focuses on the deed whereas shame—when it is over the wrong one has done—is characteristically for what is revealed about oneself. One might betray someone because one is a coward, or venal. Shame focuses on the failure of character, remorse on the betrayal. When the wrong done counts as the violation of the preciousness of a human being, then it informs one conception we have of 'evil'. I do not mean *the* concept of evil. I doubt there is such a thing, just as I doubt there is such a thing as *the* concept of goodness. We speak in many ways of good and evil. I focus on what I believe to be the deepest of them. Good and evil, as I mean them, are interdependent on each other because each is interdependent on a sense of the preciousness of every human being.

Another way of characterising remorse is to say that it is the recognition of what it means to be *guilty* of having wronged someone. That being so, there is not much difference between remorse and guilt feeling. There are differences—one hesitates to speak of a remorse trip, partly for the same reason that it comes less naturally to speak of neurotic remorse rather than neurotic guilt—but the differences are not so great. Both have many corruptions which are the cause of much of the contemporary hostility to them. Maudlin self-indulgence is the most obvious of them. Some, however, are so subtle that it is easy to lose sight of the fact that they are corruptions, and corruptions of something whose authentic forms reveal more vividly perhaps than anything else the preciousness of those whom we have wronged. To lose sight of what the corruptions corrupt and thus to become alienated from authentic forms of guilt and remorse would be to lose a sense of the full humanity of our fellow human beings. The claim that one understands the wrong one has done to another while not being seriously affected by it is as suspect, I believe, as the claim that one loves someone even though one is untroubled by their death or loss.

I am, I admit, a little embarrassed about talking, as I so often do, of the preciousness of each individual human being, not least because it can sound precious, or sentimental or soft-headed, but I can find no better way of speaking. The secular philosophical tradition speaks of inalienable rights, inalienable dignity and of persons as ends in themselves. These are, I believe, ways of whistling in the dark, ways of trying to make secure to reason what reason cannot finally underwrite. Religious traditions speak of the sacredness of each human being, but I doubt that sanctity is a concept that has a secure home outside those traditions.

Talk of the preciousness of human beings has, however, the advantage that it directs our attention to a feature of the person and to our response to the person. That is, I think, how it should be, for I believe that both the response and what it is a response to, the subjective and the objective, are interdependent here. Moreover the response—the subjective pole—is love in its many genuine forms. Were it not for the many ways human beings genuinely love one another—from sexual love to the impartial love of saints—I do not believe we would have a sense of the sacredness of individuals, or of their inalienable rights or dignity. Working together, sometimes harmoniously, sometimes in tension, our ways of loving create and are also formed by a language of love in which we record and explore the ways we matter to one another.

Plato and Kant—philosophers who in different ways haunt my thought—believed (again in different ways) that moral value is of a kind like no other and overrides everything. Their sense of its place in a human life is foreign—sometimes incomprehensible—to us now. A student once said to me that nothing mattered more than whether or not there is a God. I asked him what he would say to someone who claimed that perhaps nothing matters more than to live decently. He looked puzzled and after a considerable pause replied, 'You must be talking about morality and all that stuff.'

People say nowadays that a bit of ethics would do the professions and business some good. That is of a piece with the student's response. The very way they acknowledge the importance of morality appears to highlight its foreignness to their daily concerns. And yet I am reasonably confident that most people's ordinary living is not entirely consistent with this.

Perhaps part of the explanation about why people talk like this lies in the way in which a certain kind of moralising has entered into what we call morality. I say it that way, almost putting 'morality' in sneer quotes, because I often think that we would think more clearly about morality if we banished the word 'morality' itself. Bernard Williams, a distinguished English moral philosopher, shares this suspicion and calls this suspect notion of morality 'the morality system', claiming that it systematically distorts thought about obligation, justice, culpability and so on. He is right, I think, and such distortion is partly the cause of the curious estrangement from morality amongst morally serious people.

The most significant of the distortions of the morality system is its tendency to claim for itself all value that seriously conflicts with it. It goes very deep in us to believe that a morally serious person cannot freely and lucidly be claimed by value that conflicts with moral value. When, for example, we are told that politics sometimes clashes with morality, then we very naturally think that it can do so for a morally serious person, lucidly aware of the claims upon her, only if the political considerations are in fact moral ones. What appears to be a conflict between morality and politics is therefore claimed to be a conflict within morality itself.

Belief in the sovereignty of moral value takes many forms. Some verge on the seedy, on doing the dirt on life in the way they denigrate what appears to conflict with morality—as when, for example, they denigrate what conflicts with morality in politics as mere expedience, or when the love that conflicts with morality is dismissed as mere infatuation. Others go deep, possessing power and beauty. Plato believed that a life lived in the light of a lucid relation to the Good promised not only the reconciliation of all good things, but also a calm that would silence the voices of temptation and deny misfortune the power to drive us to despair.

The desire that Plato should be right goes deep in the human heart. It is hard to see, however, how one can love individuals— husbands, wives, lovers and friends—as one ought without sometimes being tempted to do wrong for their sakes or to protect them, and without the risk of being broken when they suffer the horrific evil human beings can do to one another, or just when we lose them. No wisdom, I think, can leave us just tempted enough to be human, but never so much as to succumb. And I doubt that anything that looks like metaphysics could generate a wisdom that guaranteed protection against the power of misfortune to make us curse the day we were born.

Plato's disagreement with that last point, about metaphysics, is at the heart of his notorious subjugation of art to philosophy. Even if it were true, however, as Plato believed, that at the highest level all good things are reconcilable, that thought is easily corrupted by moralism. If philosophy is to resist the tendency in moralism and in itself to oversimplification, then it must be responsive to art, and if art is to be 'responsive to life', as Henry James put it, then it must reveal all that makes the Platonic thought implausible—the 'appearances', as Plato would have called them. Then, even if Plato's doctrine is true, it will never be secure. Plato knew it, and that, more than a general disposition to totalitarian politics, was why he was so hostile to art. If the Platonic doctrine is true, art will always obscure our vision of it because it is obliged to be just to things which conflict with it.

Plato was, however, right to believe that morality is never merely the servant but always the judge of our interests and purposes. Thus, we cannot commandeer it to our purposes, not even when morality and the world are tragically mismatched. We cannot always find a solution (even in principle) to dilemmas which are in part caused by the claims of morality. The most serious cause of conflict within morality and between morality and other values is caused by the fact that our various ways of loving condition our sense that human beings are precious beyond reason and beyond merit. Some of those loves are in conflict with one another and with morality. Morality is, therefore, in tension with what conditions its most fundamental concept.

Awareness of such tensions is in accord with much of the modern temper which is disposed to emphasise the plurality of values and the possibilities of tragic conflict. But the modern temper is also inclined to reductionism and with that I am quite out of sympathy. To emphasise that morality is *sui generis*—that it is not fully explicable by facts which are not themselves moral facts—and to display it as such in its various manifestations, especially in political life, is one of the main aims of *A Common Humanity*. In this respect I am at one with Plato and Kant.

And so morality can have a value not reducible to our desires and interests and other forms of value. Fidelity and justice, for example, are not reducible to the material or psychological advantages they bring. Neither are they separable from them. When we say, 'It's not the money it's the principle. You betrayed me,' we mean that the loss, the hurt, the affront is not explicable only by reference to material losses and to psychological trauma. But, of course, no one seriously believes that theft or betrayal would matter as they do to us if they did not characteristically cause such losses and such trauma. It is important to note and to do justice to the fact that when someone is a victim of an attempted murder she usually responds differently than when she has a brush with death in a car accident. It would, however, be absurd to say that the evil of what she suffers has nothing to do with the fact that she would be dead if the attempt had been successful.

There is a tendency in modern thinking to say that a conception of morality such as I have outlined is ill-suited to politics. In politics, the argument goes, a prudential or consequentialist ethics is best, for these are more likely to allow politicians the flexibility to secure for their constituents goods such as wealth, security and perhaps even happiness, insofar as one thinks of happiness in ways that could be understood by anyone whether or not morality mattered to them. I believe this view is very badly mistaken.

Justice is a value which straddles the moral and the political realms. In politics, or at any rate in political theorising, it is often restricted to considerations of equity, to the distribution of and access to goods and opportunities, and to law, where it is sometimes reduced to procedural considerations. When we are not theorising, however, we speak naturally of justice in contexts where the fairness of legal procedures is not at issue—of a just war, for example. We also speak of justice when equality of respect rather than fairness is at issue. 'Treat me fully as a human being, fully as your equal, without condescension'—that is not primarily a plea to have access to certain goods, although goods may accrue if the plea is successful and sometimes must if it has been acknowledged and understood. If I am right to claim that the High Court's judgment on Mabo was the acknowledgment in law of the full humanity of the Aborigines, the acknowledgment that they, like the white settlers, had relations to the land that would make dispossession a terrible crime; and if I am also right to claim that acknowledgment to be an act of justice, then it is justice whose nature could only be parodied in the claim that the Aborigines had at last been treated fairly.

Concern for justice as the acknowledgment that all human

beings are owed inalienable respect goes deep in our system of criminal justice. We insist that criminals be brought to justice for many reasons, but two of them are particularly important. First, because we owe it to the victims that the wrong they suffered be acknowledged by their community. Secondly, because we owe justice to the criminals, and our insistence that it is owed to them no matter what they have done is the insistence that they remain members of our community no matter what they have done. That partly defines the kind of community we are and what it means to be a member of it.

Its significance becomes apparent in extreme cases in which criminals are so evil, their deeds and character so foul, that it is natural to want to shoot them in the street like mad dogs. There are, of course, prudential reasons why we do not do that, reasons that focus on the fear that such actions might be the thin edge of the wedge. But such prudential reasons do not capture our sense that justice forbids that any human being should be killed or even banished in the spirit of ridding the world of vermin. When human beings are treated in that spirit, then although they are denied due process and worse, it would be ludicrous to say that the injustice of their treatment consists in that fact, or in the fact that they were treated unfairly.

Those who believe that justice is owed only to 'human beings who behave like human beings' would not be moved by arguments about fairness which presuppose exactly what such people deny, namely that radical evil-doers still belong to the constituency in which considerations of fairness are relevant. The insistence that even the most foul criminals are owed unconditional respect, that even they belong to the constituency in which they may intelligibly press claims for fair treatment and due process, is the acknowledgment of our human fellowship with them. Our insistence that they be granted due process is an expression of justice that is deeper than anything that can be captured by the notions of proper procedure or fairness. Justice

Landau, the judge presiding over the trial of Adolf Eichmann in Jerusalem, was moved to say, against those who wished the trial to be no more than a show trial, that it had only one purpose, and that was to do justice. He meant, amongst other things, that it had to do justice to Eichmann for Eichmann's sake because it was owed to him as a human being. This is the most sublime aspect of our legal tradition.

The need for wrongs to be acknowledged, and the need for material reparation to be made in a spirit true to that acknowledgment, is fundamental to us as moral beings, and also as political beings. We acknowledge the wrongs our fellow citizens have suffered at the hands of criminals, and we think of those wrongs as a harm distinct from the otherwise identical harm (death, injury, or the loss of property, for example) they might have suffered in the ordinary course of nature. For the same reason, the wrongs done to the Aborigines must be acknowledged in appropriate ways. The systematic character of the wrongs and their connection with civic and governmental institutions shames the nation, and this too should be acknowledged in ways appropriate to the institutions of government. In some quarters the call for such acknowledgment has been disparaged with astonishing ferocity.

To respond appropriately to the wrongs suffered by our fellow citizens, we must give the right name to those wrongs. *Bringing Them Home*, the report on the official practice, from late last century until the late 1960s, of government agents taking children of mixed blood from their Aboriginal parents, describes the practice as genocide. There can be little doubt that genocide was committed during periods of Australian history, according to accounts of genocide that are for the most part uncontroversial. In my judgment there can be little doubt that the crimes against the children and their parents sometimes constituted genocide according to the United Nations Convention on the Prevention and Punishment of the Crime of Genocide of 1948. There are, however, reasons for believing the definition offered by the convention is seriously inadequate. The question, therefore, is whether the crimes against 'the stolen generations' can be counted as genocide according to any conception of it that is not mocked by the fact that the Holocaust is rightly our paradigm of it.

Sometimes a question of this kind can be answered by finding a definition that will suit our legal and political purposes. I think this cannot yet be done with the concept of genocide which is a concept intended to make sense of something relatively new in our moral and political experience. Paradigms that involve mass murder have inclined us to think that genocide must involve murder. Hypothetical examples—the forcible sterilisation of a people with the intention of making them extinct is but one— should make us resist that inclination. The hypothetical nature of such examples is not a reason for suspecting that they have little relevance to reality. Through them we explore the concepts with which we describe reality.

Many people would now agree that the destruction of a people's culture constitutes a wrong against them whose nature and gravity we have only recently acknowledged in any general way in our political and legal discourse. That fact alters our sense of the past, of how we must write it if we are to be truthful. For similar reasons we must become clearer about the nature of genocide and whether we have committed it. To do that we must distinguish it from its paradigms which involve mass murder and at the same time resist the temptation to reduce it to the crime of destroying a culture and, therefore, to the absurd proposition that assimilation is genocide. Reflection on the stolen generations reveals, I think, that the moral and legal structure of the concept of genocide has not yet been settled in ways that are true to what we want it to capture.

Our desires and interests, including our political desires and interests, are in part morally constituted. It matters to us, as individuals and as members of political communities, that we are just and honourable, that our institutions are decent in ways that are not explicable entirely by other things that matter to us—safety, security and happiness, for example. Far from being explained by our need and desire for such things, moral considerations qualify what kind of safety or security we will accept, and to some degree actually define what we will count as real happiness and real flourishing. If we find it difficult fully to accept that justice is preferable to material comfort, that honour is better than safety and even sometimes better than life itself when life can be secured only at the expense of dishonour, then we flatter ourselves if we think that to be the expression of a healthy scepticism. We have merely fallen away from values which the ancient Greeks took for granted to be possessed by anyone wishing to live a full human life.

Many terrible events of our century, including the crimes against the Australian Aborigines, have forced us to acknowledge that, even in politics, our need of truth goes deep. Yet we are afflicted by a corrosive cynicism about the very possibility of truth in politics. At a more theoretical level, long before postmodernism became influential in cultural and other studies, journalists were asking 'What is truth?' in a tone intended to belittle any aspiration to impartial, objective reporting. Not all of them, of course, but enough of them for it to be a cultural phenomenon.

Again, I confess myself unable to understand the many and different kinds of causes of this professed (though seldom practised) scepticism about truth and objectivity that in some people's eyes has assumed the proportions of a cultural crisis. One of its principal theoretical causes is, I think, a misunderstanding about what it means to take seriously the fact that our thought is inescapably *in medias res*, in the thick of things.

According to its less radical meaning we are, inescapably but only contingently for all that, creatures whose cognitive capacities intimate higher destinies than we can achieve, burdened as we are by our bodies and the requirements of practical living. Taken that way, our concepts—or many of them and especially those which determine understanding of what it is to think well or badly, our understanding of 'rational inquiry' as we often put it, parsimoniously limiting the kinds of understanding we seek—are believed not to be conditioned by any particular form of living. This can be an edifying ideal of thinking, as it would be for any rational being. It can verge on the mystical, invoking an idea of transcendence which was beautifully symbolised in Plato's philosophy. Less poetically but powerfully it is to be found in Gottlob Frege's essay 'The Thought', and in the young Wittgenstein's *Tractatus Logico Philosophicus*. An older Wittgenstein was to reject this dimension of his earlier work and to give the most powerful reasons for thinking that the denial that our concepts are constituted by and can only be mastered in the living of certain kinds of life is, as the American philosopher Stanley Cavell aptly puts it, philosophy's longstanding and deeply motivated 'denial of the human'. In the philosophy of the later Wittgenstein we find a deeper, more radical meaning of what it means to think in the midst of things.

Acknowledgment that our concepts (rather than merely our beliefs) are conditioned by our human ways of living will alter our sense of what we mean in the many ways we use the term 'human being'. Most philosophers recommend the concept of a person as more suitable than that of a 'human being' when talk is of more than the species *homo sapiens*. The concept of a person is tailor-made to prescind from the living of any particular form of life. Angels are persons, God is a person, perhaps some animals are persons and some machines will be. From this point of view, when we speak of respect for human beings we express a moral position that we would express better if we spoke of respect for persons.

Persons, rights, obligation—they are concepts at the centre of one way of thinking about morality. Human being, human fellowship, love and its requirements are concepts at the centre of another. While I favour the latter, nothing I say finally proves that I am right to do so, and nothing prevents a determined translation of the latter into the former. But if I am right about the place love plays in the constitution of our moral concepts, in my claim that talk of inalienable rights and so on is dependent on the language of love, and if love is dependent on our responses to the human form and its expressive possibilities, then my case will at least seem plausible, and perhaps even convincing.

I had wondered whether to call this book *A Common Humanity* or *A Common Understanding*. The former more accurately conveys what is central to it, even when I am explicitly concerned with the forms of common understanding, because it emphasises the dependence of the latter on the former. None of these forms, but especially not those dependent on the ways we construe the meaning of our lives, is between persons, or rational beings contingently living the life of human beings. They are between human beings whose characteristic embodiment—that we have faces, for example—and whose ways of living give us not only something to think about, but condition the concepts with which we think, including those with which we think, as philosophers must, about how we think.

The concerns of this book therefore sometimes take one to the deepest problems of philosophy, and sometimes to the critical examination of assumptions deep within the subject. Its engagement with those assumptions makes it, I hope, an original contribution to the discipline, even though it is addressed as much to the educated reader as it is to philosophers. As universities impose increasingly lunatic requirements on academics to publish more than is good for anyone, but only in the approved refereed journals, the space into which a book such as this can be published is rapidly diminishing. As fewer academics are prepared to write for the educated reader, that reader tends to become less educated, and, sadly, less prepared to think as hard as is necessary to discuss responsibly many of the issues that are of public intellectual concern. Of these issues, those raised by the streams of thought that are often called postmodernism are most obviously in need of disciplined attention. Profound and very difficult matters about the relations of thought, language and truth to one another are now impossible to avoid for almost anyone who thinks, but they require patience and stamina.

Philosophy is at its heart always a meta-activity, stepping back to think about thinking. It thinks not only about what our obligations are, but also about the concept of obligation; not only about what is just, but also about the concept of justice; not only about what it is rational to do or believe, but also about the concept of the rational. This makes it difficult for some people to find their feet with philosophy, and it makes them impatient of it. To them, I repeat Wittgenstein's advice concerning how philosophers should greet one another. He said they should say, 'Take your time.'

Goodness
beyond Virtue

In the early 1960s when I was seventeen years old, I worked as a ward-assistant in a psychiatric hospital. Some of the patients had been there for over thirty years. The ward was an old Victorian building surrounded by a high iron fence. White gravel lay on all sides between the fence and the building. There was no grass. One or two scraggy trees provided mean shade. It reminded me of some of the enclosures at Melbourne zoo. When patients soiled themselves, as some did often, they were ordered to undress and to step under a shower. The distance of a mop handle from them, we then mopped them down as zoo-keepers wash down elephants.

The patients were judged to be incurable and they appeared to have irretrievably lost everything which gives meaning to our lives. They had no grounds for self-respect insofar as we connect that with self-esteem; or, none which could be based on qualities or achievements for which we could admire or congratulate them without condescension. Friends, wives, children and even parents, if they were alive, had long ceased to visit them. Often they were treated brutishly by the psychiatrists and nurses.

A small number of psychiatrists did, however, work devotedly to improve their conditions. They spoke, against all appearances, of the inalienable *dignity* of even those patients. I admired them enormously. Most of their colleagues believed these doctors to be naive, even fools. Some of the nurses despised them with a vehemence that was astonishing.

It probably didn't help their cause for the psychiatrists to speak of the inalienable dignity of the patients I described. Natural though it is to speak this way, and although it has an honoured place in our tradition, it is, I believe, a sign of our conceptual desperation and also of our deep desire to ground in the very nature of things the requirement that we accord each human being unconditional respect. To talk of inalienable dignity is rather like talking of the inalienable right to esteem. Both are alienable; esteem for obvious reasons, and dignity because it is essentially tied to appearance. Like the protestation of rights to which it is allied, it will survive only if one is spared the worst. Those who are not spared, those whom Simone Weil described as having been 'struck the kind of blow which leaves a being struggling on the ground like a half crushed worm', depend on the love of saints to make their humanity visible. That is why Weil also said that when compassion for the afflicted is really found 'we have a more astounding miracle than walking on water, healing the sick, or even raising the dead'.

One day a nun came to the ward. In her middle years, only her vivacity made an impression on me until she talked to the patients. Then everything in her demeanour towards them—the way she spoke to them, her facial expressions, the inflexions of her body—contrasted with and showed up the behaviour of those noble psychiatrists. She showed that they were, despite their best efforts, condescending, as I too had been. She thereby revealed that even such patients were, as the psychiatrists and I had sincerely and generously professed, the equals of those who wanted to help them; but she also revealed that in our hearts we did not believe this.

The time, as I said, was the early sixties—the time when thoughts about what life could mean were about to be shaped by the optimism of the 'beautiful people' and their discovery of self-realisation. Later, reflecting on the nun's example, I came to believe that an ethics centred on the concept of human flourishing does not have the conceptual resources to keep fully amongst us, in the way the nun had revealed to be possible, people who are severely and ineradicably afflicted. Only with bitter irony or unknowing condescension could one say the patients in that ward had any chance of flourishing. Any description of what life could mean to them invited the thought that it would have been better for them if they had never been born. Later, such thoughts about such lives were commonly voiced, first in discussions of abortion and then in discussions of euthanasia. It would be no fault in any account of ethics if it failed to find words to make fully intelligible what the nun revealed, for she revealed something mysterious. But there are philosophies that leave or create conceptual space for such mystery, and there are some which close that space. Most do not even see the need for it.

I do not know how important it was that she was a nun. One is inclined, of course, to say that her behaviour was a function of the depth of her religious beliefs. Perhaps it was, but typically beliefs explain behaviour independently of their truth or falsity: a person's false beliefs explain his behaviour as effectively as his true ones. Seeing her, however, I felt irresistibly that her behaviour was directly shaped by the reality which it revealed. I wondered at her, but not at anything about her except that her behaviour should have, so wondrously, this power of revelation. She showed up the psychiatrists, but if I were asked how, exactly, then I would not elaborate on defects in their character, their imagination, or in what would ordinarily be called their moral sensibility.

Of course her behaviour did not come from nowhere. Virtues of character, imagination and sensibility, given content and form by the disciplines of her vocation, were essential to her becoming the kind of person she was. But in another person such virtues and the behaviour which expressed them would have been the focus of my admiring attention. I admired the psychiatrists for their many virtues—for their wisdom, their compassion, their courage, their capacity for self-sacrificing hard work and sometimes for more besides. In the nun's case, her behaviour was striking not for the virtues it expressed, or even for the good it achieved, but for its power to reveal the full humanity of those whose affliction had made their humanity invisible. Love is the name we give to such behaviour.

If the nun were questioned she might have told a religious or theological or metaphysical story about the people to whom she responded with a love of such purity. But one need not believe it or substitute any other metaphysical story in its place to be certain about the revelatory quality of her behaviour. That certainty is not a blind refusal to acknowledge the possibility of a mistake. It rests on the fact that there is no clear application here for the concept of a mistake as it would normally be understood in connection with claims about the metaphysical or empirical properties of the people in question. The purity of her compassion ruled out for me speculation about whether it was justified. Not, however, because it alerted me to natural or supernatural facts about the patients which justified her demeanour beyond possible doubt. To speak of those patients as 'fully our equals' is not, even implicitly, to pick out something about them that could be known or even specified independently of this kind of love.

My assent to what her love revealed did not, therefore, depend on my acceptance of an hypothesis about the grounds of that love. That is one of the great differences between goodness and, for example, great courage. One can acknowledge that beliefs which one judges to be false have inspired great heroism. The heroism is beyond doubt, but it gives no support to the beliefs which inspired it.

The nun almost certainly believed that the patients with whom she dealt were all God's children and equally loved by Him. One might therefore be inclined to say her behaviour no more supports that belief than the courage of martyrs supports their beliefs in what they died for. That is half true. The purity of her loving behaviour proves something, but not any particular religious faith or doctrine.

If the revelatory quality of her loving demeanour towards those patients depended upon her belief in a metaphysical fact about them, in something that could, quite independently of her love, become a focus for speculation, then her love would have no greater power to reveal reality than inspiring courage has. I do not say, flatly, that it would be wrong to say that her love of God and her belief that the patients were all God's children inspired her behaviour. After all, as I have acknowledged, she would probably say something like that herself. It can, however, be misleading because it can suggest that those words gesture towards describing some fact of the matter towards which one could take a speculative stance.

What is wrong with adopting such a stance? This, I think. Whatever religious people might say, as someone who was witness to the nun's love and is claimed in fidelity to it, I have no understanding of what it revealed independently of the quality of her love. If I am asked what I mean when I say that even such people as were patients in that ward are fully our equals, I can only say that the quality of her love proved that they are rightly the objects of our non-condescending treatment, that we should do all in our power to respond in that way. But if someone were now to ask me what informs my sense that they are *rightly* the objects of such treatment, I can appeal only to the purity of her love. For me, the purity of the love proved the reality of what it revealed. I have to say 'for me', because one must speak personally about such matters. That after all is the nature of witness. From the point of view of the speculative intelligence, however, I am going around in ever darkening circles, because I allow for no independent justification of her attitude.

Nothing I can say will diminish this affront to reason. Love, goodness, purity and beauty—the last being, as Simone Weil said, the word that comes first to mind when we think of saintly deeds—these have recurrently come together in a (rather marginal) strand of our philosophical and religious tradition with talk of reality and truth in spiritual and moral matters. That part of the tradition is right, I think, provided one understands these notions to go together with a distinctive concept of reality. They do not refer to peculiar epistemic routes to a reality for which, as speculative metaphysics would have us believe, factual reality is proto-typical. Reality and truth are words we use in many ways.

The nun's love was unconditional. So too is parental love. I mean that parental love is defined by the requirement that it be unconditional, not that it always or even mostly meets that requirement. Both forms of love are unconditional but they are not unconditioned. Their existence depends upon certain practices and customs as much as it informs them, and also upon certain facts of the human condition. Neither is universally an ideal amongst the peoples of the earth, and even in cultures such as ours where they are (or have been) celebrated, people's hold on them is often fragile. They are, I believe, dependent upon one another. I doubt that the love expressed in the nun's demeanour would have been possible for her were it not for the place which the language of parental love had in her prayers.

Theology and philosophy, both being discursive disciplines, seek ways of formulating the relation between the nun's behaviour and her religious beliefs which are more abstract and more tractable to a certain conception of reason. Elaborating on Kant's claim that the commandment to love one's neighbour could not be taken literally because love cannot be commanded, a philosopher recently argued that the philosophically perspicuous rendering of the biblical command is, 'Always act so that you respect every human being, yourself and another, as a rational creature.' Such formulations will not find their way into books of prayers and hymns. Philosophers and theologians are, for reasons that go deep in their disciplines, inclined to say that the language of prayer and worship, anthropocentric and often poetic, merely makes moving and therefore psychologically accessible to less than perfectly rational beings, things whose intellectual content is more clearly revealed in the abstract deliverance of theological and philosophical theories. I suspect that the contrary is closer to the truth—that the unashamedly untheoretical, anthropocentric language of worship has greater power to reveal the structure of the concepts which make the nun's behaviour and what it revealed intelligible to us.

For us in the West, the claim that all human beings are sacred is the one that bears most directly on the question of how to characterise the nun's behaviour. Only someone who is religious can speak seriously of the sacred, but such talk informs the thoughts of most of us whether or not we are religious, for it shapes our thoughts about the way in which human beings limit our will as does nothing else in nature. If we are not religious, we will often search for one of the inadequate expressions which are available to us to say what we hope will be a secular equivalent of it. We may say that all human beings are inestimably precious, that they are ends in themselves, that they are owed unconditional respect, that they possess inalienable rights, and, of course, that they possess inalienable dignity. In my judgment these are ways of trying to say what we feel a need to say when we are estranged from the conceptual resources we need to say it. Be that as it may: each of them is problematic and contentious. Not one of them has the simple power of the religious ways of speaking.

Where does that power come from? Not, I am quite sure,

from esoteric theological or philosophical elaborations of what it means for something to be sacred. It derives from the unashamedly anthropomorphic character of the claim that we are sacred because God loves us, his children. Its significance will be evident to anyone who reflects on family life. Children come to love their brothers and sisters because they see them in the light of their parents' love. Often, we learn that something is precious only when we see it in the light of someone's love.

Sometimes parental love has powers of disclosure similar to the nun's love. When their love is pure, parents who love a child who has become a vicious and vile adult remind us that this person, whose deeds are evil and whose character appears irredeemably foul, is fully our fellow human being. The requirement on parents to love their children unconditionally is not an external standard imposed from elsewhere. It is one of the standards internal to that love itself, standards which determine its real as opposed to its counterfeit forms. It is also fundamental to an account of the way in which the child appears as precious to its parents if their love is pure—that is to an account of why the child appears to them as precious, period.

But the power of parental love to reveal that even this evil and foul character is fully our fellow human being—its having *that* to reveal—depends, I think, on the impartial love of saints. Were it not for the love saints have shown for the most terrible criminals, were it not for the generalising authority of such love which we take to apply to all human beings, the love of mothers for their criminal children would appear to be merely the understandable but limited love of mothers. Because of the place the impartial love of saints has occupied in our culture, there has developed a language of love whose grammar has transformed our understanding of what it is for a human being to be a unique kind of limit to our will. We express our sense of that limit when we say that human beings are owed unconditional respect, or that they have inalienable rights, and similar things. These ways of speaking express a disposition to find a basis for what love has revealed which is more steadfast than love itself is believed to be and which will make the fruits of love's work more secure to reason.

The greatest philosophical expression of that disposition is found in Immanuel Kant's *Groundwork of the Metaphysic of Morals*. He is virtually alone amongst the great philosophers to emphasise the importance of our sense of the individual to the authority which morality claims over us. It is captured in his famous injunction that one act so that one always treats a person as an end and never merely as a means, and in his ideal of rational beings fully and unconditionally respectful of each other in the Kingdom of Ends. The first part of that injunction has great rhetorical power and has been influential well beyond philosophy despite the obscurity of the second part which tells us to treat people as ends of action. Kant also said, as I noted earlier, that because we cannot love on command, the biblical command to love one's neighbour could not be taken literally. He took it as a rhetorical way of expressing the duties whose nature he believed he had revealed more clearly in the abstractions of his philosophy. Magnificent contempt was all he would accord the position I argue in this book:

> Against the slack, or indeed ignoble, attitude which seeks for the moral principle among empirical motives and laws we cannot give a warning too strongly or too often; for human reason in its weariness is fain to rest upon this pillow and in a dream of sweet illusions (which lead it to embrace a cloud in mistake for Juno) to foist into the place of morality some misbegotten mongrel patched up from limbs of very varied ancestry and looking like anything you please, only not like virtue, to him who has once beheld her in her true shape.

It is not, however, straightforwardly true that love cannot be commanded, if that means that we cannot be required to love better. Love has its standards and lovers must try to rise to them.

Rush Rhees, one of Wittgenstein's most eminent students, said that there would be no love without the language of love. There cannot be love without certain ways and tones of speaking of what we love, without argument about what is appropriate or even intelligible to love, about whether something is worthy of our love and whether what we feel really is love. The standards intrinsic to love in all its forms are partly an expression of respect for the independent reality of the beloved. To the eye of a moralist, that can look like a straightforwardly moral requirement, independent of love as a passion. It is half true. We would not have a sense of the independent reality of the beloved if we did not think of her as someone who could be wronged. But we would not have the sense of her as someone who could be wronged, if we did not have a sense of her as precious in a way that has largely been conditioned by the language of love. The requirements of love and those of morality are, I believe, interdependent and, as we shall see, sometimes conflicting.

It is true and important, as Kant insisted, that we have obligations to those whom we do not love. We misconstrue its importance, however, if we follow Kant in imagining that we would acknowledge obligations towards people we believed to be beyond the possible reach of the love of someone like the nun or, to take a more public example, Mother Teresa. We would not find it even intelligible, I think, that we have obligations to those whom we do not love unless we saw them as being the intelligible beneficiaries of someone's love. Failing that, talk of rights and duties would begin to disengage from what gives it sense. One of the quickest ways to make prisoners morally invisible to their guards is to deny them visits from their loved ones, thereby ensuring that the guards never see them through the eyes of those who love them. That is a fact of considerable importance to reflection about the nature of morality. Our talk of rights is dependent on the works of love.

Our sense of the preciousness of other people is connected with their power to affect us in ways we cannot fathom and in ways against which we can protect ourselves only at the cost of becoming shallow. There is nothing reasonable in the fact that another person's absence can make our lives seem empty. The power of human beings to affect one another in ways beyond reason and beyond merit has offended rationalists and moralists since the dawn of thought, but it is partly what yields to us that sense of human individuality which we express when we say that human beings are unique and irreplaceable. Such attachments, and the joy and the grief which they may cause, condition our sense of the preciousness of human beings. Love is the most important of them.

The readiness of lovers to disregard prudence, to love and to suffer for it despite status, class, race, nationality and moral merit, conditions and awakens in us a sense of the mystery and preciousness of human beings. The loves that form our sense of the preciousness of individuals are therefore not only the more edifying kinds. As well as the nun's love, there is Othello's destructive love for Desdemona. To deny that the latter is real love because of the ideals implicit in the former would be as misguided as to deny (as Kant did) the moral importance of both in the name of obligation. When we are tempted to say that Othello did not really love Desdemona whom he was destined to murder, we should consider whether such moralisation of the standards by which we distinguish real love from its semblances might not undermine the very thing on which such judgments depend, namely, our sense of other human beings as irreplaceable.

Love takes many forms, some of which are in tension with one another and some of which are in tension with morality. The reasons why love commends itself to morality are also reasons why it offends it. Moralists will try to resolve this tension by moralising our understanding of what love really is and by declaring Othello's passion to be many things but never love. If they were to succeed in denigrating all love that conflicts with morality as false love, then they would undermine what is best in our morality—the faith that human beings are precious beyond reason, beyond merit and beyond what most moralisers will tolerate.

Evil beyond Vice

Does the concept of evil mark out a distinctive moral reality? Or does it merely record an inclination to demonise severe moral transgression? Here is one way to get a grip on the question. We distinguish different ways in which things are terrible for us. Pain, suffering, loss, death and disease are terrible in one way. Murder, torture, cruelty and a malevolent will are terrible in another. Let the first category go unnamed for the time being. The second answers to the name of morality. So one way of rephrasing my opening question would be to ask: does evil mark out a distinctive and irreducible kind of moral terribleness? The question is often in the air when there is discussion of the atrocities of our century. During such discussions some people speak without hesitation of the evil of those atrocities. Others, and sometimes the same people at other times, show themselves uneasy with talk of evil.

It is not want of moral sensitivity that makes people doubt that the concept of evil makes an interesting and distinctive contribution to our moral understanding. Inga Clendinnen says in her book *Reading the Holocaust* that she has no use for the concept, yet page after page of her book reveals a profound moral sensibility. People like Clendinnen are not inclined to stand in front of a fire engine and ask why one would call it red. Once scepticism about the concept of evil has seriously set in, pointing to horrific examples of it will achieve nothing.

What prompts this kind of scepticism? Leaving aside the reasons that underlie a general moral scepticism, there are two that I want to discuss. First, there is the belief that serious use of the concept of evil requires metaphysical or religious support. Secondly, its use is often associated with the kind of moralising we now call judgmentalism. Many people believe that serious use of the concept betrays a blindness to complexity and nuance, a tendency to simplification and to arrogant judgment. Thoughts of black hats and white hats are not far off. For the moment I will discuss the first reason. Discussion of the second must wait.

Imagine someone—call him N—whose route home from work takes him past destitute homeless people sleeping in the doorways of shops. They are not young homeless, but old, ruined by drink, unable ever to get a job, without family and friends. If any one of them were to die, no one would care. If N were to hear that one to whom he occasionally gave money had died that evening, he might think on it for a few minutes and then his mind would pass to other, perhaps quite trivial, things. No one would do more. Now imagine that one of the homeless people asks N for money, abuses him when he refuses to give it, and stands aggressively in his path. In a fit of temper N pushes him aside, off the kerb and, unintentionally, into the path of an oncoming car. The beggar is killed.

So far I have said nothing about N to rule out any of a number of ways that he might respond to what he has done. But there is a response that I want to comment on just because it is probable and so easily recognisable. N might be overcome by remorse, experiencing it as the pained realisation of the meaning of what he had done. Pained bewilderment is the most natural expression of remorse. 'What have I done? How could I have done it?' These questions express a shocked realisation of the meaning of what one has done, a shocked realisation that anything could have that meaning. To the extent that they are taken as questions, their answers—at any level of description that would interest a court—are generally obvious. Insofar as they carry an implication that one did not fully know what one was doing, then such ignorance is not of the kind suffered, for example, by Oedipus. Nor is it of the kind that leads us to say that the criminally insane do not know what they do or that they do not 'know right from wrong'. Just as the contact with the goodness of the kind shown by the nun inspires the wonder that there could be such a thing in the world, so remorse makes us painfully aware of the reality of evil, and of the way remorse differs from natural suffering, from the afflictions of Job, and also from shame and dishonour, though we might feel these too.

We know that N's remorse might haunt him all his life, blighting it. At times—especially early on—he might even say that he cannot live with himself, and although he would be unlikely to kill himself in his grief, the thought might come to him. Many would be critical of such suicidal thoughts, but we all find them understandable, and that is important, because our finding it so partly conditions our sense of the seriousness of this kind of wrongdoing. The bewildered grief of remorse supervenes on, transforms and deepens our sense that human beings are precious as that is given to us through our natural attachments and their consequences. Our grief over the loss of those we love partly conditions our sense that they are precious, not just to us, but *überhaupt*. Grief purified of self-indulgence is a pained awareness of the independent reality of those we have lost. That sense of the reality of another is partly morally conditioned, most importantly by the individuating work of remorse which ensures, when it is pure, that our victims remain with us in all their individuality, haunting us. Were it not so, we would not find it intelligible that someone should contemplate suicide for killing a person whose life meant nothing to anyone, and whose death would go unnoticed were it to occur naturally.

N's grief and his suicidal thoughts make sense only if we see them as responses to the moral dimensions of what he has done. Those dimensions are often characterised by terms like 'rules', 'taboos', 'transgressions' and so on. If such terms are the main ones informing our sense of the nature of morality, then we are likely to diminish the significance of the fact that our wrongdoings have victims. N's sense of the terribleness of what he did depends on the way his remorse focuses on his victim in all his individuality. He is not haunted by the principles he betrayed or by the Moral Law he transgressed; he is haunted by the particular beggar he killed. 'My God, what have I done? I have transgressed most terribly! I have violated my principles! I have shattered the ancient taboo against killing! I have transgressed against the Moral Law! I have done what would reduce social life to tatters if too many people did it! I have broken the Social Covenant!'

These are parodies of his remorse because they are insufficiently attentive to the particularity of his victim—a particularity, which as I noted in the previous paragraph, is itself partly morally conditioned. Reflection on remorse takes us closer, I believe, to the nature of morality and of good and evil, than reflection on rules, principles, taboos and transgressions can.

Dostoyevsky makes the point powerfully in *Crime and Punishment*. Raskolnikov kills the old money-lender to prove to himself that he is one of those rare individuals who can do evil fully knowing what he is doing, yet be unaffected by it. Only after he kills the money-lender and her sister, when remorse threatens, does Raskolnikov understand that his project was incoherent.

Even more astonishing for him is his intermittent realisation that to kill a 'louse' and a 'parasite'—he never retracts these descriptions of the money-lender—is as terrible as to kill a saint.

Aristotle (who is often praised by modern moral and literary theorists for his humane commonsense) would have found that last thought absurd. He would also have found it absurd that someone should contemplate suicide because he had unintentionally (or intentionally) killed a beggar whom no one cared for and who was of no use to anyone. There are prudential reasons why it would be bad not to condemn such killings severely—reasons that focus on the likely consequences of not doing so—but N's remorse is informed by none of them. His response, like Raskolnikov's, is saturated by the realisation of the unconditional preciousness of his victim.

The affirmation that each human being is unconditionally precious is responsible for a feature of remorse which is fundamental to it, but which is so strange that it tempts us into a reductionism of a psychological or socio-biological kind. Remorse is the only form of suffering that cannot legitimately seek comfort in a community of the guilty or in the hope that time will heal it. If we lose someone we love, for example, then we may be haunted by them all of our lives, but we often rightly seek comforting fellowship with others who grieve as we do. With remorse other things must come into play—atonement, forgiveness, perhaps punishment. The many and infinitely subtle corruptions of remorse—almost always forms of self-indulgence or self-obsession—can obscure that from us because attention to the plight of others and (sometimes) therapy is the cure for those corruptions. But when the neurotic and corrupt dimensions fall away one is alone with the bitter knowledge of what one has done, and then no comfort can legitimately be found in a fellowship of the guilty. That being so, the lucid refusal of consolation in such fellowship is not a form of pride and is not morally or psychologically unrealistic. It is not a consequence of setting standards that are too high, nor is it the expression of a severe and persecutory superego. It is merely the acknowledgment that such is the nature of guilt. Why is remorse as it is? How could there be such a phenomenon? These questions are no more an invitation to psychological inquiry than is the bewildered cry 'How could I have done it?'

If we understand guilt-feeling to be a pained acknowledgement of the wrong one has done, then there is no significant difference between guilt-feeling and remorse. Contemporary hostility to remorse has been fuelled by a vivid sense of its corruptions, and we have, like Nietzsche who brilliantly (if venomously) diagnosed the pathologies of remorse, failed to see that they are, after all, corruptions. Some of those corruptions—the ones that focus on a destructive sense of self-hatred and worthlessness—are often the result of confusing guilt and shame. Guilt focuses on what one has done. The moral focus of shame is on what one has been revealed to be in doing it. If, in order to avoid such corruptions we seek to escape the severity of lucid remorse, then unless we are saints, we will estrange ourselves from one of the most effective ways of retaining a sense of the unconditional preciousness of each human being. To try to retain it without remorse is like trying to retain a capacity for love while exorcising all vulnerability from it.

Our sense of the reality of others is partly conditioned by our vulnerability to them, by the unfathomable grief they may cause us. It is also conditioned by our shocked and bewildered realisation of what it means to wrong them. Remorse is that realisation. It is interdependent with a distinctive concept of evil. It is the perspective in which the meaning of what one has done, what one has become through doing it, and what one's victims have suffered, are inseparable. If that still raises the suspicion that a remorseful concern with what one has become competes with a proper concern for one's victim, then it might help to think of other examples. Grief, when it is not self-indulgent, is a heightened form of the awareness of another, but hardly anyone would say that the pain of grief must distract our attention from the person over whom we are grieving. The astonishment that there could be such a state as guilt and such suffering as remorse, has its counterpart in the wonder that other human beings whom we might otherwise not care for, and whom we might otherwise despise, could matter so to us.

More than anyone this century, perhaps, Sigmund Freud persuaded us to seek an understanding of morality in a reductionist moral psychology. He often spoke in debunking tones about morality, especially in his 'philosophical' works such as *The Future of an Illusion*, *Civilisation and Its Discontents* and *Totem and Taboo*. The conception of morality that provoked that tone was, essentially, Kantian. More than once he spoke with derision of the Categorical Imperative (an imperative of duty which does not depend upon an appeal to our desires and interests), identifying it with morality with a capital 'M'. He had a number of reasons. The most interesting of them is that he thought that morality conceived that way rested on an illusion.

The illusion, according to Freud, was to think that morality could be *sui generis*—more than an expression of our enlightened interests and desires. He believed that only metaphysics could secure such a status for morality and that metaphysical claims were always false and almost always the expression of superstition. That being the case, he reasoned, the nature of morality is to be explained by things that can be characterised independently of its categories. His official view was that morality is a system of rules whose rational justification we make perspicuous when we reveal how those rules serve our enlightened interests. Those interests, he believed, could all be described without using moral terms. Some of them are interests like safety and security, the kind to which reductionist theories of morality have always appealed. Freud's contribution was to offer an account of the deep needs of the psyche.

Accounts of morality which appeal to the pre-moral purposes that moral rules serve in order to deny that the categories of morality are *sui generis* are commonplace. Freud added a compelling dimension when he argued that moralists failed to understand the degree to which unconscious mechanisms which we only dimly understand determine much of the content of morality and—more importantly—our sense of its nature and authority. He would see in the account I sketched earlier of the radical singularity of the guilty a mere phenomenology of appearances as they are structured by bad philosophy and religion, each supporting the other. The singularity of the guilty would be for him a psychological echo of the religious belief that sinners will be alone at the last judgment, which he thought to be an illusion whose nature psychoanalysis would make plain. In fairness to Freud, many of his opponents thought much the same about the metaphysical presuppositions of any conception of morality as *sui generis*, except they endorsed the metaphysics he rejected.

The claim that many of the categories of morality, including those of good and evil, are *sui generis* need involve no mysteries. It means merely that an important aspect of morality can never be fully explained by reference to facts which are not themselves moral facts. Take the concept of nobility which was so important to Aristotle. He believed it revealed what was most glorious in courage. We can agree while also noting that there are many practical reasons why we prize courage. It is necessary for individuals if they are to achieve their ends, whatever they may be, and it is obvious why societies should encourage bravery in their members. Yet, these good practical reasons for praising and prizing courage do not take us to an appreciation of its nobility. That appreciation supervenes on the practical reasons, as a distinct category of appraisal, related to but not reducible to them. It is not at all mysterious that in addition to prizing courage for its functional role in individual lives and in society, we should also prize it for its nobility.

Another example. Assume that someone betrays a good friend, perhaps to his friend's enemies, but that no natural consequences attend the betrayal. Assume also that the betrayed friend does not know that she was betrayed, that her betrayer is deeply remorseful and that we have every reason to believe that he will never do such a thing again. Even so, we might pity the person who was betrayed. If someone were to ask why might we pity her, since nothing has happened and she suffered no harm, then we can say, and surely would say, that the harm consists simply in the fact that she was betrayed, a harm distinct from and not reducible to whatever other harms it causes in the natural course of things. Our pity could be denied to be appropriate, I think, only by someone who dogmatically insists that betrayals which result in no other harm, material or psychological, cannot, strictly speaking, be a form of harm. Of course, betrayal undermines friendship and friendship is a human good. But betrayal undermines friendship because betrayal is a terrible thing. It is not a terrible thing because it undermines friendship and the natural good it brings.

That morality is *sui generis* is no more mysterious than the fact that language is not reducible to the function of communication, or the aesthetic appreciation of artefacts to the functions which define them. Imagine a caveman who carves his spear, always in ways to improve its utility. One day he carves notches which have no functional value. He looks at the spear and takes a different kind of delight in his handiwork. To press here for reduction of the aesthetic to the functional, to insist that if such reduction fails we have a phenomenon offensive to reason, is a blank refusal to accept that something new has come into the world. Some people are like that. They are incapable of acknowledging the new except as a fully explicable variation of the old. Their handicap should not be elevated into a requirement of reason.

The examples I have just given show that the claim that morality is *sui generis* is consistent with the claim that it is entirely of human origin. But one should not slide from this acknowledgment to thinking that we can, individually or together, change it at will in the service of our enlightened desires. That slide is not justified by logic and its conclusion is not true, though we are encouraged to believe it by the thought that if morality is of human origin it must be an artefact, something we have made. Morality is not the servant of our desires and interests, but their judge. We cannot commandeer it into our service. That is why talk of the will as obedient to necessities whose nature is different from force (psychological or physical) has been fundamental both to morality and art.

It would, however, be disingenuous for me to rest there. Resistance to reductionist accounts of morality need entail no appeal to mystery, but there *is* something mysterious in our sense, to the degree that we still have it, of the preciousness of each individual human being. When I gave examples of it, in this chapter and the previous one, I emphasised how astonishing they were. There is nothing to make reason uneasy in the fact that we prize virtues and despise vices in ways that are not reducible to functional accounts of their value. But it is deeply unnatural to reason to affirm that no human being, however evil their deeds and however foul their character, should be denied our unconditional respect, or be treated as though they are filth, having forfeited all right to justice. And it is even more deeply unnatural to affirm that people in severe and ineradicable affliction, who appear to have lost all that gives life meaning, should be fully our moral equals. Two thousand years of religious tradition which has taught that life is sacred has accustomed us to these things, dulling our sense of how astonishing they are. The religious tradition has given them their first expression, but that does not mean they make no sense of it. What grew in one place may take root elsewhere.

The need to affirm what reason finds offensive makes me speak of mystery, but not because I believe our limited understanding is defeated, that perhaps other beings with vastly superior intelligence and knowledge could better comprehend these things. I mean by mystery something which no powers of understanding can penetrate, not because it is so difficult that even God would be perplexed, but because the mystery of good and evil is not contingent on our limited cognitive powers.

A French woman, who saw a young Nazi officer send train-load after trainload of children to the death camps, said in an interview in the 1970s that every day she asked herself how it was possible for him to do it. She did not mean that sociology, history, philosophy, psychology and political science had not yet delivered an answer to her question, but perhaps one day they might. She might have known, perhaps, that that particular soldier had merely been too afraid to disobey his superiors. At one level that is a sufficient explanation. Even if one believes it requires deeper social or psychological probing, no distance we travel in that direction will take us towards an answer to her question. Hers was a question without answer, and someone who offered her an answer would fail to understand the nature of her bewilderment.

Call those mysteries which are contingent on our limited cognitive powers 'contingently mysterious', and those which are not, 'essentially mysterious'. Good and evil are essentially mysterious, which is why no metaphysical or religious explanations will penetrate their mystery. To offer such explanations is to misunderstand the mystery of good and evil in much the same way as someone who offers the French woman a psychological (or other) answer to her question, 'How could he have done it?'

The matter is so important and so often misunderstood, that it deserves further development. Nothing I have said about the mystery of evil implies a kind of mysticism. Elie Wiesel once said, 'Evil more than good suggests infinity.' In another place he writes, 'I have always placed the Holocaust on a mystical level, beyond human understanding.' I do not want to be taken as saying anything like that.

Hannah Arendt was more sober. 'Evil never has depth,' she wrote in a letter to Mary McCarthy, and to the distinguished scholar of Judaism, Gershom Scholem, she wrote that 'evil is never "radical"...it is only extreme and...possesses neither depth nor any demonic dimensions'. 'A report on the banality of evil' is the subtitle of her book *Eichmann in Jerusalem*, which grew out of her account of Adolf Eichmann's trial for the *New Yorker*. Somewhat disingenuously she said that she offered no theory of evil, merely a 'factual' observation on a phenomenon 'which stared one in the face at the trial. Eichmann was not Iago and not Macbeth, and nothing would have been further from his mind than to determine with Richard III "to prove a villain". Except for an extraordinary diligence in looking out for his personal advancement, he had no motives at all.'

In later works Arendt explored further the terrifying thoughtlessness that she attributed to Eichmann, a man so overcome by the 'winged words' he spoke immediately before his execution that he forgot he was at his own funeral. At no stage did she offer a theory of evil—not when she wrote *Eichmann in Jerusalem* or later. The claim that evil never has depth, however, is obviously not a factual observation.

Arendt's remarks on the banality of evil and on the banality of Eichmann's character have often been developed—contrary to her own belief—to deny that evil is a distinctive moral phenomenon. At the time she wrote *Eichmann in Jerusalem* she was also writing *On Revolution* where she makes the remark which provides the first two chapter titles of this book, namely that the men of the eighteenth century did not know that there exists goodness beyond virtue and evil beyond vice. She did not mean that the people of that time did not understand good and evil in their lives. She meant that such understanding was not reflected in their philosophies and, more strongly, that the central concepts of their moral and political philosophies tended to undermine a proper understanding of good and evil as distinct from virtue and vice.

Along with many others, Arendt was sometimes inclined to say that the political crimes of our century have impressed on us moral categories that the enlightenment could ignore. That inclination compromises the force of her observation about 'the men of the eighteenth century'. It is not the mass murders of our century that make us speak of evil as a distinctive form of the morally terrible. Without an antecedent sense of the preciousness of all human beings, the crimes of our century would appear only different in degree from crimes that Aristotle knew well enough. What Arendt said of the men of the eighteenth century could even more surely be said of him. Yet Aristotle knew only too well the variety of human vices, particularly malevolent cruelty.

We tend to associate evil with a malevolent will, particularly malevolent cruelty. Raskolnikov's killing of the money-lender expressed such a will and so we think that is why we call it evil. N's killing of the beggar did not express such a will and so we think that is why we do not call it evil. Our sense of a malevolent will, however—of what it is and the deeds in which it issues—will be different according to whether or not we have a conception of the preciousness of each individual human being against whom that will is directed. Only if we have it will our sense of a malevolent will also be that of an evil will.

Goodness and virtue, evil and vice, do not, therefore, exist separately side by side. Conceptions of virtue and vice, justice and injustice, of strict obligation and of moral necessity are transformed by a sense of the inalienable preciousness of each individual human being. That transformation gives us a distinctive understanding of good and evil—to my mind the deepest. For many reasons we are becoming estranged from the conception of the individual with which it is interdependent. That is one reason why some people are sceptical of talk of evil, and it is why pictures of corpses in Nazi death camps will not diminish their scepticism.

Arendt thought that her belief that evil has no depth ran counter to the conception of evil that has dominated our Western tradition. That tradition, however, has many parts, and Arendt's understanding of evil belongs to a part of it that has a long history.

Some theologians and philosophers have for centuries claimed that evil has no reality, that it is a negativity. Dostoyevsky gives literary expression to a thought similar to Arendt's when Ivan Karamazov meets the devil. Expecting the glorious Prince of Darkness, 'Satan with scorched wings', Ivan meets instead a slightly ridiculous, slightly vulgar figure afflicted with rheumatism, wearing check trousers 'of an excellent cut, but a little too light in colour and a little too tight, such, in fact, as were no longer worn and the same was true of his fluffy felt hat which was certainly not in season'. In a similar vein again, Simone Weil wrote:

> Nothing is so beautiful and wonderful, nothing is so continually fresh and surprising, so full of sweet and perpetual ecstasy, as the good. No desert is so dreary, monotonous, and boring as evil. This is the truth about authentic good and evil. With fictional good and evil it is the other way round. Fictional good is boring and flat, while fictional evil is varied and intriguing, attractive, profound, and full of charm.

These are not examples of identical conceptions of the banality of evil, but they bear a family resemblance to one another. Putting my own view Platonically, I would say that evil can only be understood in the light of the good, which means, amongst other things, that it cannot lucidly be an object of fascination, competing with goodness for our allegiance. That thought is foreshadowed in my account of remorse as a realisation of the meaning of what one has done.

Sadism is a phenomenon that is often invoked to refute decisively the claim that evil cannot clear-sightedly be the object of fascination and desire and, together with that, the Socratic claim that no one does evil fully understanding what they do. But the sadist is no more powerful a counter example than are more ordinary thugs, thieves, traitors and murderers. Let me try to explain why.

Plato's artistry gives us a compelling portrait of a Socrates who has spent his philosophical life astonished by his discovery of the existence and meaning of good and evil, a discovery he expressed in various ways—that it is better to suffer evil than to do it, that no one does wrong fully understanding what they do, and, at his trial, that a good man cannot be harmed. He believed that ordinary virtuous Athenians, who thought this all to be nonsense, mistook a partial understanding of the ethical for a full one. Even when a full understanding is attained, however, it waxes and wanes, a fact that Plato expressed beautifully when he said that those who seek wisdom are clinging in recollection to wonders they had seen.

The bewilderment characteristic of remorse—What have I done? How could I have done it?—gives some support to the idea that we are often only partially aware of the nature of good and evil and its proper place in our lives. There is no reason to think that remorseful sadists would express themselves differently. *Prima facie*, the expression of such bewilderment about the meaning of what one has done implies that we did not fully understand what we were doing when we did it, although this failure of understanding (of knowledge, as Socrates would have said) is not of a kind that would interest a court. It would not enable one to enter a plea of diminished responsibility for a crime. The law is not wrong about this. It has different purposes which require a different understanding of what counts as 'knowledge of right and wrong'.

No tension exists between the lessons of remorse and what rightly distinguishes sadists from ordinary brutes. Sadists appear to have a refined sense of human dignity and they take self-conscious pleasure in its violation. But that is quite evidently consistent with the Socratic thought that the sense of human dignity that gives pleasure to their cruelty is a false semblance of a genuine understanding of it. If Socrates is right, then the sadist fails fully to understand what he does, just as the ordinary brute does.

When Callicles, one of Socrates' interlocutors in *Gorgias*, hears him say repeatedly that it is better to suffer evil than to do it,

43

he is moved to say, 'Tell me, Socrates, are you serious or are you joking? For if you are serious and what you say is true, then human life must be turned upside down.'

His astonishment was justified. The sense of good and evil, and of its reality and place in our lives that is expressed in the tradition to which I assimilated Arendt's remark that evil never has depth, does indeed turn upside down the world of ancient Greece as it is represented in Homer and also in Aristotle. But if we take Callicles' justified astonishment as a sign that we would be right to reject the conception of good and evil that provoked it, then we should remember that the idea that individuals are precious—as that shows itself in the affirmation that the radically and incurably afflicted are our equals and that the most foul evil-doers are owed just punishment—is what turns human life upside down. We should then ask ourselves whether we are ready to abandon it.

If it is true that evil cannot be an object of fascination, and that one cannot do it—as Raskolnikov sometimes fantasised that he could—just in order to be an evil-doer, then there are few circumstances in which appeal to an evil intention or to an evil character will explain a person's actions. Not, at any rate, if the concept of an evil person is partly that of someone who assaults the preciousness of another human being.

An apparently strange state of affairs, I admit. After all, the concept of evil is often invoked as much to explain certain deeds as it is to characterise or judge them. On the other hand, people often rightly complain that such explanations are vacuous. To the extent that evil actions are explained by appeals to a person's failure to be moved by certain moral considerations (either because she fails fully to understand them, or because she cannot act upon her understanding of them), the appeals are generally to concepts which can be possessed by someone who has no distinctive sense of good and evil. Even when a distinctive concept of evil informs the characterisation of what is to be explained, it seldom figures in the explanation of it.

Take as an example the hypothetical motive I attributed to the young officer in the French woman's story. He did evil and the reason (and I stress again that his having this reason and its being sufficient to explain his action has no bearing on the nature of her bewilderment) is that he was a coward. In other examples, say, of real brutality that occurred in the death camps, what needs to be explained is not why its perpetrators failed to see the *evil* of what they did, but why they were unmoved by its brutality. One doesn't need a sense of goodness beyond virtue and evil beyond vice in order to be appalled by cruelty and brutality.

Consider for example this characteristic passage from Homer's *Iliad*:

> Meges in turn killed Pedaios, the son of Antenor,
> who, bastard though he was, was nursed by lovely Theano
> with close care, as for her own children, to pleasure her
>   husband.
> Now the son of Phyleus, the spear-famed, closing upon
>   him
> struck him with a sharp spear behind the head at the
>   tendon,
> and straight on through the teeth and under the tongue
>   cut the bronze blade,
> and he dropped in the dust gripping in his teeth the cold
>   bronze.

In these wonderful lines Homer conveys the horror of war in all its bitterness and the irreplaceable importance human beings have in the lives of others who love them and will grieve for them. Each—the horror and the sense of the soldier's preciousness to his loved ones—deepens our sense of the other. This is not the preciousness that I have been arguing is interdependent with a sense of good and evil, but the latter would not exist without it. And it is more than enough to inform our response to brutality. Evil is seldom done because people lack a distinctive understanding of it, and never done for that reason, I think, in cases of great cruelty where we are most inclined to appeal to it for an explanation. It is therefore not a concept which enables one to up the moral ante. One can't say, 'I see that you are unmoved by the brutality of what you are doing. Let me explain the evil of it to you. Perhaps that will stay your hand.' The same is true of the concept of the sanctity of human life. 'Don't you see this person is sacred, the child of God,' cannot function as an exhortation intended to trump, 'Don't you see, this is a fellow human being.' Only if we were moved by the latter could we understand the former.

My point is not a general one about moral concepts. Many do play substantial explanatory roles, positive and negative. A person's perception of a good *sui generis* can explain why she pursues it; her perception of an action's brutality can explain why she avoids it, and her failure to see the brutality, the dishonour, the ignominy, the treachery and so on, in what she does can explain why she does it.

In limited circumstances, the same is true of the concept of evil. Some philosophers do not believe that all human beings are unconditionally precious, and attack the claim that they are. That explains why they recommend, and, perhaps, perform certain actions—infanticide and euthanasia—in circumstances inconsistent with that claim. From the perspective from which I have been arguing, they will sometimes do evil, but from no sane perspective are they therefore evil people. The circumstances in which the absence of a sense of evil explains what people do are the circumstances in which we are least inclined to appeal to it. One might therefore savour the irony that the moral concept that is thought to be most guilty of exciting the impulse to moralism—the concept of evil—is the one most unfit for the task. If the concept cannot explain actions that especially provoke us to appeal to it, then it will not serve moralising interests well.

The fact that the concept of evil has no explanatory power just when we feel most need of it does not mean that it is inessential to our understanding of what happens even then. Our need to understand is not exhausted by our need to explain why things occur. We sometimes need the concept of evil to describe adequately what we are confronted with and also to characterise adequately our responses to certain actions, as their perpetrators, their victims or as spectators of them.

In a challenging discussion of an example from Primo Levi's *If This Is a Man*, Inga Clendinnen takes issue with Levi, partly, I think, because she believes that if the concept of evil is to play a part in our understanding of events it must play a part in explaining them. The event she discusses is a football match between SS guards and the Jewish *Sonderkommandos* whom they force to work in the crematoria as accomplices to the Nazi crimes, administering the death 'showers', pushing corpses into ovens and extracting gold from their teeth until their time comes to endure the same fate. For reasons I have elaborated I think she is right to believe that the concept of evil does not explain why the SS acted as they did. But because she appears to think that it is therefore unimportant in the moral descriptions of what they did and what their victims suffered, she fails, I think, properly to understand her disagreement with Levi.

This is how Clendinnen describes that disagreement:

> The Hungarian doctor Myklos Nyiszli, pathologist to Dr Mengele's researches and medical officer to all the men of the *Sonderkommando*, reports a particularly eerie example of comradely fun: an impromptu twilight football match between scratch teams from the 'SS' and the 'SK', with much shouting and laughter from players and onlookers alike.
>
> When Primo Levi read Nyiszli's account he was utterly repelled, precisely for what it indicated about the comradeship between the SS and the veterans of the *Sonderkommando*. He heard the echo of 'Satanic laughter' in this game played 'as if on a village green and not at the gates of hell', seeing in it Nazism's final triumph over the Jew:

'You are like us, you proud people, dirtied with your own
blood, as we are. You too, like us and like Cain, have killed
the brother. Come, we can play together.'

We can see what he means, and why he feels it. It is
possible, however, to read the game differently—as men
being allowed to recognise each other, even if briefly, as
fellow humans.

Later Clendinnen says: 'I would claim...only that some small sense
of community and some recognition of the other as a comrade,
seems to have bloomed in that unlikely place, and in that
blooming lightened one corner of the darkness that was
Auschwitz.'

How does one settle a disagreement such as this? How does
one determine whether the football match expresses a sense of
common humanity or, as Levi believes, a grotesque parody of it?
To try to answer that I will look at other examples where I would
speak without hesitation of the emergence of a sense of common
humanity in circumstances which had extinguished it or which
threatened to do so.

George Orwell expressed it in 'Looking Back on the Spanish
War', when he explained why he could not shoot an enemy
soldier who was running holding up his trousers. 'I had come here
to shoot at "Fascists"; but a man who is holding up his trousers
isn't a "Fascist", he is visibly a fellow creature, similar to yourself,
and you don't feel like shooting at him.' Similar stories came from
the trenches of World War I.

A slightly different example comes from the film *The Confes-
sion* by Costa-Gavras. Made immediately after the invasion of
Czechoslovakia it is an account of the Soviet show trials of 1952.
Old and loyal party members accused of counter-revolutionary
activities are arrested and brought to trial on trumped-up charges.
The judge, who knows he is presiding over a show trial, shouts his
charges and questions to the prisoners. During this brutish inter-
rogation, one of the prisoners moves his hand which had been

holding up his trousers, his belt having been confiscated in the cells. His trousers slip, not to the floor, but sufficiently for him to count as a man who has lost them. Frightened even more than before, he looks at the judge. Neither knows how to respond. Nor do the other prisoners. The judge begins to laugh, first mocking the prisoner, but then sympathetically. When the tone of his laughter changes, the other prisoners laugh. The wretched man who has lost his trousers laughs too.

Although the judge is a major participant in a grievous injustice against the prisoners, the laughter of everyone in the courtroom expresses a sense of a common humanity amongst men who know they are caught in a system in which no one is secure from punishment merely because they are innocent. Their laughter is a lament for their common vulnerability. The outcome of the trial is fixed. Today the judge will find guilty men who only yesterday were high party functionaries. Tomorrow he may be the prisoner. Bertolt Brecht described the reversal of fortunes common amongst high functionaries in the communist world with a precise bitterness. The prisoner has been interrogated and is told:

> We know you are our enemy. Therefore we shall now put you against a wall. But in consideration of your merits and virtues, it will be a good wall, and we shall shoot you with good bullets from good guns, and we shall bury you with a good shovel in good soil.

We have no hesitation, I think, in accepting Orwell's response and the laughter in the court as spontaneous expressions of a sense of human fellowship in circumstances which tended to extinguish or radically weaken it. In fact they could serve as paradigms of such a response. One could confidently appeal to them to explain to someone what one means by speaking of a spontaneous expression of a sense of common humanity.

The footballers in Auschwitz are not like that. The reason,

of course, is because of the morally terrible circumstances surrounding the game. Yet it is just because the game is played in those circumstances that Clendinnen finds the story so interesting. The question therefore is, what reading of the circumstances will support or erode Clendinnen's interpretation of the meaning of the football match? That meaning cannot be read straight off from the behaviour of the players. Behaviour which in some circumstances would express camaraderie would in others express servility or despair. The difference will not necessarily be determined by what is in the mind or heart of the person whose behaviour is being interpreted. It is more likely to be determined by the circumstances in which he behaves. Perhaps he is the victim of sadism.

The point applied to Levi's example can be dramatised like this. Imagine one of the prisoners, overwhelmed by a sense that the game is grotesque, stops and cries, 'What are we doing!' The judgment that the football game expresses a sense of common humanity, rather than a grotesque parody of it, must be reflectively answerable to a challenge concerning its meaning. The cry, 'What are we doing' has an inexpungeably moral dimension. An answer to it may extend our sense of morality—of the nature of moral phenomena. It may even subvert some its categories. But it will be no answer if it seeks to avoid moral categories. Clendinnen would agree, I am sure.

One wants to say, and I think it is right to say, that everything in the death camps was saturated with their evil, and that this distinguishes them from the labour camps in the Soviet Union, for example. That is one of the reasons why the death camps are emblematic of the distinctive evil of the Holocaust, the kind that inclines people to say that it was unique. I don't say they are right to say this, but Clendinnen respects, as I do, the strong disposition to say it. Any gesture of kindness by the guards, and especially by the SS, seems sullied by the terrible realisation of their role in the death camps. But of course, to say that everything in the camps is saturated by their evil does not explain why no actions on the part of the perpetrators of that evil can survive being sullied by it. It is just to record that judgment.

Simone Weil writes in her fine essay, 'Human Personality':

> What is it, exactly, that prevents me from putting that man's eyes out if I am allowed to do so and if it takes my fancy?... What would stay [my hand] is the knowledge that if someone were to put out his eyes, his soul would be lacerated by the thought that harm was being done to him.
>
> At the bottom of the heart of every human being, from earliest infancy until the tomb, there is something that goes on indomitably expecting, in the teeth of all experience of crimes committed, suffered, and witnessed, that good and not evil will be done to him. It is this above all that is sacred in every human being.

The harm Weil speaks of is not primarily physical or psychological. It is the harm of being wronged. Confronted by someone who wrongs us, especially if it is a terrible wrong, we need a sign that he understands the wrong he has done, if there is to be anything between us that counts as a sense of common humanity. He must show that he hears the cry that Weil says is at the bottom of every human heart, even if it shows only in the way he turns away.

That cry was not put on hold during the football match. If it had been, the prisoners who played in it would not be capable of a human response, and therefore no sense of common humanity could exist between them and the SS. Simone Weil sometimes speaks as though the effects of terrible affliction can turn a human being into a thing. But if that cry was not extinguished in the members of the *Sonderkommando*, then it accompanied everything they did. Nothing in the behaviour of the SS shows that they heard it. Playing football and laughing with their victims does not of itself show they did, except perhaps as sadists do, which is why Levi says the game is demonic.

Perhaps someone could elaborate further and show that Clendinnen is right. I think it unlikely, but I do not want to insist that it could not be done. My purpose has been to show that any attempt to do so is answerable to the moral dimensions of the situation, and that the moral dimensions are sometimes only adequately represented by a distinctive concept of evil.

The first point does not depend on the second. It does depend, however, on the belief that a reading opposed to Levi's of what the football game means is answerable to the moral concepts that must be used in any adequate description of the circumstances in which the game is played. There are, of course, ways—moralistic ways—of using moral concepts which subvert any attempts to gain a deeper understanding of the situations in which they are deployed, but such corruptions no more speak against the need for moral concepts than reductionist psychological theories speak against the need for a psychological understanding that could inform a rich moral psychology.

Our sense of ourselves and others is partly morally conditioned because our ways of responding to others—our joys, our sorrows, and the many forms of our attachments—are answerable to the requirement that we are responsive to their independent reality, which means that we must acknowledge them as limits to our wills of the kind we record in concepts of obligation and moral necessity. Distinctions we draw between real and counterfeit love, grief or remorse, for example, are answerable to a sense of the independent reality of the other, which is in considerable part structured by those and other moral concepts. We do not need to moralise love in order to acknowledge that we would not count something as love—because we would not find it consistent with an acknowledgment of the independent reality of the beloved—if the lover found it unintelligible that the beloved could be wronged. Love asks to be celebrated and such celebrations should not be a black mass.

A similar story can be told about most, if not all, aspects of the inner life. Later I will develop the point. For the present I will merely note that as with those values we naturally call 'moral', so with the states that compose the inner life—our sense of them will be radically different according to whether or not we have serious use for a conception of the individual as unconditionally precious.

If we have it, we can hardly think of human life without it. Nor will we be able to think of human life without thinking of ourselves as essentially constituted by our relation to good and evil. Incredible though it may sound, that is the consequence of accepting that a conception of individuality, interdependent with a sense of good and evil, is central to our sense of the Other, and that our sense of the Other is central to our application of the distinction between the real and the counterfeit to our inner states. If that distinction is fundamental to the very being of those states, then it follows that the self is morally constituted and that it is constituted by a particular conception of good and evil for anyone who has a sense of the unconditional preciousness of each human being.

If that is so, then nothing which aims to deepen our understanding of the human condition—be it psychology, philosophy or art—can ignore the morally conditioned character of the inner life. No radical separation can legitimately be drawn between moral judgment and what Henry James called 'responsiveness to life', between moral judgment and a descriptive psychology of the inner life, or between moral judgment and the desire for understanding.

Any psychological account—be it empirical or novelistic—of the inner lives of the camp guards must acknowledge the ethically conditioned grammar of appearance and reality as it applies to the inner life, and also acknowledge the way it undermines favoured contrasts between description and judgment. We are ethically constituted. That is not a metaphysical or biological fact. In some sense of this dangerous phrase, it is dependent upon what human beings have historically *made of themselves*. But we cannot radically prescind from the ethical constitution of our inner lives without becoming unintelligible to ourselves. As things stand, for us to try to describe the inner life without reference to good and evil would be like trying to describe it without reference to our mortality or our vulnerability to misfortune.

Reminders that the death-camp guards were human beings and not monsters can mean more than one thing. It is a mistake flatly to endorse such reminders. Some human beings *are* monsters, in this sense: their deeds and their characters are so foul that there rightly appears no space in the characterisation of their lives and feelings in which one could imagine remorse to grow. It is a mistake to think that there *must* be something in their lives and characters which a psychologist or novelist could show to be the reason why we should acknowledge them as fully our fellow human beings. If we insist that the existence of such facts is a condition of that acknowledgment, then realism will eventually force us to condemn some of them as beyond the reach of our sense of a common humanity.

Justice Landau, the judge presiding over Adolf Eichmann's trial in Jerusalem, insisted to those who wished to make a show trial of it, that justice was its one and only purpose. From one perspective Justice Landau's point was about the procedures necessary to preserve the integrity of the court. From another (and of course these perspectives do not conflict) he gave voice to one of the sublime features of our system of criminal justice. Justice was owed to the man in the glass booth, not just for the sake of the court, or for the sake of future legal or political goods, but because it was owed to him as a human being, even though there was no doubt about his identity and about his terrible guilt. Only if justice were done for that reason, amongst others, would the integrity of the court be uncompromised.

So I read Justice Landau's remarks. I am able to do so because, wonderful though his protest was, it also expressed a commonplace of legal practice—namely, that no criminals are so foul that they may be denied justice. In its turn, that is an expression of the affirmation that all human beings are owed unconditional respect. The forms of that respect vary. In this case it consisted simply in insisting that the proper procedures of the court be followed against the very understandable temptation to do something that seemed much more important—to teach the world a lesson about the terrible significance of the Holocaust. In Kant's words, even Eichmann must be treated as an end in himself and never merely as a means to an end, however worthy it may be.

Some people were outraged by Justice Landau's rebuke to the Israeli prosecutor. Perhaps they will be by my words. I sympathise with them and believe that I understand their anger. I would go so far as to say that the belief that Eichmann should have been shot like a mad dog in the streets of Buenos Aires where he was captured by Israeli secret agents is a natural response of anyone who fully understands the terribleness of his deeds. Perhaps the temptation to it is even a criterion for such understanding.

Yet there is an irony here that is perhaps too terrible to be edifying. Anyone who fully understands the evil of Eichmann's deeds will understand why some people are inclined to say that the Holocaust is unique and unprecedented in its evil. It may be wrong to say that, but any account of why it is will be unconvincing unless it is morally faithful to what has driven many people to say it. Any account, whether it justifies or deflates that inclination, will, I believe, be inadequate unless it sees in the Holocaust a relentless and unprecedented assault on the preciousness of human beings, an assault that is partly conscious of its nature even when its victims are treated like vermin. If that is so, then a vivid appreciation of what drives some people to say that people like Eichmann should be shot like the vermin they believed the Jews to be, requires that we acknowledge such people as fully our fellow human beings, owed unconditional respect.

Beyond all sense and reason, beyond all the discoveries of science, literature and philosophy, that acknowledgment insists that we keep amongst us those evil-doers in whose lives and characters we can find no empirical basis for the assertion that they are fully our fellow human beings.

Racism:The Denial
of a Common Humanity

James Isdell was Protector of Aborigines in Western Australia in the
first decade of the twentieth century. Commenting on the forcible
removal of Aboriginal children of mixed blood from their parents,
he said that he 'would not hesitate for one moment to separate any
half-caste from its Aboriginal mother, no matter how frantic her
momentary grief might be at the time. They soon forget their
offspring.' When I read this in *Bringing Them Home*, the report on
the 'stolen children', I was reminded of a woman I knew when she
was grieving over her recently dead child. I shall call her M.

M was watching a television documentary on the Vietnam
War which showed the grief of Vietnamese women whose children were killed in bombing raids. At first she responded as
though she and the Vietnamese women shared a common affliction. Within minutes, however, she drew back and said, 'But it is
different for them. They can simply have more.' That remark could

mean different things in different contexts. Coming from her I knew it to be a racist remark of a kind I trust is easily recognisable. Isdell said much the same of Aboriginal mothers. M did not mean that whereas she was sterile they were not. Nor did she mean that as a matter of fact Vietnamese tended to have many children. Hers was not an anthropological observation. She meant that they could replace their dead children more or less as we replace dead pets.

Taking her remark as the expression of her racism we ascribe a certain kind of generality to it. We know it applies not just to Vietnamese women and their relation to their children, but to other aspects of the lives of the women and also of the men. It would not be so if we took it simply as an empirical remark, an anthropological observation for example, to the effect that Vietnamese have many children and tend to look upon them as replaceable. Treating what M said as an empirical remark, we would draw no inference about what it means. It could have racist implications of the kind I have been drawing out. Or, it might simply mean that for a variety of cultural reasons, that is how it now is with them and their children. Sometimes war, famine and other conditions cause people to treat children in that way. It need say nothing deep about their sensibility that it should be so. But because we take M's remark as expressive of her racism, we see immediately that it applies to all aspects of the inner lives of the Vietnamese.

We would misunderstand M's sense of the difference between herself and the Vietnamese women if we thought that she did not believe they suffered. After all, just like Isdell, she sees their 'frantic grief' and hears their anguished wailing. Her sense of difference centres on how she conceives what suffering may *mean* to the Vietnamese. She fails to see that it could mean anything deep and she takes this attitude to their entire inner life, to all their hopes, fears and joys whatever these may centre on. To be sure, she will admit that some of 'us'—the shallow ones amongst us—act as though their children are replaceable. When their children die they may actually have more in the spirit in which she thinks she cannot. Unlike the Vietnamese, however, they can be called upon to rise to the potentiality they have for something deeper. Unless, of course, they are incapable of it because they are, for example, mentally deficient. But then they are still one of 'us', contingently incapacitated, the victims of ill fortune.

In M's eyes, the Vietnamese are not contingently unable to rise to the requirements that are inseparable from the possibility of a deepened inner life, as might happen to a people if they suffer great hardships. To her, that is how they *essentially* are. That the shallow ones amongst us can be called upon to be true to a deeper potential is a conceptual condition of their being judged to be shallow, in the same way that it is a conceptual condition of being judged to be irrational that one could be called upon to rise to the requirements of reason. But M does not judge the Vietnamese mothers to be *shallow*. She responds to them as being *outside of the space of possibilities* which gives sense to judgments of depth and shallowness.

Peter Winch, a fine English philosopher, remarked that 'treating a person justly involves treating with seriousness his own conception of himself, his own commitments and cares, his own understanding of his situation and of what the situation demands of him.' That implies that to take seriously a person's conception of his commitments and cares is to be able to find it intelligible that he should explore those commitments and cares with an increasingly deepened understanding. It is to find it intelligible that he could have a rich or impoverished inner life. It is to see him as a potential partner in that conversational space in which we are answerable to the demand or to the plea that we try to invest our thoughts and words with the authority of an individually achieved lucidity. That lucidity is what we refer to when we speak of people finding their own voice, of 'having something to say'. Failing all that, we can have, at best, only an attenuated sense of what it is seriously to wrong them. If 'they' can 'simply have more', then if we rape them or kill their children or forcibly take their children from them, we cannot wrong them in the way we wrong one another.

There could be no serious discussion between M and a Vietnamese mother whose child had been killed about death, about sexuality or about motherhood. Neither could call upon the other to make herself adequate to what she is trying to fathom in her grief. Dostoyevsky prayed that he would be deserving of his sufferings. If M could find it intelligible that Vietnamese mothers could do the same, then she would no longer say, 'It's different for them.' The examples I have given of what lies beyond discussion for M and the Vietnamese—motherhood, sexuality, death and grief—are obvious ones. As soon as one reflects on what they imply, it is evident that it includes virtually everything that we would discuss in response to questions about life's meaning, or to the question, how should one live?

Victims of racism often say they are treated as 'sub-human'. In many cases—perhaps the majority—that is not even slightly an exaggeration. We can see from what I have been saying about M how radically demeaning her attitude is, how literally dehumanising—because it denies its victims any possibility of responding with depth and lucidity to the defining features of the human condition. In a natural sense of the word 'human'—when it is not used to refer simply to the species *homo sapiens* and when it is not explicitly morally inflected, as when we exclaim, 'What a human being!'—those who are deemed incapable of an inner life of any depth and complexity are rightly said to be treated as less than fully human, as sub-human.

I have emphasised that M finds it *unintelligible* that the sufferings of the Vietnamese mothers could go deep. The kind of incomprehension I have in mind may become clearer if we reflect on why we could not cast someone with the kind of face caricatured in 'The Black and White Minstrel Show' to play Othello. Most accounts of racism assume that if racists are sincerely (if self-deceivingly) mistaken about the objective characteristics of, say, blacks or Asians, and if that error is connected with how (physically) they appear to them, then those appearances constitute only a contingent psychological obstacle to racists objectively appreciating how things really are.

The 'Black and White Minstrel Show' face presents more than a merely psychological obstacle, however, to our acknowledgment that behind such a face there might be a soul capable of all the magnificence and misery of Othello. We cannot, I think, so radically divorce our conception of an inner life from the forms of its expression. We would be bewildered by the suggestion that we are unduly influenced by mere surfaces—by the expressive possibilities in faces or in voices or in the inflexions of the human form. Tempting though it is, I am sure that it is wrong to believe that we would be bewildered because we have become so accustomed to certain forms of expression or to certain matchings of forms of expression with psychological states that we are merely resistant to new forms and new matchings. If that were true, then we could at least *try* to overcome our prejudices and to accept that someone whose features we believe are justly caricatured by the 'Black and White Minstrel Show' face could feel as Othello does. But that we cannot even try to do, because even to try presupposes a degree of dissociation of feeling from expression which this example shows to be impossible.

The 'Black and White Minstrel Show' face was a caricature which revealed how many whites saw Afro-American faces. As reflected in the caricature, those faces did not appear to white racists as only accidentally incapable of expressing anything deep, as the face of a white person who was terribly disfigured in an accident would. The racist's thought is 'that is how they look', *essentially*, and the fact that they look like that to him is fundamental to what makes them 'them' and to why he finds it inconceivable that they should be treated as 'one of us'.

We find this hard to accept because we have deep prejudices

against attributing anything important to people on account of how they look. We think that is superficial. Our resistance has deep philosophical as well as moral and religious roots. Faces, we think, belong to the surface. The soul is deep below all surfaces. That is why we accord undue weight to the empirical, sometimes pseudo-scientific, rationalisations racists offer in defence of their attitudes. We accord such weight to them, not because we believe them or even take them seriously, but because we think they make racist behaviour more intelligible than it would be if it were essentially a response to how someone looks. Not even racists can be that superficial, we think.

Most psychological theories of racism assume that all forms of racism are basically the same and that racists recognise the full humanity of those they denigrate, but that they rationalise the complex and deep causes of their hostility in stereotypes which suggest that they don't. It is almost commonplace in psychological studies of racism that racists do not really believe what they say when they try to justify their attitudes and behaviour. Study after study of racism tells us that the rationalisations racists offer to support their attitudes towards those whom they denigrate are not vulnerable to argument and to evidence in ways that reckless generalisations and careless inferences usually are.

Complex and deep psychological causes, we are told, drive racists to evade evidence that bears on their stereotypes, unless of course they consider it to be favourable. It goes with this way of looking at the matter to suggest two consequences of the way blacks appear to white racists. Either those appearances tempt racists into sincere but false beliefs of an empirical kind (no one who looks like that has the brain power to do physics; anyone who looks like that must have uncontrollable sexual desires, for example). Or those appearances reinforce and deepen the psychological incapacity of racists to attend, with even a semblance of objectivity, to the evidence. Put more generally, it is assumed that how blacks look to white racists constitutes only a contingent—

though often overwhelmingly powerful—psychological obstacle to racists objectively appreciating how things really are.

It is often true. The sense of difference that really drives the kind of racism that I have been describing—expressed by M when she said, 'They can just have more'—is necessarily vague. 'They' can do and feel almost everything we can except not as we do, not as deeply we do. We grieve, but they 'grieve', we are joyful, they are 'joyful', we love and they 'love', we feel remorse, they feel 'remorse' and so on. And through this denigration of their inner lives runs a denigration of how it is possible for them to think and reflect, because central to our conception of the states that compose the inner life is a distinction between their real and false semblances. We distinguish real love from infatuation, real grief from maudlin self-indulgence, and that we do so is fundamental to our sense of the kinds of states they are—to their very existence. The inner lives of blacks and Asians are placed in inverted commas by white racists because they cannot believe there could be any depth in them.

Impressed by the necessary vagueness of how racists seem to think 'we' differ from 'them', we are inclined to think those characterisations are not really important and cannot be what is at the heart of racist attitudes. We might think M and Isdell cannot mean what they say. That would be a mistake. They mean it, although such is the effect of anti-racist sentiment that many racists might now mean it a little unsurely. Their incredulity at the suggestion that one could wrong 'them' as we can wrong one another is genuine. James Isdell would have been sincerely incredulous at the suggestion that an Aboriginal mother's soul could be lacerated by the loss of her child.

Racists are themselves sometimes embarrassed by all this and fall back with some relief on more determinate factual claims to support their denigratory attitudes. Blacks have lower IQs. They smell. They are lazy. They have uncontrollable sexual appetites and so on. These are often called stereotypes, and in the psychological literature they are usually treated as rationalisations both in the sense of rendering rational and in the sense of using reason to hide rather than to reveal the truth. Occasionally, especially when racism becomes an ideology, those stereotypes are elaborated in pseudo-scientific theories.

Achieving a clear understanding of this is difficult partly because of serious ambiguity in the concepts we use to characterise racist attitudes. We say, for example, that racists are mistaken about the psychological and intellectual capacities possessed by those whom they denigrate, and that their mistake can be demonstrated by the disciplines which study these things, psychology, biology and so on. We point out that, given the right kind of experiences, racism can fall away.

Words like 'capacity' (or 'property'), 'empirical' and 'experience' can, however, take our thoughts to very different places. If racists say that blacks are not as intelligent as whites, then they may mean something which could be shown to be true or false by a study of their comparative achievements on IQ tests. But racists may mean that blacks are incapable of the kind of understanding they would need to understand what Othello says and feels. In the former but not in the latter case, it makes sense to speak of gathering evidence and of deploying such evidence—from psychological or sociological studies, for example—in argument. When I say that it is intelligible I mean that those concepts get some purchase, that they are appropriate concepts even though the psychology of racism may convince us that it would be pointless to deploy them in argument with racists. In the latter case, where a racist asserts that blacks do not have the kind of understanding which would enable them to play Othello, that essentially they are the kinds of beings who lack it—experience may show him that he is mistaken, but, for reasons I hope to make convincing, it is not experience as we speak of it when we speak of the empirical results of scientific studies.

We naturally take it, and we are encouraged by most psychological accounts of racism to take it, that the denigratory claims made by racists are of a kind that can be assessed by social scientists, perhaps with help from biologists, that their results could be recorded in journals and books and, if they are sufficiently corroborated, in encyclopaedias. It is a corollary of this way of looking at the matter that we can come to see how things stand in reality with a racially denigrated people by reading books about them. For psychological reasons, we may think, some of us—the racists amongst us—may be deeply reluctant to accept these findings, but it is possible, at least in principle, for a person to say truthfully that extensive reading of reputable authorities convinced her that none of the stereotypes she had believed about blacks are true. The theory, then, is basically that racists are hostile to their victims for deep psychological reasons which are often instinctively exploited by politicians, and that racists rationalise (both in the sense of making rational to themselves and in the sense of hiding from themselves and others) the nature of their hostility by appeal to stereotypes which have the form of empirical generalisations about the nature and capacities of their victims.

Such an account of racism directed against people whose skin colour and whose facial features are significantly different is mistaken, at least when racism is not on the defensive (as all forms of it now are) in the face of widespread anti-racist sentiment. It is mistaken, moreover, in a way that it obscures the degree to which such racism is a denial of the full humanity of its victims.

If racists cannot accept arguments against their stereotypes because the psychological obstacles which prevent them are so powerful, then it must make sense, even if it is unrealistic, to urge them to try to be more open to reality, perhaps not directly, but by means of a strategy. Why must it? Because that is part of what we mean by calling an obstacle 'psychological', distinguishing it, for example, from moral or logical obstacles. By contrast, if someone says that morally she cannot give out certain information because it would amount to betraying a trust, then one would have misunderstood what she had said or be cruelly cynical if one replied,

'Why don't you try? Let me help you devise a method to make it easier.' Imagine saying that to Luther when he declared, 'Here I stand. I can do no other.' And if someone were to say, 'I must conclude, after agreeing that all men are mortal and that Socrates is a man, that Socrates is mortal,' then only in a Monty Python or Goon Show script would we hear the reply, 'Don't be such a wimp. Try not to.'

The kind of impossibility we encounter when we realise that we cannot cast faces that look like the 'Black and White Minstrel Show' face to play Othello, because it is unintelligible that such a face could express the necessary depth of feeling, is neither a moral nor a logical impossibility. But like those forms of impossibility, it makes nonsense of any suggestion that those who experience it should try to overcome it. Therefore, it is not psychological difficulty, of the kind that might be caused by complex defence mechanisms. Nor is it a psychological difficulty of the kind that might be caused by contingent limitations in our understanding. Not even God could make sense of the claim that the 'Black and White Minstrel Show' face has the expressive possibilities needed to play Othello. No more than He could make sense of the proposition that there are square circles. Once we see that, we understand that the generality expressed in the belief that a face like that cannot play Othello is not an empirical generalisation. We see too that M was not expressing an empirical generalisation when she said 'They can just have more.'

When a racist points to a black or an Asian face and says (implicitly) that someone who looks like that can easily replace her children when they die, is not expressing an opinion that has been built up, by him or by others, from observation of similar instances. It is true that racists sometimes give up such denigratory beliefs because they have had certain experiences, generally because they have lived with the people they had denigrated. But 'experience' is a tricky word, just as 'capacity' is a tricky word. For complex reasons we assimilate it to the concept of the empirical as that lends itself to the idea of building up understanding by means of generalisations supported by confirming instances. But coming, through living with a people, to see dignity in faces that had all looked alike to us, to see the full range of human expressiveness in them, to hear suffering that lacerates the soul in someone's cry or in their music, or to see it in their art, to hear all the depth of language in sounds that had seemed merely comical to us—all or any of that is quite different from coming to acknowledge that they score well on IQ tests. We do not discover the full humanity of a racially denigrated people in books by social scientists, or not at any rate if those books merely contain knowledge of the kind that might be included in encyclopaedias. If we discover it by reading, then it is in plays, novels and poetry, in other words not in science but in art. For such books to be published, however, and for them to reach a reasonably wide audience, the days of that kind of racism must be numbered.

I hope it is now clear how carefully we must attend to the language used by racists and of the language we use in reflecting on them. Racists are, assuredly, 'mistaken about how things are'; in some sense of that tricky expression they are mistaken about the 'facts of the matter'; in some sense of that tricky expression 'experience' might teach them to see things differently. But if we regiment what we might mean with those expressions under a prototype that makes science the perfection of factual knowledge, of knowledge gained through experience, then we will fail to understand the most important aspect of some kinds of racism. We will fail to see the difference between the racist claim that blacks have little brainpower and the claim that having children and caring for them cannot mean to them what it means to us.

Not all racism is of the kind I have been describing, although reflection on why one could not cast a 'Black and White Minstrel Show' face to play Othello sheds light, I believe, on the nature and importance of caricatures in all racist propaganda—caricatures of the kind to be found for example in *Der Stürmer*, the infamous

Nazi propaganda magazine. Anti-Semitism is, I am sure, a more complex phenomenon than the racism of white against black, and I suspect it is not just one kind of thing over its shamefully long history. As the philosopher Tony Skillen has observed, 'If Jewish people are a paradigmatic object of racist hate, Black people are standard targets of racist contempt. (English Nazis proclaim that they don't hate blacks, because they are like children manipulated for purposes of world domination by the wicked Jews!)'

During historically the most evil manifestation of anti-Semitism, the indescribably cruel humiliations that the Nazis inflicted on the Jews appeared to presuppose exactly the depth of inner being that white racists deny their black victims. Here is an example amongst countless others in the Holocaust literature. It is from Chaim Kaplan's *Warsaw Diary*:

> A rabbi in Lodz was forced to spit on a Torah scroll that was in the Holy Ark. In fear of his life, he complied and desecrated that which is holy to him and to his people. After a short while he had no more saliva, his mouth was dry. To the Nazi's question, why did he stop spitting, the rabbi replied that his mouth was dry. The son of the 'superior race' began to spit in the rabbi's mouth, and the rabbi continued to spit on the Torah.

To do what he so clearly intended with exquisite sadistic refinement, the Nazi had to understand what it means to the rabbi to spit on the Torah. He did not think the rabbi had only an inverted commas understanding of what it means for something to be holy.

Different though anti-Semitism may be from racism directed against colour, at least when such racism is not defensive, as it almost always is nowadays, these forms of racism share an important feature which I suspect inclines psychologists to believe that all forms of racism have a common psychological structure. I have remarked on it before, and it distinguishes racism from ethnic hatreds of the kind shown between many Serbs, Croats and Muslims in the former Yugoslavia.

Recall that in most accounts of racism it is a commonplace that the reasons racists give to explain their attitudes and behaviour are not the reasons that actually motivate them. Anti-Semites might give a number of reasons why they hate Jews. The reasons are of a kind that would make hatred of Jews understandable in anyone who accepted them. But the radical imperviousness of these beliefs to evidence and to reason makes it clear that they do not stand to the attitudes and actions of anti-Semites as beliefs normally do to the attitudes and actions they explain. This is so even when in the normal—that is, non-anti-Semitic—case the beliefs combine with a hatred so deep that they make the person who feels it invulnerable to reason.

Some Serbs, Croats and Muslims feel this kind of hatred towards one another. A mixture of half-truths, sustained by lies, enlisted into the support of a murderous hatred by cunning leaders, their beliefs are hardened against reason by the ravages of war. But even then they remain in principle open to evidence and to reason. It was so in the past and, I am confident, it will be again. Oversimplifying a little, only passion stands in the way of the combatants seeing for what they are the half-truths and lies they believe, and which, unlike the stereotypes professed by racists, genuinely motivate them. In this we have a familiar, if dismaying, manifestation of a common relation between beliefs and passions. It may be astonishingly naive, but it would not show a misunderstanding of the psychological nature of what one is confronted with, to adopt strategies to calm someone in the grip of ethnic hatred so that they could stand back from their beliefs in order to assess them rationally.

Occasionally something similar to ethnic hatred, different from anti-Semitism, occurs in relations between Jews and Gentiles. It occurred in 1995 in Australia during the Demidenko debate. Helen Demidenko's novel *The Hand That Signed the Paper* was about Ukrainian participation in the Holocaust, and many Australians—Jews and others—felt it was anti-Semitic. Naturally Jews were hurt and shaken that such a novel should be honoured by receiving the Miles Franklin Award, the country's most distinguished literary prize. The subsequent fuss, reported and inflamed almost daily for a period of three or so months, became one of Australia's longest and most bitter literary controversies. It took a bizarre twist when the author, who had called herself Helen Demidenko, and claimed to be the descendant of Ukrainians murdered by 'Bolshevik Jews', turned out to be Helen Darville, born in Scunthorpe, Yorkshire, with no connections whatsoever with the Ukraine.

Amongst some of the intelligentsia the controversy took the lid off long-standing irritation with Jews caused, I think, by distaste with what some make of the Holocaust, and with the antics of a politically influential Jewish lobby. The irritation expressed itself in half-truths and ill-informed generalisations whose content was unnervingly similar to anti-Semitic stereotypes. Context often enabled one to tell the difference, but sometimes it was difficult and so, in my judgment, what was not anti-Semitism was often taken to be that. This irritation with Jews had essentially the same psychological structure as ethnic hatred, although it was not nearly so nasty. It was actually motivated by the partially rational beliefs that expressed it, beliefs which consisted of half-truths, reckless generalisations, and which were, for a time, beyond the reach of reason because the conflict generated such strong emotions. If one did not see the difference between this and anti-Semitism one might assimilate anti-Semitism to it and think that an anti-Semite is someone who stubbornly sticks to his rationally ill-supported beliefs, partly because he knows no better and partly because his passions are inflamed.

Reduction of anti-Semitism to a form of ethnic hatred, at least in the Ukrainians, is indeed the didactic purpose of Darville's novel—a purpose I think Australian Jews instinctively recognised and feared. According to Darville, Ukrainian hatred of the Jews was understandable, perhaps even justified, as a response to the role Jews allegedly played in the Bolshevik oppression of the Ukrainian people, especially to the role they played in the great famine in which over five million people perished. Darville invites us to attribute the lusty participation of Ukrainian peasants in the murder of hundreds of thousands of Jews at Babi Yar and Treblinka to their hasty and extensive generalisation of things they knew and had seen, generalisations they believed intensely because of what they had suffered and which were exploited by the Nazis. She makes no mention in her novel of the long and murderous history of Ukrainian anti-Semitism.

The significance of that does not lie in the mere fact that Darville's novel is untruthful about when Ukrainian hatred of Jews started. It lies in the fact that, in suggesting that it started when Ukrainians came to believe that Jews were massively implicated in Bolshevik oppression, she denies the hatred was the expression of anti-Semitism. She thereby sidetracks the otherwise obvious thought that Ukrainian vulnerability to the stereotype of the Jewish Bolshevik was not the cause of a Jew-hatred which was like the ethnic hatreds in the former Yugoslavia, but the expression of their anti-Semitism.

The fact that anti-Semitic hatred does not relate to the stereotypes which are offered to justify it, as ethnic hatred relates to the beliefs cited to justify it, is why anti-Semitism and other forms of racism fascinate psychologists. It has been said that if Jews did not exist anti-Semites would have to invent them. The thought is that anti-Semitism and other forms of racism serve deep psychological and social needs which one will never understand if one approaches them equipped only with the conceptual resources needed to understand ethnic hatred.

Nothing I have said is fundamentally at odds with this insight about the nature of most forms of racism. Nor, I think, is it at odds with the importance, of which the philosopher Tamas Pataki convinced me, of giving an account of the many psychological needs which racism satisfies. An adequate psychology of racism, especially of racism when it is defensive, will explain many things that cannot be explained by the account I gave when I elaborated on M's response to the Vietnamese. One should not assume, however, when constructing theories to account for the nature of racist rationalisations, that racists must really know in their hearts that their victims are fully human. Such theories will distort the nature of racism directed at people whose skin colour is different and the difference of such racism from anti-Semitism, as in fact they often have done. The assumption that racism is a psychologically motivated denial of the empirical characteristics of those who are its victims makes one blind to that difference and it closes the door to the understanding afforded by reflection on M's racism.

Anti-racism is one of the great movements of the postwar period. It can hardly be doubted that the world is a better place for it even though foolish things have been said and done in its name and even though unjust accusations of racism have actually contributed to racism. Like feminism, to which it has been both aligned and compared, it has expressed a concern for equality which cannot adequately be captured in talk of equal access to goods and opportunities. Treat me as a person, see me fully as a human being, as fully your equal, without condescension—these are not demands for things whose value lies in the degree to which they enable one to get other things. These are calls to justice conceived as equality of respect, calls to become part of a constituency within which claims for equity of access to goods and opportunities may appropriately be pressed. It is justice of the kind often called social justice because of its insistence that our state and civic institutions should, to the degree that is humanly possible, reveal rather than obscure the full humanity of our fellow citizens.

Justice beyond Fairness:
Mabo & Social Justice

In 1992 the High Court of Australia granted Australian Aborigines native title to some lands taken from them when the continent was settled. The court's decision was in response to Eddie Mabo's petition for native title in part of the Meriam Islands, off the coast of Queensland. The case is now generally referred to as 'Mabo'.

The High Court's principal conclusions were these. First, that many of the applications of *terra nullius* (to the mainland of Australia and elsewhere) were the expressions of a racist blindness to the depth of the indigenous peoples' relationship to the land. Secondly, and following from the first, that at the time of settlement the relation to the land of many of the Aboriginal peoples would render unjust all property laws which depended on the assumption that the land was *terra nullius*. Thirdly, that the resulting injustices which were committed and perpetuated in Australian law were within the court's legitimate power to rectify.

The court rejected previous applications of the concept of *terra nullius* because those applications assumed a conception of ownership that was too narrow. In a lecture to the Samuel Griffith Society that was much admired and whose arguments were often borrowed by conservative critics of Mabo, S. E. K. Hulme, QC, gave a clear statement of that narrow conception of property. *Terra nullius*, he said:

> ...meant that the soil was the property of no one, either because there was no one there at all, or more normally because the people who might from time to time pass over it or hunt on it had no concept of individual ownership of it. It was the soil, not the country—there was no 'country' yet—which was not 'occupied'; was not 'settled'. Nothing turned on the reason for that, but the usual one was that the nomadic and hunting life of those who were from time to time present had never created the need for such a concept.

Such a conception of property informed earlier rejections of petitions for native title. Justice Blackburn's judgment in the early 1970s is particularly interesting in this connection. He relied on a conception of ownership similar to Hulme, but in his judgment he recorded a deeply respectful appreciation of the Aborigines' relation to the land:

> The spiritual relation is well proved...The evidence seems to me to show that the aboriginals have a more cogent feeling of obligation to the land than of ownership of it. It is dangerous to attempt to express a matter so subtle and difficult by a mere aphorism, but it seems easier, on the evidence, to say that the clan belongs to the land than that the land belongs to the clan.

A fascinating tension lies at the heart of this judgment. Justice Blackburn acknowledged that the Aboriginal peoples' spiritual relationships to the land are deeper than can be conveyed by the notion of ownership as he took it to be defined in common law. Yet he would not accept that those relationships to the land entailed a 'burden' on the Crown. But, for reasons I give below, to acknowledge the depth of the relationship is to undermine the power of the doctrine of *terra nullius* to *justify* settlement, and therefore to undermine the legitimacy of many of its applications.

Few would now deny that people suffer a grave injustice if they are forced from land to which they have the kind of relationship Justice Blackburn described. As far as I know, Justice Blackburn did not deny it. The nature of that injustice is revealed by (amongst others) the concept of dispossession as we normally use it outside legal contexts. Legal definitions of land ownership will, therefore, justify settlement that forces indigenous peoples from land in which they have invested their spiritual substance, only if those definitions are answerable to those concepts whose use in ordinary speech *is interdependent with* our understanding of justice. Definitions which condescend to the use of such concepts in our ordinary ways of speaking will rightly be accused of legalism in the pejorative sense of that term. Because they refuse to be answerable to a conception of justice that transcends the narrowly defined observance of legal practices, those definitions will also debase the law into a system for rationalising the brute exercise of power.

Of course there are many people who say that that is what the law essentially is; and there are others who say that that is what it all too often is. But unless one takes the former nihilistic view, one will need to acknowledge that the doctrine of *terra nullius* could effectively rationalise and disguise imperial interests only if it was not seriously offensive to a sense of natural justice. A lucid sense of natural justice should be offended unless ownership and the sense of dispossession which ordinary speech marks as a grave injustice are mutually defining. And that is the source of the tension in Justice Blackburn's judgment. Once he had acknowledged the depth of the indigenous peoples' relationship to the land, he had effectively acknowledged their dispossession in the full moral sense of that term. The only way then to rescue the law from complicity in grave injustice would be to reject the narrow conception of property assumed in previous applications of *terra nullius*.

Justice Blackburn's judgment therefore pressed to its limits the tension between the acknowledgment that indigenous peoples may have a relationship to the land as deep as he described it to be, and appeal to the doctrine of *terra nullius* to justify settlement of lands which they had occupied. Our sense of the authority and dignity of law, by virtue of which we consent without servility to its jurisdiction over us, depends on our seeing it as answerable to a conception of justice that transcends and guides its practices and proscriptions. The die was cast for Mabo.

Such, broadly, seems to have been the view of Justices Brennan, Deane and Gaudron, the most prominent of the six High Court judges who found in favour of Eddie Mabo. The concept of native title expresses the acknowledgment that justice required that the Aboriginal peoples' relationship to the land be seen as 'a burden on the Crown's radical title'. In his dissenting judgment Justice Dawson claimed that the law permitted the Crown to 'treat the land as its own to dispose of without regard to such interests as the natives might have had prior to the assumption of sovereignty'. Land rights granted to the Aborigines on *that* assumption would be inconsistent with proper acknowledgment of their dispossession. That is why the substance of native title is rightly defined by the laws and customs of the Aboriginal peoples concerned. Those laws and customs both constitute and express their relationship to the land, a relationship we acknowledge when we acknowledge their dispossession. Justices Deane and Gaudron expressed this when, in support of a Privy Council judgment that 'traditional interests of the native inhabitants...[may be]...of a kind unknown to English law', they characterised native title as *sui generis*. Justice Brennan did the same when he said that 'Native title, though recognised by the common law, is not an institution of the common law.'

The Justices argued, forcefully and without a trace of ambiguity, that the applications of *terra nullius* to determine the land-holding relations between indigenous and non-indigenous Australians resulted in grave injustices which had shamed the common law. Justice Brennan, for example, said:

> According to the cases, the common law itself took from indigenous inhabitants any right to occupy their traditional land, exposed them to deprivation of the religious, cultural and economic sustenance which the land provides, vested the land effectively in the control of the Imperial authorities without any right to compensation and made the indigenous inhabitants intruders in their own homes and mendicants for a place to live. Judged by any civilized standard, such a law is unjust and its claim to be part of the common law to be applied in contemporary Australia must be questioned.

That questioning entailed an inquiry into the way *terra nullius* had been applied to analogous cases—although, of course, which cases *were* analogous was itself part of the inquiry. Obviously the application of *terra nullius* depended upon assumptions about the customs and institutions of the relevant indigenous peoples. It is common knowledge that in some cases those customs and institutions were profoundly misunderstood because of a racist blindness to what they might mean. Such misunderstandings were an expression of what Justice Brennan called 'discriminatory denigration'. He quoted Lord Summers speaking for the Privy Council in 1919 about Southern Rhodesia:

> The estimation of the rights of aboriginal tribes is always inherently difficult. Some tribes are so low in the scale of social organization that their usages and conceptions of rights and duties are not to be reconciled with the institutions or the legal ideas of civilized society. Such a gulf cannot be bridged. It would be idle to impute to such

people some shadow of the rights known to our law and then to transmute it into the substance of transferable rights of property as we know them.

We love, but they 'love'; we grieve but they 'grieve' and, of course, we may be dispossessed but they are 'dispossessed'. That is why, as Justice Brennan said, racists are able 'utterly to disregard' the sufferings of their victims. If they are to see the evil they do, they must first find it intelligible that their victims have inner lives of the kind which enable the wrongs they suffer to go deep. But that is exactly what they do not find intelligible. I think that is what Justice Brennan had in mind when he spoke of discrimination that 'denies the *capacity* [my emphasis] of some categories of indigenous inhabitants to have any rights or interests in land'. As I understand them, Justices Brennan, Deane and Gaudron believed that the law that was invoked to determine the case of the Meriam Islanders could only have become the settled law of Australia because of racially conditioned blindness to the fact that the land was not *terra nullius* at the time of its settlement. That same blindness prevented the law from coming earlier to that point of tension which makes Justice Blackburn's judgment such an interesting one.

To summarise this part of my argument. The significance of the High Court's judgment lies in its acknowledgment that Aborigines had lived under property laws that were based on a doctrine whose application dispossessed them of their lands. Worse, it effectively denied their full human status because it denied the depth of moral and spiritual being which alone makes dispossession such a terrible affliction and, thereby, a terrible injustice. For that reason, the concept of native title is essentially the acknowledgment of the meaning of the Aboriginal peoples' dispossession. In the historical context of Australia, that is no less than a belated recognition of their full humanity, because it is the recognition that they are beings with inner lives of the same depth and complexity as 'ours' and that therefore they can be wronged as seriously as we can be. Justice Brennan made the point explicitly when he said that in many cases the application of *terra nullius* denied 'the capacity of some categories of indigenous peoples to have any rights or interests in land'; it expressed a perception of them as beings so 'low' and 'barbarous' (Lord Summers) that their claims could be 'utterly disregarded'.

For many of the settlers, the Aborigines were not the kind of limit to our will, to our interests and desires, that we mark when we speak of respecting someone's rights, or treating them as ends rather than as means, or of according them unconditional respect, and so on. Of course, not all the settlers were like that, nor was such racism always expressed in the acts and institutions of the colonial government. The acceptance of *terra nullius* as a concept, however, which could justify settlement in Australia and elsewhere was, I believe, the expression of the kind of racism that finds literally unintelligible the thought that its victims could seriously be wronged.

We are now in a better position to understand aspects of the High Court's 1992 judgment which excited much hostile comment. Critics asked why a case about the Meriam Islanders was applied to the Aborigines of the mainland and, also, why so little factual detail about either the Islanders or the mainland Aborigines was treated as relevant to the judgment.

The answer to both questions goes roughly like this. According to the majority of the Justices, the settled law relevant to the Islanders was tainted by the racist application of *terra nullius* to the mainland and elsewhere. If, as the Justices claimed, this was the expression of a blindness to the full humanity of those whose dispossession had been justified by the application of *terra nullius*, then it would be odious to call for evidence to determine whether the Islanders were relevantly different from those whose claim to native title had been rejected.

Justice Brennan saw with admirable clarity that comparisons between the Islanders and the Aborigines on the mainland would amount to an attempt to determine whether the Islanders were 'higher' in the scale of humanity than the mainland Aborigines. It cannot be the business of a court in a civilised community to inquire into how people stand in relation to others who had been deemed less than fully human. The only decent thing to do was to jettison the doctrine of *terra nullius* and to change whatever law was infected by its racist applications. When the justices invoked contemporary values they assumed no more than agreement on this. Critics from the right have warned that the Justices were mistaken to count on such agreement. God help us if that is so.

In her essay, 'Human Personality', Simone Weil writes:

> If you say to someone who has ears to hear: 'What you are doing to me is not just', you may touch and awaken at its source the spirit of attention and love. But it is not the same with words like 'I have the right...' or 'you have no right to...' They evoke a latent war and awaken the spirit of contention. To place the notion of rights at the centre of social conflicts is to inhibit any possible impulse of charity on both sides.
>
> Relying almost exclusively on this notion, it becomes impossible to keep one's eyes on the real problem. If someone tries to browbeat a farmer to sell his eggs at a moderate price, the farmer can say: 'I have the right to keep my eggs if I don't get a good enough price.' But if a young girl is being forced into a brothel she will not talk about her rights. In such a situation the word would sound ludicrously inadequate.

Weil's point, and my argument thus far, has serious implication for the tendency to theorise justice as essentially a species of fairness. The Aborigines were certainly the victims of terrible injustices. Yet it would have been ludicrous for them to express the affliction they suffered through their dispossession by protesting that they had been treated unfairly—as ludicrous as the protestation of her rights by the young girl in Weil's example. It would also have been absurd in the same way if they had protested that it was unfair that some of the laws of their country were based on the assumption that they were not fully human.

Acknowledgment of someone as fully human is an act of justice of a different kind from those acts of justice which are rightly described as forms of fairness. Fairness is at issue only when the full human status of those who are protesting their unfair treatment is not disputed. When they centre on the distribution of goods or access to opportunities and such things, concerns about equity presuppose a more fundamental level of equality of respect. If you are taken as fully 'one of us', then your protestation that equity demands that you receive higher wages or be granted better promotion prospects, for example, is probably an appeal to justice as fairness. If, however, you are regarded as subhuman, then it would be ludicrous for you even to consider pressing such claims, unless as a device to dramatise the radically different kind of equality that is really at issue.

Avishai Margalit, an Israeli philosopher, made known, perhaps, to many Australians by the praise Martin Krygier bestowed on him in his Boyer Lectures, calls a 'decent' society one whose institutions do not humiliate. Margalit is onto something important, but the quasi-technical meaning he ascribes to 'decency' prevents him from catching it. He fails, I think, because he assumes that justice as a political concept, describing relations between citizens and between citizens and their institutions, is a species of fairness and he therefore cannot capture what he is after. But if I am right in claiming that Mabo was the acknowledgment in law of the full humanity of Aborigines, the acknowledgment that they, like us, had relations to the land that would make dispossession a terrible crime; and if I am also right in claiming that acknowledgment to be an act of justice, then it is justice of a kind that could only be parodied in the claim that the Aborigines had at last been treated decently.

The justice done by Mabo is deeper than anything that can

be captured by concepts of equity as they apply to people's access to goods. It brought indigenous Australians into the constituency within which they could intelligibly press claims about unfair treatment. How much or how little land should be given was not, therefore, what was most seriously at issue when the High Court sat. The need to grant native title would have been as important and as urgent if it were clear that hardly any land claims would be lodged, a fact that was somewhat obscured, even by those who appreciated it, by talk of the 'symbolic value' of the rejection of *terra nullius*. 'Symbolic value' is a woefully inadequate expression, for it invites contrast with what is substantial and practical. But if what is practical has to do with what is important, then it was a matter of urgent practical concern to change laws which implicitly denied some citizens the respect which is unconditionally owed to all human beings.

Talk of the symbolic value of native title makes many supporters of Mabo nervous. To many of them symbolic value appears to be *merely* symbolic. That is partly because they find it hard fully to accept justice as a good *sui generis*—at least when they reflect on the matter. By 'justice as a good *sui generis*' I mean that the value of justice, what we prize—and indeed cherish—in it, can never entirely be accounted for in terms of the natural benefits it brings. And the terribleness of injustice—the *kind* of terribleness that it is—can never entirely be explained by the natural harms attendant on it. Those who are the victims of injustice suffer not merely certain determinate forms of natural harm—physical or psychological damage, for example—but also the injustice of their infliction, which is a distinct and irreducible source of torment to them. Simone Weil expressed it beautifully in her essay 'Forms of the Implicit Love of God' when she said that:

> …the just must be thanked for being just, because justice is so beautiful a thing, in the same way as we thank God because of his great glory. Any other gratitude is servile and even animal.

The only difference between the man who witnesses an act of justice and the man who receives a material advantage from it is that in such circumstances the beauty of justice is only a spectacle for the first, while for the second it is the object of a contact and even a kind of nourishment.

That should alert us to something deeply wrong about the discontent amongst many modern conservatives with the concept of social justice. It was clearly expressed by the English political philosopher John Gray, in his influential book *Beyond the New Right*. Gray says, 'The bottom line in political morality is thus never justice or rights, but instead the individual well-being which they protect and the common form of life in which it is realised.' He quotes an eloquent formulation of the point by an Oxford colleague, Joseph Raz:

> What makes us care about the various inequalities is not the inequality but the concern identified by the underlying principle. It is the hunger of the hungry, the need of the needy, the suffering of the ill, and so on. The fact that they are worse off in the relevant respect than their neighbours is relevant. But it is relevant not as an independent evil of inequality. Its relevance is in showing that their hunger is greater, their need more pressing, their suffering more hurtful, and therefore our concern for the hungry, the needy, the suffering and not our concern for equality makes us give them priority.

Gray and Raz have in their sights those who insist on a distributivist conception of justice in ways that blind them to the fact that significant structural inequality in a society does not entail that anyone is wronged by it. I think that they are right in that. The harm suffered by victims of injustice, however, is never merely material or psychological harm. And the harm which is the injustice—distinct from and irreducible to the kinds of harm Gray and Raz have in mind—is suffered (albeit differently) by the victim and by the community of which that injustice is a structural feature (if it is that); and also by the community that is systematically blind or indifferent to the wrongs suffered by its members. Someone who is murdered, for example, suffers the natural harm of death, and the evil of having been murdered. If his community is indifferent to this, then he also suffers the injustice of that indifference and the community suffers the shame of it. To the extent that the legal, political and civic structures of society encourage its members effectively to ignore the suffering of those who are racially denigrated, the homeless or the unemployed, for example, then to that extent their suffering is often compounded by injustice. In the essay from which I have already quoted, Simone Weil quotes the words of a Spanish song: 'If anyone wants to make himself invisible, there is no surer way than to become poor.' She then says, 'Love sees what is invisible.'

A concern for justice in a community should be, in critical part, a concern that its institutions enable and encourage us always to see, and in seeing to be responsive to the full humanity in each of our fellow human beings. That is why this kind of concern is called a concern for *social* justice and it is why it is so often connected with compassion. It is true, I think, as the right has often claimed, that compassion is not a virtue that can be exhibited by the state, and that only in a secondary sense of the word can compassion be a virtue of a community. But justice is a virtue attributable to states and to communities. In the kinds of examples I have been considering, it partly consists in the creation of institutions which ensure, to the extent that it is humanly possible, that our state and civic institutions should not be the cause of such suffering in our fellow citizens that we should be ashamed of our ourselves if compassion were fully to reveal it to us.

That is why justice in a community is valued beyond the ways in which it serves our material and psychological needs. We desire justice because often it serves our needs and interests, but we desire it also because, as Simone Weil says, it is 'so beautiful a thing'. It is, therefore, not true that all that matters morally, or should matter, is that the hungry no longer be hungry, the homeless no longer be homeless, the unemployed be employed and so on. When poverty and homelessness are the expression of injustice they matter differently and more to us than when they are not. Communities take pleasure and pride in the fact that injustices have been acknowledged and overcome, and that reparation has been made when it is possible. Such pleasure in justice is necessary if people are lucidly to love their community, country or nation.

Love is never of what is merely useful, no matter how vital to us that use may be. A love of the past is always more than a prudential concern for how knowledge and preservation of it may serve our present and future interests. And the love of a language is never for it merely as an instrument with which to express ourselves, but depends on the recognition that our thoughts and feelings are made by language as much as they are expressed in it. These are analogies but they are also more, for love of the language and of the past of one's people nourishes the deepest forms of communal identity. For those who enjoy them, the blessings of such love are partly constitutive of that dimension of their identity which they attribute to their membership of community. It will be fundamental to what they understand about what it means to be human and, therefore, of anything that counts as 'human well being'.

Guilt, Shame
& Community

In most of its forms love is, as Plato saw, tied to things which are (ethically) good even when it is not actually directed upon them. But the conditions that make love possible are inseparable from those which make shame and guilt possible.

The history that supports Mabo and the conclusions of *Bringing Them Home,* the report on the 'stolen children', have been a source of deep shame for many Australians, and for some a source of guilt. Such responses—shame especially—often express acknowledgment of a collective responsibility, sometimes directly *for* the wrongs done, but more often *to* those who were wronged by our political ancestors. It amounts to the acknowledgment that we are rightly called to a communal responsiveness to those who are the victims of our wrongdoing or the wrongdoing of those who preceded us.

Others have responded differently. They have mocked an

historically deep sense of shame, calling it a 'black armband' view of history. They often say something like this. The practical—and therefore the *really* moral—thing to do is to stop brooding on the alleged wrongs committed against the Aborigines in the past and to get on with the task of providing them with land, health, education and other benefits. This (the thought continues) should not be done in response to the divisive idea that their history entitles them to it, but in response to their present needs assessed equitably alongside the needs of all their fellow citizens.

Such a position, a slightly cruder version of the one advanced by Gray and Raz, is seriously mistaken. Amongst other things, it treats as morally and politically irrelevant the fact that the Aborigines are landless because they were dispossessed rather than because of a natural catastrophe. More generally, it treats as irrelevant that their suffering is saturated by a justified sense that they have been terribly wronged. To ignore that, to insist high-mindedly that *real* moral concern focus on the present and the future rather than the past, is to compound their humiliation and our shame.

Justices Deane and Gaudron saw that quite clearly. When they said so in their judgment, they were accused of subverting the integrity of the court by their use of irresponsibly emotive language in the service of a transparent political intent. Here is their language at its strongest: 'An early flash point with one clan of Aborigines illustrates the first stages of the conflagration of oppression and conflict which was, over the following century, to spread across the continent to dispossess, degrade and devastate the Aboriginal peoples and leave a national legacy of unutterable shame.'

Later, when they justified their re-examination of 'the validity of fundamental propositions which have been endorsed by long-established authority and which have been accepted as a basis of the real property law of the country for more than one hundred and fifty years', they said:

> The acts and events by which that dispossession [of the Aboriginal peoples of most of their traditional lands] in

legal theory was carried into practical effect constitute the darkest aspect of the history of this nation. The nation as a whole must remain diminished unless and until there is an acknowledgment of, and retreat from, those past injustices.

Anticipating criticism of their language, the Justices acknowledged what would provoke it. To explain themselves they wrote:

> we have used language and expressed conclusions which some may think to be unusually emotive for a judgment in this Court…the reason which has led us to describe, and express conclusions about, the dispossession of Australian Aborigines in unrestrained language is that the full facts of that dispossession are of critical importance to the assessment of the legitimacy of the propositions that the continent was unoccupied for legal purposes and that the unqualified legal and beneficial ownership of all the lands of the continent vested in the Crown.

When they acknowledged that their language was 'unrestrained', however, they did not mean that it was undisciplined and unsuited to a dispassionate appraisal of the facts and their relevance. A dispassionate judgment is not one which is uninformed by feeling, but one which is undistorted by feeling. This fact separates legitimate use of the words 'emotive', 'emotional' or 'rhetorical' as terms of criticism from illegitimate insistence that objective thought must always be separable from feeling.

Perhaps another, more dramatic example, will make the point clearer. The descriptions of the Holocaust by Martin Gilbert and by Primo Levi are written with disciplined restraint. Those descriptions are dispassionate in the sense I claimed for the prose of Gaudron and Deane: though informed by feeling, they are not distorted by it. We know when we read them that they are written by men whose souls were lacerated by what they knew. It shows in their prose which we read, as Nora Levin put it, with bleeding eyes. There is no other way to read them with understanding and no other way they can convey the reality of the evil they describe. This kind of truth and reality can only be understood by an informed heart. We see that immediately if we compare the reports of the murders with SS reports which are reports of the killing without any sense of its evil. Those SS reports are dispassionate, in the sense of being uninformed by feeling. The effect is not to disclose reality objectively, but to obscure it.

Justices Deane and Gaudron claimed to speak as they did, so that the 'full facts of the dispossession' and their significance to the legitimacy of previous judgments might be appreciated. By the 'full facts of the dispossession' they meant the full meaning of it which can only be conveyed in prose that reveals its moral reality. It is not sober and truthful speech which they (implicitly) contrasted with their own, but speech in which a falsifying kind of restraint is mistaken for disciplined impartiality. One may dispute the accuracy of their descriptions and one may claim that, in its actual application, their language obscures rather than reveals the facts in their 'full significance'. But only specious assumptions about the distinctions between description and evaluation, fact and value, or emotion and reason can support the claim that the words of Justices Deane and Gaudron are intrinsically unsuited to dispassionate appraisal of the facts and their significance.

Justices Gaudron and Deane were also accused of sacrificing the integrity of the law for the sake of (perhaps morally worthy) political purposes. As far as I am able to judge that is not merely false, but the very opposite of the truth.

It is clear that the justices desired a change in the law. It is also clear that they believed that those changes would benefit Aborigines. From that it does not follow that their primary intention was to change the law for the benefit of Aborigines. Their primary concern, as it shows in their judgment, was not with the effects of injustice on Aborigines, but with its effect on the law. Concern for the Aborigines is mediated and constrained in their judgment by that primary concern for the integrity of the law.

Justices Gaudron and Deane made more explicit than the other Justices the connection between that concern for the integrity of law and the realisation that the 'nation as a whole must remain diminished unless and until there is an acknowledgment of, and retreat from, those past injustices'. That is why they were so severely criticised.

There need, however, be no conflict between concern for the integrity of law and a desire to redeem the nation's shame. The law is the most important element in the definition of the political *persona* by virtue of which a person may have a national identity of which he or she may be proud or ashamed or, as is likely, both. In redeeming the law from the injustices in which it had become complicit the Justices were at the same time, and to some degree, redeeming the 'national legacy of unutterable shame'.

My reply, then, to those who say that Mabo and the persistent threat of (allegedly) irresponsible claims issuing from it are a threat to the national interest is as follows. One should not, as critics of Mabo tend to do, restrict the notion of the national interest to economic interests and the interest of having an undivided body politic. If the dispossession of the Aboriginal peoples is one of the 'darkest chapter[s]' in Australian history, then the Justices may reasonably have hoped that, acknowledging this, their fellow citizens would accept the material costs to the nation of the court's concern to purge the law of its complicity in the 'national legacy of unutterable shame'.

Mabo should, therefore, not be contrasted with the national interest. It should be seen as an expression of the kind of concern with law and justice which is essential to any conception of the national interest informed by an appreciation of the difference between patriotism and jingoism. Realpolitik and other infatuations with 'political realism', applied nationally and internationally, create unnecessary tension between the demands of justice and the national interest.

We are, inescapably, moral beings. No adequate concept of

our interests or of our well-being should ignore or diminish that fact. Justices Deane and Gaudron saw quite clearly that our communal and national interests include living justly and with a pride that we can honestly celebrate because we have acknowledged our shame. Shame is as necessary for the lucid acknowledgment by Australians of the wrongs the Aborigines suffered at the hands of their political ancestors, and to the wrongs they continue to suffer, as pain is to mourning. It is not an optional emotional addition to the recognition of the meaning of their dispossession. It is, I believe, the *form* of that recognition.

It was the burden of the previous chapter to argue that societies which acknowledge the injustices they sanction or the evils they encourage must acknowledge them as distinct from, and not reducible to, the natural suffering they cause. The spirit in which such suffering is ameliorated must, therefore, be informed by the acknowledgment that those who suffered it were wronged—that to be wronged is a distinctive and irreducible form of harm. Pained acknowledgment of the wrongs we have committed or in which we are in other ways implicated is, according to the circumstances, either guilt or shame.

Who then is answerable to the call to acknowledge collective responsibility, and in what way? Those who are guilty by deed or omission and those sufficiently close to them in time to feel obliged to bring them to justice. Also those who are related to the guilty in such a way that they rightly feel ashamed. Finally, those who are related to the guilty in such a way that they should seek an appropriate figure—usually the head of an institution or of government—to apologise on their behalf and to acknowledge other responsibilities, generally, the responsibility to make reparation.

Obviously this last group will include many members of the first and second, but it may also have members who are not guilty and who are not ashamed because they do not have the kind of attachment to the country which would make shame appropriate. They might think of themselves merely as citizens of their nation, acknowledging certain rights and duties, but unable yet to appropriate the distinctive use of the first person plural characteristic of those who are rooted in their country, who love it and who are nourished by its historically deep traditions. National shame requires an historically deeper and more intense attachment, perhaps a more *defining* attachment, to country than citizenship.

Discussion of these issues is sometimes muddied by the conflation of shame and guilt. Because remorse—which I take to be the pained acknowledgment of one's guilt—is taken as a paradigm of the acceptance of responsibility, people sometimes think responsibility must be restricted to what one has done or omitted to do. Moral guilt is indeed so restricted; the guilt of others can be the occasion for one's own guilt only if one failed to do something to prevent their deeds or at least to protest them. Perhaps that is why collective responsibility is so often taken to mean collective guilt rather than national shame. It is, after all, tempting to say that one's omissions must reasonably be judged to stand in some causal relation to the wrong deeds of others if one is justifiably to be held responsible together with their perpetrators—roughly, that one must reasonably judge that one could have played a part in stopping them.

That temptation should be resisted. If one soberly judges that one's actions could achieve nothing, one might nonetheless rightly feel obliged to protest, perhaps so it be known that, or merely so it be true that, at least someone cared that wrong was done to people. But in such cases, one must be in sufficient proximity to the deeds to give sense to the guilty thought that evil was done and one did nothing to stop or to protest it. That is not a thought that can justifiably occasion guilt in later generations, although they may rightly feel guilty for not responding, in ways appropriate to them, to the fact that their ancestors did wrong, because they have not offered reparation, for example.

Important though the distinction is between guilt and shame, it is not always sharp. There are borderline cases as, of course, there are with any concept. More importantly, there is a condition which is neither guilt nor shame and which is not a state borderline between them. Ron Castan, a QC who played a prominent part in securing native title legislation, alerted me to it in discussion when he described the response of Adolf Eichmann's son to the fact that he was the child of one of the architects of the genocide of the Jews and gipsies. The oppressive and ineradicable gloom of that condition was neither shame nor guilt, but more like the condition the ancient Greeks described in their tragedies as 'pollution'. The fact that there is such a state which has aspects of shame and aspects of guilt and is not a borderline state but a distinctive condition of its own, and the fact that it burdens people caught up in the evil deeds of others, may together explain why there has been such a confusion in public debate about the appropriate way to acknowledge the wrong done to our indigenous peoples.

Guilt and collective guilt seem simpler in their conceptual structure than national shame. That appearance should be trusted, on the whole, but there is an interesting complication to guilt, which may help us understand shame. It makes itself felt when one reflects on the response that many people have to Sophocles' play *Oedipus Rex*. Oedipus killed his father and married his mother. He did both unintentionally because of ignorance for which he was not culpable. Or, so I read Sophocles. When Oedipus realises what he has done, his horror is of the kind we would naturally call 'remorse'—its character is determined by his sense of the evil-doer he had unwittingly become:

> Now, shedder of father's blood,
> Husband of mother, is my name;
> Godless and child of shame,
> Begetter of brother-sons;
> What infamy remains
> That is not spoken of Oedipus?

The chorus does not doubt that Oedipus did evil: it shows in the quality of its pity for him:

> And now, where is a more heart-rending story of affliction?
> Where a more awful swerve into the arms of torment?
> O Oedipus, that proud head!
> When the same bosom enfolded the son and the father,
> Could not the engendering clay have shouted aloud its
>   indignation?

When reading Sophocles' play, and even more when watching it, few people would doubt that Oedipus and the chorus respond appropriately. Many question it on reflection, however, suspecting it is irrational, the expression of superstitions of times long past, but psychologically understandable even now. In fact, as the philosopher Bernard Williams has pointed out in his book *Shame and Necessity*, urging that we must distinguish what we actually believe from what we think we believe, we are not so distant from such ways of thinking as we sometimes sincerely profess to be. He cites our law of torts as an example where responsibility is assigned and compensation demanded from those who played no causal role in the suffering of the litigants.

I do not, however, intend to argue for the rightness of Oedipus' response. To those who concede there is at least a case for it, I shall outline the more generous conception of responsibility that beckons even with something as severe as guilt. It shows in the response of the chorus. It doesn't blame Oedipus. That would indeed be irrational unless it judged his ignorance to be culpable, which it rightly does not. The stern pity of the chorus ensures that Oedipus does not evade his guilt by pleading, as he does in a later play, *Oedipus at Colonus*, that he was not culpable. Holding him in that way responsible, as properly responsive to the moral significance of his deeds, conditions what is morally possible between Oedipus and the chorus in the future. It is the exercise of a responsibility that Oedipus and the chorus have to the community which has been polluted by his deeds. Importantly, the chorus's pity is conditioned by a judgment which is severe but not 'judgmental'. It does not turn away from Oedipus in disdain, but towards him, expressing its sorrow for what he has (morally) become.

In *Romulus, My Father*, I ascribe a similar attitude of, if I might put it this way, utterly non-judgmental moral severity to my father. The response to the book, the way people have been moved by it and to this aspect of my characterisation of him, convinces me that whatever we may say reflectively under the influence of a moralistic conception of morality, a conception we have inherited partly from Aristotle, our practice is thankfully more lucid. This is a passage from my book.

> People argue about whether suffering ennobles. There is another and different thought, which is that only suffering makes one wise. Of course, people can suffer the most horrific experiences and emerge even more superficial than they were before. Some kinds of wisdom, however— the kinds that show themselves not only in thoughts, but in the integrity of an authoritatively lived life—are given only to those who have suffered deep and long. His affliction gave authority to much of what my father said, gave power to his language, rich in peasant imagery, and spared his harsh moral judgment from any tinge of moralism in the pejorative sense of that term which implies an ever-present readiness to point the finger at others and to turn one's back on them.
>
> In one way, my father was a fierce moralist. Not about the big and controversial issues of the day, but about simple moral requirements such as honesty and concern for one's neighbour. If he thought you were a liar or a cheat or had acted unkindly, then he would say so to you without a trace of euphemism. But there was never anything in his judgment which implied you should be shunned by decent people. Though fierce and uncompromising, his judgments were not what we now call 'judgmental'.

Even his most severe judgments were made in many tones. If he called you an incorrigible liar he might do it angrily, scathingly, sorrowfully or, strange as it might sound, matter-of-factly, but never in a tone that suggested he would turn his back on you. You were always welcome at his table, to eat and more importantly to talk; always to talk. But he believed that it was essential to decent conversation that one not pretend to virtues one did not possess—as essential as being truthful about one's identity. Only then could conversation be true to its deeper potentialities and do its humanising work of opening up the possibilities of authentic human disclosure.

Such a non-moralistic desire severely to hold someone to their responsibility is, I think, what people express when they say that in calling for a national apology they do not thereby wish to lay blame. Sometimes they say they want merely to express their sorrow, even their grief. The trouble, however, is that the connections in our understanding between morality and blame are so close, that people then think such an expression of sorrow is not a moral response or, more precisely, that it is not a response which allows a moral description of what one sorrows over. It then seems irrelevant to the sorrow felt for the Aborigines that their suffering is largely a consequence of the fact, and is saturated by their awareness of the fact, that they were wronged rather than victims of a natural catastrophe, and that it was our political ancestors who wronged them.

Pollution is a good metaphor for the way the guilt of its members can affect an entire community, including those who are not guilty. The crimes of the Nazis estranged some German poets and novelists so deeply from their country that they could no longer write creatively in its language. Here it does seem as though the streams that nourish national identity, the love of country and its culture, have been poisoned, depriving them of the power fully to do so, at least for those with a certain kind of moral sensibility.

Response to such pollution can of course be in various ways self-indulgent. The maudlin self-abasement that gives point to talk of black armband brigades is an example. But any distinction between authentic and unauthentic forms of such responses will depend on whether and in what way they are conditioned by a sense that one is answerable to the victims of the polluting crimes.

To talk of political ancestors is, of course, to rely on another metaphor, one whose task is to bring national shame within the conceptual ambit of familial shame. Sometimes the shame of parents for the deeds of their children depends on what they did or failed to do for their children, but it is not always so, and one would have desperately to be committed to the causal connotations of responsibility to believe (facilitated by, for example, a theory of unconscious projection) that it is generally so when children are ashamed of what their parents have done. But reflection on familial and national shame brings into focus the deep and sometimes intense attachments to groups which form part of a person's sense of identity.

The role of the metaphor of ancestry in bringing national shame within the conceptual ambit of familial attachments is perhaps a function of what Bernard Williams has called the 'bonding interactive effects of shame'. In this respect shame is quite unlike moral guilt. Severe remorse is, as I noted in chapter two, radically individualising. Remorseful suffering seems to be alone amongst the forms of human suffering in its need to resist the consolation which comes from the recognition that others suffer as we do. The commonplace fact that we may be consoled by the knowledge that we do not suffer alone informs Isak Dinesen's insight that 'all sorrows can be borne if you put them into a story, or tell a story about them'. Her point is not merely that stories characteristically are ways of making sense of the lives of their heroes. It is that they do so against a compassionate sense of a common human condition.

None of which means, however, that one should not speak of

national guilt, as people did of the Germans after World War II. Such talk refers basically to the consequences for a sense of national identity, of the fact that so many in the nation are guilty by deed or by omission. Although such people may have done their evil deeds under the inspiration of a corrupt nationalism, and although they were together complicit in the institutions which enabled the evil to be done and often disguised or denied, they cannot lucidly face the meaning of what they did in their capacity as members of a particular nation and in guilty fellowship with their compatriots. They can face it lucidly only as individual human beings.

Pride and shame, on the other hand, are fundamental to the kind of fellowship that makes community possible. It is a fellow- ship whose nature is determined by the way joys and sorrows change when they are shared. When that fellowship shows itself historically—as happens when people say, 'we of this nation'— then it is inseparable from the desire to celebrate achievements which shape an historically deep sense of communal identity. But if we are right to be proud, then sometimes we are obliged to be ashamed. The wish for national pride without the possibility of national shame is an expression of that corrupt attachment to a collective whose name is jingoism. Hugh Morgan, chairman of Western Mining Corporation, gave a good example of it when he responded to Mabo. 'Despite their high office, these people seem ashamed to be Australians. They seem to have no pride in their country and they strive mightily to melt it down and recast it, furtively, in a new self deprecating and much diminished mould.'

Explaining to Frank Brennan why John Howard could not apologise in his capacity as prime minister though Howard had offered his personal apology, the minister for employment, workplace relations and small business, Peter Reith, wrote: 'The government does not support an official national apology. Such an apology could imply that present generations are in some way responsible and accountable for the actions of earlier generations.'

No explanation was offered of why the prime minister believed he needed to apologise personally.

How should we respond to the thoughts Peter Reith expressed in that letter and to the claim that, so long as one works to relieve the present misery of the Aborigines, there is no need to brood on past wrongs?

Imagine someone who says that he fully understands the wrong he had done in swindling a friend, and who also says that, while he is more than ready to make up his friend's losses, he feels no remorse and no need to apologise. Suppose he then indignantly denies that this compromises his claim fully to understand what he had done. He says that remorse is a useless and often destructive emotional addendum to the full understanding of what it means to be a wrong-doer. Such understanding, he goes on to say, entails only the desire to make good the damage to whatever degree one can. Now imagine the other extreme of this misunderstanding—someone who often and tearfully expresses remorse, but is never prepared to make reparation. Few people would deny that these characters have a desperately thin moral understanding. In the first the connection between remorse and understanding the wrong he has done has come apart. In the second, the connection between remorse and reparation has come apart in the same way.

Is the same true of shame? Up to a point it is. The similarities are sufficient to yield a reply to those who say that protestations of shame unaccompanied by serious attempts to ameliorate the effects of the wrong done are self-indulgent and in the end harmful to the Aborigines. Would anyone deny it? Would anyone seriously say that shame is of itself an adequate response to the terrible plight suffered by most Aborigines, or that shame amounts to anything when it is separated from a serious concern with reparation? Relief of the material and psychological misery of many of the Aborigines will not count as reparation, however, unless the spirit in which that relief is given is informed by a recognition of the wrongs they have suffered. That is part of what we *mean* by 'reparation' and it is why we distinguish reparation from other actions which would bring the same material benefits to those who have been wronged.

Acknowledgment of those wrongs as a source of torment distinct from and not reducible to their material or psychological consequences is, I believe, what the Aborigines desire when they ask for a national apology. One can debate whether remorse and shame constitute *forms* of understanding as I claimed in my discussion of the remarks by Justices Deane and Gaudron, or whether their existence is a *criterion* for understanding. My argument does not depend on the stronger claim. The weaker one—that they are criteria for understanding the wrong one has done or been implicated in—will suffice.

Thus far the analogy with remorse goes through. But can one go on to say that those who declare that they know full well the terrible wrong their political ancestors did to the Aborigines, but feel no shame, have broken the connection between shame and understanding in the same way as the character in my example broke the connection between remorse and understanding?

Yes, provided one adds the qualification that the persons involved must have the kind of attachment to Australia that could make shame possible for them. Clearly, people from other nations and citizens with no deep attachment to the country can acknowledge the wrong done to the Aborigines, and acknowledge it in the sense that implies—as mere recognition does not—that they are morally responsive to a claim on them. But that would not be shame. The attachment that makes shame appropriate and sometimes called for is inseparable from the desire to celebrate achievements which shape an historically deep sense of communal identity. The pained, humbled acknowledgment of the wrongs committed by their ancestors, of those who are rooted and nourished by their country, who feel as do Justices Deane and Gaudron, that those wrongs constitute a stain on their country, and whose joy in its achievements is thereby sometimes blighted—that acknowledgment I take to be one of the forms of shame. If it is not, then I do not know what to call it.

Peter Reith's claim that we cannot be held responsible for the crimes of our ancestors is true, therefore, only if one takes him to mean the kind of responsibility expressed in remorse, that is, in the pained acknowledgment of one's guilt. We can rationally feel remorse (feel guilty) only for what we have done or failed to do. But as well as, or perhaps instead of, feeling guilty, we may feel ashamed, and that suggests a different notion of responsibility. Or, perhaps not a different notion so much as a different aspect of the same notion.

Martin Buber, a great Jewish religious philosopher, wrote: 'The idea of responsibility is to be brought back from the province of specialised ethics, of an "ought" that swings free in the air, into that of lived life. Genuine responsibility exists only where there is real responding.' In remorse we respond to what it means to wrong another, which involves a new and terrible shock at their reality. Far from being intrinsically self-indulgent, lucid remorse makes one's victim vividly real. Corrupt forms of remorse, of which there are infinitely many, do the opposite. When our shame is the lucid expression of collective national responsibility for the wrongs done by our ancestors, we have risen in truthful response to the evil in our history—of the fact that it is *our* history. Because it is an acknowledgment of the fact that we must rise in truthful moral responsiveness to the meaning of what we have been caught up in, often through no fault of our own, it is rightly called an acceptance of responsibility.

It is a matter for argument in what way and to what degree the Aborigines may hold the non-Aboriginal community of Australia responsible for what happened in the past—some of it two centuries ago. But the fact that some of the crimes of our political ancestors were committed long ago does not mean that their victims should not require costly reparation of us. Nor does it mean that they should not call us to a sober acknowledgment of the responsibilities that determine our moral relations to them, and whose truthful acknowledgment is a precondition of our becoming, together, fully equal members of one political community. We may judge some of their claims to be excessive or foolish or even offensive. But such disagreements we must have with them—fully together with them—in the knowledge that we cannot unilaterally set the agenda, nor unilaterally proclaim what is reasonable and what is not. None of this means that non-indigenous Australians should descend into maudlin self-abasement. Nor does it mean that they cannot vigorously criticise indigenous proposals for reconciliation, or corruption in Aboriginal institutions and culture.

Long ago Yasser Arafat warned that the Palestinian problem was not merely a humanitarian problem, that its most serious dimensions could not be addressed by food and medicines sent to the refugee camps. Their deepest need, he argued, was for the political realisation of their identity as a distinct people. That realisation has now been agreed to be a Palestinian state. The Aborigines too are saying that theirs is not merely a humanitarian problem to be solved by better housing, schools and health services. They are saying that, as important as these matters may be, they must be dealt with in forums that acknowledge their need to find political identities which would be adequate to their history. Such claims were pressed before Mabo, but Mabo enhanced them and strengthened the demand for discussion of political structures that would best express the Aborigines' complicated relations to the Australian body politic—discussion of the kind found, for example, in recent books by Henry Reynolds (*Aboriginal Sovereignty*) and Nonie Sharp (*No Ordinary Judgment*).

Much of the exploration of those new structures is guided by the concept of self-determination. The vagueness of that concept has made it vulnerable to uncharitable attack. Its vagueness is not itself the expression of intractable confusion, however, even if there is plenty of confusion in its discussion. The vagueness of the concept is the expression of the fact that the Aborigines—together with indigenous peoples in other parts of the world—are exploring forms of political identity and association which would adequately express the meaning of their dispossession. This exploration is radical and often novel to the classical traditions of Western political thought. Unavoidably, talk of self-determination does little more than gesture towards an outcome whose full conceptual character is unforeseeable. Such exploration of cultural and political identity is now necessary to the Aborigines' self-respect. Openness to it and to its unforeseeable outcome is a necessary condition of respect for them.

Simone Weil said that if one saw others as another perspective on the world, as one is oneself, one could not treat them unjustly. That means that we must be open to the distinctive voice of others, and that in turn means that we must encourage the conditions in which those voices can form and be heard. When people's souls have been lacerated by the wrongs done to them, individually or collectively, openness to their voices requires humbled attentiveness. When one's nation has committed those wrongs, shame is the form that humbled attentiveness takes. Without it there can be no justice.

There is little evidence of such attentiveness in the claim that historically we have little to be ashamed of and that, on balance, our history is a fine one. If we put together the thoughts that we have little to be ashamed of and that our history is 'on balance' a fine one, the relative weightlessness in these scales of the evil done to the Aborigines becomes apparent. The alternative need not be to conclude that on balance our history is a shameful one. It may be to resist such summing up. But if we insist on summing up, then we should not be surprised when Aborigines are insulted by the implication that the evil done to them should be treated as lightly as it is by those who sneer at 'black armbands'. Nor should anyone be surprised if they take such judgments as merely the further expression of the fact that they have always been, and continue to be, only partially perceptible to the moral faculties of most Australians.

We must therefore not be sentimental about reconciliation. We should resist especially the kind of sentimentality expressed in 'Sorry Day', which good-hearted though it may be, really hides from us the terrible evil the Aborigines have suffered and our responsibilities to them. More often than not, talk of reconciliation assumes that the road will be relatively smooth and the end welcome to all people of goodwill, if only indigenous and non-indigenous Australians will really listen to one another with an open heart. It might be so. But it might not. The assumption that it *must* be so, if minds and hearts are truly open, is inconsistent with anything that could seriously be called reconciliation. Anything really deserving of the name will be the result of an openness to the other which denies us the capacity always to predict what will be consistent or inconsistent with an open heart and mind.

In 1998 Noel Pearson was moved to call some members of the Coalition 'racist scum'. This was at the time when the Queensland government together with the state's pastoralists steamrolled the federal government into treating a technical High Court judgment that native title could co-exist with pastoral leases (a judgment supported by a black-letter judge) as though it were a piece of gung-ho social engineering. They thereby made a High Court judgment an extreme position in an acrimonious political debate. Seen against the action of the Queensland government (in its own way a naked and brutish display of political force), against the history of black–white relations which informed native title legislation, and against the fact that the court ruled that, in case of conflict, pastoral rights prevail over native title, the indignant response to Pearson's outburst appeared prissy if not disingenuous. It shows, I think, that we are not yet ready to hear the full truth about the evil done to the Aborigines and to bear the pain of it.

An emasculated notion of conversation applied to politics enables us to hide this from ourselves. Michael Oakeshott, the most profound conservative political philosopher of the postwar years, celebrated the idea of conversation as a way of understanding the life of the mind and of politics in his enchanting essay 'The Voice of Poetry in the Conversation of Mankind'. He insisted that strident, and even passionate, voices will destroy conversation. Even in academic life, however, that point has its limits. What is one to do with the many shrill voices in our intellectual history? How are they to speak to us? Must one first 'civilise' them? Civilise Plato, Augustine, Nietzsche, Schopenhauer and Kierkegaard?

The rhetorical force of those questions becomes more powerful when they are directed to our attempts to converse with those whom we or our political ancestors have brutally wronged. If we enter such conversations with a determinate idea of what counts as their civilised forms, then we are bound to shut our ears to what we do not wish to hear. It happens often in personal relations. More often than not the injunction 'Try to be civilised' is a cruel reproach to those we have hurt, telling them not to make us too uncomfortable by showing their pain. We then add humiliation to their pain.

Martin Buber was wiser about this. He said that the basic difference between monologue and 'fully valid conversation' was 'the otherness, or more concretely, the moment of surprise'. His point is not merely that we must be open to hearing surprising things. We must be open to being surprised at the many ways we may justly and humanly relate to one another in a spirit of truthful dialogue. It is in conversation, rather than in advance of it, that we discover, never alone but always together, what it means really to listen and what tone may properly be taken. In conversation we discover the many things conversation can be. No one can say what will happen when we fully acknowledge the evil done to the indigenous peoples of this land and when they see and accept that we have acknowledged it. More importantly, no one can say what should happen.

Genocide &
'The Stolen Generations'

Kim Beazley, leader of the federal opposition, cried when he first spoke to parliament about *Bringing Them Home*, the report on 'the stolen generations'. I don't think many people were embarrassed by his tears, as they sometimes had been by those of former prime minister Bob Hawke. Enough of the report had been in circulation for people to know something of the terrible stories it contained. And most people knew in their hearts that they should have known them long before. Beazley's tears were for the children and their mothers. They were for the Aborigines. And they were for the nation.

Heartbreaking stories are to be found on most pages of *Bringing Them Home*. An official tells how children were taken. It was not always as he tells it, but it seems often to have been so:

The assembled children were loaded into the truck very suddenly and their things thrown in hastily after them. The suddenness and the suppressed air of tension shocked the mothers and the children and they realised something was seriously wrong...Children began to cry and the mothers to wail and cut themselves...The tailgate was slammed shut and bolted and the truck screeched off with things still hanging over the back and mothers and other children running after it crying and wailing.

Millicent, a child taken to Sister Kate's Home in Western Australia, tells this story:

> ...it was a terrifying experience, the man of the house used to come into my room at night and force to me have sex...
>
> When I returned to the home I was feeling so used and unwanted. I went to the Matron and told her what happened. She washed my mouth out with soap and boxed my ears and told me that awful things would happen to me if I told any of the other kids. I was so scared and wanted to die. When the next school holidays came I begged not to be sent to that farm again. But they would not listen and said I had to.
>
> This time I was raped, bashed and slashed with a razor blade on both of my arms and legs because I would not stop struggling and screaming...
>
> When they returned me to the home I once again went to the Matron. I got a belting with a wet ironing cord, my mouth washed out with soap and put in a cottage by myself away from everyone...I ate rat poison to try and kill myself but became very sick and vomited. This meant another belting.

Another victim testifies, 'I've seen girls naked, strapped to chairs and whipped. We've all been through the locking up period, locked in dark rooms.'

Racism, sometimes gross, brutal and individually enacted, sometimes more subtle and institutional, was common and was at the heart of the policy of removing Aboriginal children from their families during at least most of the time it was enacted, from roughly the end of last century until the 1960s:

> There was a big poster at the end of the dining room and it used to be pointed out to us all the time when religious instruction was going on in the afternoon. They had these Aborigine people sitting at the end of this big wide road and they were playing cards, gambling and drinking. And it had this slogan which they used to read to us and point to us while they're saving us from ourselves and giving our souls to the Lord. It had, 'Wide is the road that leads us to destruction', which led up into hell. The other side they had these white people, all nicely dressed, leading on this narrow road, and 'Narrow is the road that leads us into the kingdom of life or the Kingdom of God'.

Another witness puts it more bluntly: 'These are people telling you to be Christian and they treat you less than a bloody animal. One boy, his leg was that gangrene we could smell him all down the dormitories before they finally got him treated properly.'

Page after page is the same. I have quoted at length to convey a small part of the experience of reading this report of over 600 pages. Sometimes it is different:

> I was very fortunate that when I was removed, I was with very loving and caring parents...my foster parents were the type of people that always understood that I needed to know my roots, who I was, where I was born, who my parents were and my identity...I remember one day I went home to my foster father and stated that I had heard that my natural father was a drunk. My foster father told me you shouldn't listen to other people: 'You judge him for yourself, taking into account the tragedy, that someday you will understand'.

Such acceptance was rare, if one is to believe the report. It doesn't say so directly, but it gives that impression. In the months and years to come this question will be debated, as it should be. *Bringing Them Home* is no substitute for an informed history. One hopes that there are many more stories like that last one than the report suggests. If there are, they will to some degree redeem this period of Australian history, but they will not diminish the terribleness of the crimes that were committed. On the contrary, stories of kindness towards the children or their parents tend to undermine the claim that the brutalities merely expressed the values of the time. In a letter to the *Age,* a son tells of how his father, a policeman, cried bitter tears when he came home after taking children from their mothers. I imagine the tears were not only compassionate tears for the pain he caused, but also remorseful ones for the evil he had done. The fact that he was a good man who had it in him to cry such tears does not diminish the evil he did.

Bringing Them Home has had a profound impact on many Australians, partly because it alerted them to other dark parts of Australian history, but mostly because it has forced on them the terrible realisation that even in their own lifetimes Aborigines were the victims of brutal racism. The report's accuracy, and even the honesty of those who produced it, have been questioned. Nothing, however, has emerged which should make one doubt that thousands of children were forcibly removed from their parents, racially abused, treated harshly and sometimes brutally.

Bringing Them Home also accuses the Australian government of genocide. An unnerving silence has met this serious charge, which at first seems astonishing given its seriousness and given the response to the cruelties detailed in the report. The silence has not been an expression of people's uncertainty about the facts. They are, after all, the facts to which so many of them responded with anger, sorrow and shame. Many on the left accepted the facts and took the accusation of genocide in their stride. They had for so long used the concept carelessly, even frivolously, that they appeared to have become inoculated against its serious meaning. The right, on the other hand, took the charge to mean that

Australia had been guilty of the same crime that the Third Reich had committed against the Jews and gipsies and so thought it ridiculous, for just that reason, long before any of its number had claimed to show the report to be irresponsible and dishonest. Journalist and publisher, Michael Duffy, wrote in his column in the *Australian* that to take the charge of genocide seriously is to think that Paul Hasluck and Robert Menzies should occupy the same circle of hell as Hitler and Himmler.

Leaving aside the fact that the times when the absorption programs could most plausibly be described as genocidal preceded the periods when Menzies and Hasluck held office, Duffy's rhetoric relies on the apparent moral absurdity of comparing the crimes committed by Hitler and those committed even during the worst periods of the absorption programs. That presupposes—rightly in my judgment—that no account of the nature of genocide can extend beyond its moral reach. The concept has an inexpungeable moral dimension. It is not a morally neutral concept in a value-free social science, nor in a conception of law which would radically separate law and morality. That being so, it is assumed, naturally enough, that there can be no serious account of genocide whose moral reach can extend from the Holocaust to even the darkest periods of the absorption programs. Or, to put the assumption another way: the crimes committed against the Aborigines and the crimes committed against the Jews and gipsies cannot legitimately be brought under the one concept if it requires them to be morally commensurable.

It is no accident that Duffy selects the Holocaust to work up his rhetoric. Although Raphael Lemkin had explored the concept of genocide as early as 1944, it was the difficulty of understanding the crimes that define the Holocaust that prompted the most intense reflection on it. It is now impossible to think about genocide without thinking about the Holocaust because the Holocaust is the purest example of it. The Holocaust, however, has features which make some people call it a crime different in kind from other acts of genocide, as they occurred for example against the Armenians, or in Rwanda or Cambodia. Those features incline some people to say that the Holocaust is unique. One can therefore think of the Holocaust as unprecedented for two reasons. First, because it has features that make it different in kind even from other acts of genocide and which prompt people to say it is unique. Secondly, because no other preceding act of genocide (or subsequent act, for that matter) has exhibited such a pure genocidal intention, prosecuted so relentlessly. It is therefore not surprising that these aspects get mixed up and that discussions of genocide become confused when the Holocaust is (rightly) held up as its paradigm. In the next chapter I will discuss this more fully.

Confusion about the Holocaust is, however, not the only reason why some people think it is absurd to bring under the same concept the crimes against the Aborigines during the period covered by the report on the stolen children and the crimes of the Nazis against the Jews. They think it equally absurd to bring the crimes detailed in *Bringing Them Home* under the same concept as the crimes committed in Rwanda or Cambodia, if one takes the latter as an instance of genocide. The reason is that they believe that genocide must involve mass murder if the concept is not to degenerate in morally frivolous and offensive ways. The examples of genocide that come most readily to mind encourage this belief and they inform one part of common usage. Nonetheless the belief will be seen as mistaken by anyone who accepts that the forcible sterilisation of a people would count as genocide according to all morally serious accounts of it.

There are, of course, great moral differences between the crimes against the children and their mothers and crimes of mass murder whether or not they constitute genocide—so great, indeed, that one might agree with Duffy that different circles of hell are sure to be reserved for their perpetrators. But there is a radical moral difference between the murder of one hundred people and the murder of one hundred thousand, yet no one denies that both are mass murder and that the former should not attract the obloquy carried by the expression. That, I acknowledge, does not settle much. But if one agrees that genocide need not involve mass murder and also that crimes which fall under the same concept may differ radically in respect of their moral seriousness, even when that concept is partly morally conditioned, then one should at least accept that one now has something to think about. The question, then, is whether the concept of genocide will tolerate the relevant moral differences between the Holocaust and what was done to the Aborigines.

Rhetoric will not settle that. Nor will appeal to ordinary usage because there is considerable variety in that usage. Some people restrict the concept of genocide to crimes involving mass murder, while others apply it freely to policies of assimilation. Should we not settle the matter then, by devising a definition suitable for legal purposes? Is it not true, as many people think, that obedience to the injunction 'define your terms' is necessary to clear thinking? Without a definition to guide it, they suppose, discussion will almost certainly degenerate into misunderstanding and obscurity.

Making many and fine distinctions while not seeking a definition is common in the kind of philosophy that is sometimes called 'conceptual analysis'. It is, therefore, not at all obvious that anyone intent on thinking clearly should seek a definition of disputed terms. The difficulties in the concept of genocide are not the difficulties of settling on a definition that might satisfy contesting parties. They are the characteristic difficulties involved in the conceptual exploration of an element of our experience that continues to baffle us. It may baffle us because, as Hannah Arendt insisted, the phenomenon itself is new. Or it may do so because, although the phenomenon is not new, our moral responses to it are, and we are not yet clear what to make of them, or of the two— the phenomenon and our responses—taken together.

Cultural genocide is a term which people use (misleadingly, I shall argue) to describe the intentional destruction of a people by destroying their culture. It is an old crime, but only recently has there been growing consensus that it is an evil whose nature we should acknowledge with a distinct concept in law. There is, however, little agreement about what kind of evil it is and, more importantly, considerable lack of clarity about it. Exploration of it is of a conceptual and moral kind which does not straightaway seek a definition, if one seeks it at all, and which would almost certainly be less subtle and go less deep if it did. The absorption programs reveal, I believe, that the moral, legal and political features of the concept of genocide are still unclear, that we have not yet adequately conceptualised the experiences that make us reach for it.

The sense that our thinking about genocide should rise to something new in our moral and political experience is one that appears to wax and wane. Mostly it seems to wane. This is partly because the concept stands in complex relation to the moral features of a situation which cause people to invoke it, which are generally easily recognised and which almost all people deplore. I have already remarked that many people were shocked by the brutalities recorded in *Bringing Them Home*. Clearly, therefore, the fact that the same people were not seriously troubled by the report's charge of genocide does not mean that they were not troubled by the crimes upon which the concept of genocide offers a new perspective. Does it matter, then, that so many people were not seriously troubled by the fact that the report accused the Australian government of genocide? If someone deplores the brutality against indigenous children and their parents and the racism that made it possible, does it matter if they refuse to call it genocide? What moral difference would it make? Inga Clendinnen asked: 'Is the guilt attaching to the intention to destroy a whole people…different in kind from the intention to kill an equal number of individuals? Does the crime of "genocide" inhabit a moral category of its own?'

The question (I take it to be one question) is important and later I will try to say something to answer it. For the moment I shall merely observe that people of all political persuasions appear to believe that to describe the absorption programs as sometimes genocidal is to level a charge more serious than one informed by even a full appreciation of the racist brutality sometimes suffered by the children and their parents. Implicitly they seem to acknowledge that the concept gives a perspective on that brutality which reveals it to be both more serious and an evil of a different kind. That does not mean that genocide is the worst of crimes. It means only that the concept of genocide can rightly make crimes, which appear relatively insignificant when measured against morally more terrible ones, more serious than they would appear if they were not seen in the light of that concept. If that is true, then the concept does serious moral (and legal) work. It would also explain why the concept tolerates great moral differences between its instances. How great those differences may be can only be determined by careful attention to its alleged instances. Clearly, however, genocide is not necessarily the worst of evils. And there were acts of genocide against the Aborigines, and other crimes against them which were not genocide, that were (morally) worse than the genocide that appears sometimes to have been committed when the absorption programs were enacted.

Even so, I do not underestimate the tendency to feel that the question of whether certain brutalities and injuries count as genocide may appear pedantic and insensitive in the face of an imaginatively realised sense of what people have actually suffered. Many people responded in the same way to the argument about which concepts most adequately revealed the distinctive character of the crimes that defined the Holocaust. Once one had seen the corpses, the death camps, the chilling application of bureaucracy and technology, had one not seen all that was morally relevant to a full appreciation of what had occurred? Why, some people asked, was there so much fuss, so much argument, so much soul searching,

about the nature of 'crimes against humanity', the name given by
the Nuremberg judges to the crimes of the Holocaust in order to
distinguish them from war crimes and from crimes against the
peace? We know what the victims suffered. Would it have made a
difference to their terror, their pain, their humiliation if they had
known their murderers and tormentors were guilty of genocide?
The rhetorical force of these questions is, I think, undeniable. On
the other hand, the instinctive sense that to call something genocide
is to acknowledge a terribleness that may not have been apparent in
an otherwise full description of what had occurred, often shows
itself when people exploit the term for political purposes and when
others are outraged that the term has been abused.

Bringing Them Home accepts the definition of genocide in the
1948 Convention on the Prevention and Punishment of the
Crime of Genocide and argues quite carefully that the crimes
against the children and their parents constituted genocide
according to that definition. The report concludes: 'The policy of
forcible removal of children from Indigenous Australians to other
groups for the purpose of raising them separately from and ignorant of their culture and people could properly be labelled
"genocidal" in breach of binding international law from at least 11
December 1946' (p.275). The argument is, I think, convincing and,
as Colin Tatz, founder of the Centre for the Comparative Study of
Genocide and a tireless campaigner on behalf of the Aborigines,
has often and forcibly pointed out, its importance to Australia
which is a signatory to the convention can hardly be denied. Yet,
when one considers the following quotation, one can see why
both the report's accusation of genocide and the United Nations
definition which supports it should be treated with suspicion:

> The Inquiry's process of consultation and research has
> revealed that the predominant aim of Indigenous child
> removals was the absorption or assimilation of the children
> into the wider, non-Indigenous, community so that their
> unique cultural values and ethnic identities would disappear,

giving way to models of Western culture…Removal of children with this objective in mind is genocidal because it aims to destroy the 'cultural unit' which the Convention is concerned to preserve.

And more explicitly: 'The continuation into the 1970s and 1980s of the practice of preferring non-Indigenous foster and adoptive families for Indigenous children was also arguably genocidal. The genocidal impact of these practices was reasonably foreseeable.'

Sadly, this muddies the waters, for it makes it seem as though depriving a people of their culture with the intention of destroying their identity as a people is of itself the same kind of crime as the genocide in Germany or Rwanda. The argument of the report suggests that these crimes differ only in the means used to realise a common intention. It suggests that the different ways the common intention is realised—sometimes by mass murder, sometimes by the destruction of a culture—is irrelevant to the essence of the crime, but because some ways aggravate the crime so dramatically we are misled into believing that we are confronted with a different kind of crime. No one could seriously deny that some forms of genocide are worse than others and that they are made so by the means chosen to eliminate a people. But that does not mean that genocide should be defined by the intention to destroy a people, as though the death camps in Germany, the killings in Rwanda and the assimilation of children of mixed blood into the white community in Australia in the 1960s were merely different ways of committing the same crime.

Indeed, it is arguable that some of the acts which the convention would count as genocidal may be morally unobjectionable, perhaps even morally necessary. The Convention defines genocide as an act against 'groups' whose identity may be religious or national. Simone Weil had a profound sense of the connection between roots and identity, and she was a ferocious critic of colonial insensitivity to indigenous culture, yet she wrote in *The Need for Roots*:

we owe our respect to a collectivity, of whatever kind—
country, family or any other—not for itself, but because it
is food for a certain number of human souls…One sack of
corn can always be substituted for another sack of corn.
The food which a collectivity supplies for the souls of
those who form part of it has no equivalent in the entire
universe…

[Sometimes it happens that] there are collectivities
which, instead of serving as food, do just the opposite: they
devour souls. In such cases, the social body is diseased, and
the first duty is to attempt a cure; in certain circumstances,
it may be necessary to have recourse to surgical methods.

One need not agree with Weil to find what she says to be at
least arguable amongst decent people. Because the convention
defines genocide as a crime against (amongst others) national or
religious groups, it appears to be vulnerable to Weil's observation
that sometimes 'collectivities devour souls' and that when they do
'surgical methods' may be necessary. The phrase 'surgical methods'
is, it is true, a chilling one, but it is necessary only to imagine
what de-Nazification would look like if the 'Thousand Year
Reich' had survived fifty years only, to see that it could sometimes
be the right one.

Nonetheless, those who say that the destruction of a culture
with the intent to destroy a people's identity is characteristically an

evil are, I believe, right. It is sometimes called 'ethnocide'. That
seems a good name for it, and should refer to a different and lesser
crime than genocide. The reason is not, as the example of forcible
sterilisation shows, because genocide must involve mass murder. It
is hard to explain why more positively and I think the difficulties
go deep. That is why it is so tempting to divide through examples
and settle for a definition that places nearly all the weight on the
intention to destroy a people. And, because a people ceases to exist
as surely when its descendants are no longer nourished by their
native culture as when they are physically exterminated, one can

see why people feel the need for the concept of cultural genocide. Others, like myself, believe it is a *reductio ad absurdum* of the definition that delivers it. It is one of the admirable features of the modern age that we now appreciate the terrible wrong done to a people when they are forcibly denied their culture. But that wrong is not genocide.

When there is discussion of how many children were taken during the absorption and assimilation programs the figure of 100,000 is often mentioned. *Bringing Them Home* expresses no opinion, but says that estimates vary from 10 per cent of children to one third. Critics have attacked the report's accuracy on this as on other matters, implying that the shock people have felt on reading it is a consequence of that inaccuracy. Only if the report were mendacious or irresponsible to a degree that no one reputable has so far suggested, however, would there be reason to believe that 5,000 is an inflated figure. I doubt that anyone reading the report and predecessor reports would believe it could be so low, but even if it were, that figure should not allow consciences to rest easy. The report would also have to be mendacious or grossly irresponsible if the children and their parents were not often the victims of the expression of racist contempt, sometimes brutally expressed.

Brutal treatment of Aboriginal parents and their children and the fact that it was often an expression of racist contempt do not, however, add up to genocide. When people acknowledged that the Holocaust was not merely the worst of the pogroms, they acknowledged that even a murderous racism is not of itself genocidal though it may claim millions of victims. We need something more if we are seriously to invoke the concept of genocide. But, given that the brutal treatment of the Aborigines was often an expression of racist contempt for them, what of the claim that its perpetrators were generally 'well intentioned but utterly misguided', as Ron Brunton put it in the *Courier-Mail* on 21 June 1997?

A person's sincere belief that his intentions are good does not make them good. If it could, then we would have to say the Nazi murderers had good but radically benighted intentions, because many of them believed it to be their duty to humankind to rid the earth of a race that polluted it. We call 'good' only those intentions that express values we can take seriously, even if we do not hold them. The allegedly good intentions of many of those who participated in the absorption programs were akin to those of some slave owners in the southern states of the USA, who wished to improve the conditions of their slaves while at the same time never dreaming that slavery itself constituted an injustice. Such a person might sincerely have condemned his slave-owning neighbour when he raped a slave girl, but we see the nature of his condemnation when we remember that he found it unintelligible to think that his neighbour wronged the girl in the way he would if he raped a white girl. Neither could believe that the girl's soul could be lacerated by this violation of her sexual being, just as many Australian racists could not believe that an Aboriginal mother could grieve all her life for her lost child.

When people say that the absorption programs were for the most part administered by men and women who were 'well intentioned but utterly misguided' they hope to persuade us that the programs were not as bad as they might first appear to be. Few people would be persuaded of this if they kept before their mind the fact that the allegedly good intentions were towards people who were believed to be of a radically different and inferior kind to 'us'—who were seen as different because it appeared unintelligible to their 'benefactors' that anything they could do or suffer could go deep, and therefore that they could not be wronged as 'we' can be.

The dehumanising nature of such racism makes the report of a conference in 1937 of the key administrators of the absorption program chilling reading. With no trace of irony the proceedings were entitled 'Aboriginal Welfare'. All the participants spoke, sincerely I'm sure, of their concern for the welfare of the Aborigines while at the same time applying eugenic categories to them as though they were animals and prescribing conditions for them which they would not dream of prescribing for whites. This looks inconsistent only until one realises that the concern for the welfare of the Aborigines expressed in the report was a concern for the welfare of people perceived to be less than fully human. The report is such chilling reading precisely because page after page expresses this conjunction of racist disdain and sincere professions of concern. Discussions in the report and its publication are acts as brutal and offensive to the dignity of the Aborigines as many of the actions it rationalised and initiated.

Many Aborigines say that they were treated as 'sub-human'. To see why that is often not even slightly an exaggeration, one need only remember that sub-human treatment need not be cruel. It can vary from the unrelievedly brutal to the treatment some 'benevolent' slave owners gave to their slaves. It is consistent with sincere, romantic admiration for the 'nobility' of the people who are treated as sub-human. Such professions of admiration were not uncommon amongst those who administered the absorption programs, and were of a piece with their sincere regret that full-blooded Aborigines were ravaged by disease and alcohol and destined for extinction. To eradicate all traces of the suspicion that such concern is inconsistent with seeing as sub-human the people to whom it is directed, one need only remember that such 'benign' treatment and professions of 'respect' were directed towards people whose inner lives were perceived to be intrinsically lacking in depth. We should remember how M perceived the Vietnamese and how Isdell perceived the Aborigines. If we also remember that to see someone as having an inner life intrinsically lacking in depth is to find it unintelligible that they should be wronged as we can be, then we will not believe that intentions which are saturated with racist disdain can excuse much.

I come now to that 'something more' which, I believe,

explains why a serious concept of genocide may be needed to characterise at least some aspects of the absorption programs. Sometimes the programs were designed to ensure the extinction of the Aboriginal peoples by breeding out those of mixed blood. *Bringing Them Home* makes this clear and it is corroborated by external evidence, notably by the report of the meeting in 1937 at which A. O. Neville, commissioner of Native Affairs in Western Australia was a powerful presence. Neville, Robert Manne tells us in his powerful essay 'The Stolen Generations', was a zealous convert to the eugenic theories which were fashionable in many parts of the world in the thirties. He had ambitious plans for their implementation in Australia. By the time of the conference he had persuaded the Western Australian parliament to create many of the enabling conditions for it. Manne comments:

> This legislation made uncontrolled sexual relations between Europeans and Aborigines a punishable offence. It required Aborigines to seek the permission of the native commissioner to marry. It more or less forbade marriages between half-castes and full-bloods. It prohibited the association of quadroons with those deemed to be 'native' under the act. Most importantly of all it gave the commissioner guardianship rights over all Aborigines up to the age of twenty-one, allowing him to remove all children, whether legitimate or not, from their families.

Keen to persuade other delegates to have a clear mind about the 'half-caste problem' and also a firm resolve to solve it in the way he thought best, Neville asked them rhetorically, 'Are we going to have a population of [1 million] blacks in the Commonwealth, or are we going to merge them into our white community and eventually forget that there were any Aborigines in Australia?'

Dr Cecil Cook, Protector in the Northern Territory needed little persuasion. He had already expressed the view that 'Generally by the fifth and invariably the sixth generation, all native characteristics of the Australian Aborigines are eradicated. The problem of our half-castes will quickly be eliminated by the complete disappearance of the black race, and the swift submergence of their progeny in the white.' Cook's optimism was sustained by the belief, shared by many at the time, that there would be no throwbacks in later generations, no sudden appearance, that is, of a black or partially black baby.

When they are taken together, the three facts I have highlighted—that the Aborigines were sometimes treated brutally, that they were often treated with racist disdain as sub-human, and that the absorption programs were sometimes explicitly intended and prosecuted to eliminate the Aboriginal peoples—should transform our sense of the evil that is already contained in the first two. The concept of genocide will express that transformation. For some time, certainly in the thirties, and in some places, certainly in Western Australia and the Northern Territory, the absorption program expressed the horrifyingly arrogant belief that some peoples may eliminate from the earth peoples they believe to be less than fully human. Enactment of that arrogance is always an evil, whatever the degree of its brutality, and the concept of genocide makes that perspicuous. The concept reveals how a denigratory racism becomes transformed into an evil of a different and more serious kind when it expresses an intention to rid the earth of people who are the victims of that contempt.

If the facts are as I have sketched them, then I am persuaded that genocide was sometimes committed against the indigenous peoples of Australia during the period when it was Australian policy to absorb mixed blood children into the white community. Again, if the facts are as I have assumed them to be, then at the very least my argument establishes that there is a serious case for claiming that the absorption programs had genocidal elements. That may sound weaker than the accusation in *Bringing Them Home*, but it is still much stronger than anything that has been tolerable to those who ridiculed the accusation as ludicrous and offensive. If the forcible sterilisation of a people counts as genocide, then in my judgment so too does the forcible, brutal and relentless abduction of a people's children for the purpose of making that people extinct. The moral difference does not strike me as significant. Their perpetrators may then find themselves in the same circle of hell, though not in the same circle as Hitler and Himmler.

More needs to be said, however, about two facts upon which I commented earlier if justice is to be done to the full complexity of the crimes against the stolen generations. The first is that there was no killing, or certainly no systematic killing, to further the aims of the absorption programs. The second is that at least some who participated in those programs did indeed have good intentions.

A fact more significant than the fact that there was no mass murder explains, I think, why some have angrily rejected the accusation that genocide was committed against the stolen generations. It is the fact that there was no mass murder because it was unthinkable that even a genocidal intention could be realised by such means. Indeed Neville, the most zealous of the administrators in his pursuit of what I claim was his genocidal intent, appears to have been sincerely outraged when he heard reports of the physical maltreatment of Aborigines. In one context, it is important, as I have stressed, to see such outrage as consistent with perceptions of Aborigines that are saturated with racist condescension. In another context, the present one, it is important to note how far such an attitude places Neville and others like him from the perpetrators of the genocides in Germany or Rwanda or Cambodia.

Even the most hair-raising stories in *Bringing Them Home* and elsewhere do not suggest that mass murder ever became thinkable as a measure of last resort. Because mass murder was unthinkable, many people feel that, however terrible the crimes against the Aborigines may have been, Australia was even then a nation different in kind from those in which murder is thinkable, even when it is rejected for political or other reasons. They are right and it is a fact of great moral and political importance. It is not, however, a fact inconsistent with genocide, not at any rate for anyone who accepts that the forcible sterilisation of a people is genocide. The fact that mass murder was unthinkable as a means to eliminating the Aboriginal peoples during the period of the absorption programs is, therefore, consistent with Australia's being guilty at the time of the same crime that was committed by nations in which mass murder was not only thinkable, but also chosen as the means to realise a genocidal intent. Perhaps it helps to get things in perspective if one knows that, although mass murder was unthinkable as a means to eliminate the Aborigines, sterilisation of those of mixed blood was not.

What then of the fact that many people participated in the programs for good motives? *Bringing Them Home* says that 'mixed motives' are not an excuse, meaning that genocide is committed even when a genocidal motive coexists with others, some of which may be good. That strikes me as broadly true, but the matter is more complex than the report allows.

Even in jurisdictions in which there existed a firm genocidal intent, the policy was not always and at all levels executed with that intent. Those on the ground who executed it had a variety of intentions. Some were straightforwardly genocidal, others were not genocidal but expressed racist contempt for the Aborigines, some were good but spoiled by paternalism, and others were good without qualification. We don't know the proportions. The important point, however (one which cuts both ways), is that people whose intentions were good without qualification may have participated in the absorption programs knowing full well that the programs were intended to hasten the end of a race, and while making that intention their own. With sincere and deep regret, they may have concluded that Aboriginal cultures were doomed and that, human nature being what it is, half castes will always be despised. That being so, some may have reasoned, Aboriginal culture was not food but poison for the soul and children needed to be rescued from it. It would be nonsense to say of the genocidal programs in Germany, Armenia or Rwanda that some people who participated in them and who knowingly served their ends were nonetheless good people with unqualifiedly good intentions. That is why some people find it absurd, even indecent, to call the absorption programs 'genocide', with all the disgrace that word rightly attracts. It is, to be sure, an extraordinary qualification on an accusation of genocide to say that some, perhaps many, people knowingly participated in it with intentions beyond serious reproach.

Do such concessions inflict a death of a thousand qualifications (to adapt the memorable phrase of the English philosopher Antony Flew) on any substantial notion of genocide? I think not. Suppose administrators who intend that their actions should cause a race whose members they treat as sub-human to become extinct. Suppose that the existence of that intention depends on a belief that the full-blood members of the race will become extinct through natural causes. Suppose that the extinction of the full-bloods is not sought and is actually regretted. And suppose, finally, that the administrators and those whom they entrust to carry out their programs have other intentions, some consistent with their intention to eliminate a people and some which conflict with, even contradict, it. Even so, with all those qualifications in place, the genocidal intention exists and is acted upon. Those suppositions, consistent with the conclusion that genocide is committed, correspond to the facts as I understand them to be recorded in *Bringing Them Home*. Important though the qualifications I have recorded are, they do not, singly or together, undermine those facts and their genocidal significance.

That being so, Australia is awakening to something truly terrible. John Howard said in response to *Bringing Them Home* that contemporary Australians should not feel guilty for what they did not do. He was reminded by Sir Ronald Wilson that the word 'guilt' did not appear in the report in any accusations by its authors. No doubt they had their reasons for their restraint. Yet Howard was right to be troubled by thoughts of guilt. Indeed, the most puzzling aspect of the report's reception is that (as far as I know) hardly anyone who has broadly accepted the facts it records and its conclusion that genocide was committed has proposed that there be criminal trials to determine who is guilty and to punish them. Admittedly, the United Nations Convention was never incorporated into Australian law and there are more than enough other practical and legal reasons to reject such a proposal, but they are not the reasons why no one has seriously suggested that a court be established. How can one say that genocide has been committed, yet ask only for an apology and compensation? How can you think genocide always to be a serious crime, yet find it unthinkable to call for criminal proceedings? Such questions can fairly be pressed against those who say that genocide was committed and that it was a terrible evil.

If anyone important—especially an Aboriginal leader—were seriously to press for trials there would a vicious backlash against the Aborigines far worse than anything expressed in Hansonism. That is in itself sufficient reason not to propose them. There is also the fact that the kind of genocidal intent expressed by protectors like Isdell, and which gave the character to much of the evil done to the Aborigines before the fifties, became at least attenuated from the early fifties onwards. Many of the thoughts which informed that intent—those that expressed the racist denigration of Aborigines and their culture and those that expressed the wish that they should disappear as a people—persisted, but they appeared no longer to harden into an explicit genocidal intention. If the intention was still there, it was residually there. So, at any rate, it seems.

Such facts speak against trials—decisively so in my judgment—but they do not explain why they are unthinkable. That they are unthinkable for most Australians is the most persuasive evidence that the significance of the crimes against the Aborigines has not been fully appreciated. If it becomes fully appreciated, as I hope it will, then it is hard to see how people will be able to resist the natural thought that the criminals who enacted the programs when the genocidal intention was firm should be brought to justice. I hope that if and when that happens, the thought will promptly be put aside under the pressure of the overwhelming reasons to do so. There are other ways we can properly acknowledge the evil done to the Aborigines and the imperatives of reconciliation. But before it is put aside a thought must first come to mind. In its application to this case, the distinction between something being unthinkable and its being thought and rejected marks the difference between a full and a partial understanding of the crimes committed against the Aborigines. Chesterton was right to say that civilisation is suspended on a spider's web of fine distinctions. Unless trials become thinkable for us, I believe we cannot claim fully to understand the moral dimensions of our past.

Just as it has been unthinkable that there should be trials, so it has been unthinkable, even to most people who passionately support reconciliation, that Australians are now obliged to examine their consciences for reasons similar to those which obliged the Germans to do so after the war. Because people are guilty not only for what they do but also for what they fail to do, the citizens of a democratic nation which is guilty of genocide cannot for long avoid asking questions about the role they played in it. What did we make of rumours? What did we know? What should we have known? The world demanded that the Germans put these questions to themselves. The evil done to the Aborigines was significantly different in degree to the evil done to the Jews and the gipsies and (in my opinion) different in kind. But the differences do not obviate the need for us to put these questions to ourselves and sometimes to others.

I would not wish to encourage sentimental expressions of collective guilt. They are distasteful and often harmful. Arendt noted caustically how protestations of collective guilt released

German youth from a sober sense of their duty to name those whom they suspected, and sometimes knew, to be guilty of mass murder. Far better to beat your breast on Anne Frank's birthday than to risk your job by naming your boss. 'When all are guilty, none are,' Arendt observed.

Her rhetoric hit its mark, I think, but one should not take her to mean that guilt by omission cannot be extensive. It is that acknowledgment of such guilt must be hard and sober if it is to be a truthful recognition of the wrong one has done and if it is to preserve the fundamental distinction between those who are guilty because, in different ways and for different reasons, they failed to respond to the crimes committed by their governments and fellow citizens, and those who are guilty in a primary way because they directly participated in those crimes.

Whatever the outcome of the painful debate that is now upon us, we can be sure that the Aborigines will not find their Daniel Goldhagen, who recently argued that many more Germans knew of and readily participated in the Holocaust than had previously been admitted. Most Australians did not know the facts contained in *Bringing Them Home*. But the reason we did not know does most of us little credit and must morally complicate whatever extenuating work can be done by the fact that we did not know. We did not know because we did not care enough. We did not care enough because the humanity of the Aborigines was not fully present to our moral faculties. The reasons for that are not different in kind from the reasons why Isdell could say that he 'would not hesitate for one moment to separate any half-caste from its mother'. The racism expressed in both is merely more virulent in the second. Australians were often culpably ignorant of the wrong done to the Aborigines because, in racist ways, they were blind to their full humanity. How extraordinary then that our current government treats reconciliation as though it were substantially a two-way affair, as though we had something serious for which to forgive the Aborigines.

Is it just hyperbole to say that many Australians are now obliged to examine their consciences for reasons similar to those which obliged Germans to do it after the war? An anecdote will show that it is not. During the late sixties many students were active in their support of the civil rights movement in the US, and often of more radical movements like the Black Panthers. During that period someone came from Queensland to speak to the Labour Club at the University of Melbourne, which was then a club of the radical left. I was amongst the thirty or more students present. The speaker said that people from the southern states of the US, disenchanted with their lives there because of the success of the civil rights movement, had moved to Queensland where they sometimes went on hunting parties in their four-wheel-drives to shoot Aborigines. That is almost certainly false, but it does not matter to the point of my anecdote, which is that, although we found the story credible, I am sure that not one of us did anything to find out whether it was true.

My fellow students and I were guilty of an appalling omission. It is, after all, no credit to us that the story was not true. How, then, could idealistic, sincerely anti-racist students be guilty of such indifference to what was alleged to be happening to their black fellow citizens? Any explanation must, I think, use the concept of racism. But it would be wrong to say, flatly, that despite our sincere anti-racist professions we were racists at heart. I don't know that we were racist at all. If we were, then the manner or degree of it would not explain why we did not inquire into what was happening in Queensland. The racism that must be invoked to explain why we failed to do anything must be located somewhere other than deep in our hearts. That place, of course, is in some of the institutions of Australian society.

Genocide &
the Holocaust

By the time of the Final Solution, it was evident that the attempt to annihilate the Jews served none of the ordinary political purposes for which crimes have been committed throughout history. Nor could it be explained by the way the human personality becomes deranged in times of war and great upheaval. Nor by elaboration of the theme that violence begets violence. The Jews were not murdered because they were enemies of the Reich, or because they were obstacles to its expansion, or because it served the Reich's purpose to scapegoat them or for any such familiar political reason. They were killed because they were judged unfit to inhabit the earth with the master race. The ruthless determination to hunt and to kill them in all the corners of the earth, if possible, distinguishes the Holocaust from other forms of genocide, as they are alleged to have occurred in colonial times. And it distinguishes the murder of the Jews from that of the gipsies and homosexuals. More chilling even than that, however, is the fact that the attempt to exterminate of the Jews was not an aberration of war. It was integral to the civic ideals of the Thousand Year Reich.

Jews threatened no one, not even religiously. They had either assimilated successfully or lived in ghettoes which caused no problems to the wider community. Yet to the Nazis and their supporters their mere existence was so offensive as to inspire the most virulent hatred. Nothing Jews could do, even in principle, could save themselves from annihilation. It is a bitter irony, therefore, that the Final Solution was not a measure taken to address what anyone could seriously call a social or political problem, not even if one added that the Jews could be a problem only for the wicked. When the mere existence of a people is supposed to constitute a problem independently of their characteristics and how they behave, then we are dealing with a degenerate application of the concept of a problem. Anti-Semitic stereotypes did, of course, cast Jews as a problem—as Bolsheviks, as capitalists, as threats to children, to culture and religion and so on. But those stereotypes did not express genuinely mistaken beliefs about the Jews which would explain the hatred of them. The stereotypes rationalised the hatred; they did not cause it.

It seems that the terribleness of the Holocaust dawned on the judges at Nuremberg only gradually. At first they were preoccupied with their determination to prosecute Germany for crimes against the peace and for war crimes. When the distinctive character of the Holocaust began to emerge for them, they were understandably overwhelmed by the horror of it and so were unable to conceptualise clearly what struck them as distinctive. Their sense that they were confronted with new crimes appeared to wax and wane—as it has done in the minds of many after them—yet it remained sufficiently strong for them to give a new name to them. They called them 'crimes against humanity'. In some ways the name is inspired but it also invites the misconception that the Holocaust was marked by its extreme *inhumaneness*, that it was the most hideous of .

the pogroms, distinguished from others by its extent and terribleness, but not in its essence. It suggests that crimes against humanity were different from others only on account of their barbarity. The crimes of the Nazis *were* distinguished by their barbarity, but considered in that aspect they were different only in degree from their war crimes, and from other abominations throughout history. A tendency to understand the concept of a crime against humanity as marking a terrible degree of inhumaneness has been one reason why the distinctions drawn at Nuremberg have largely been forgotten, even amongst Jews.

That forgetfulness shows itself in a number of ways. Consider as a first example the debates in the late 1980s over whether the Australian government should pass legislation to try people, now living in Australia, who had committed crimes during World War II. Everyone knew that most of the accused would be from Eastern Europe and that they would be charged with crimes connected with the Holocaust. Few people expected that anyone would actually be convicted in the Australian trials. Those who wanted the trials did so because they hoped they would have 'educative value'. It is ironic, therefore, that the legislation they supported should have expressed the most common and fundamental misunderstanding about the Holocaust, namely that the crimes that define it were acts of war, no different in kind from those that were committed in the former Yugoslavia.

It was, of course, the Serbs' talk of ethnic cleansing that made people speak in the same breath of their crimes and those of the Nazis. The Serbs, however, indulged only their desire to rid their territory of Croats and Muslims. Their hatred was not inspired by the thought that Croats were vermin, but by a complex history of national hatred, past fighting and atrocities. The thought that one's enemies are vermin can mean different things and show itself in many ways. When it surfaced in the minds of the Serbs, it was more a consequence of the war than one of its causes. For the Nazis, ridding the earth of the Jews was a civic ideal, which, though it developed and hardened during the war, was essentially unconnected with the war and the kinds of hatreds wars cause. The chilling bureaucratic finesse of the Final Solution was a terrible intimation of a postwar civilian world in which the death camps would continue. Had the Nazis won the war, the attempt to annihilate the Jews totally would have continued in peacetime, not in the spirit of finishing business that had started in wartime and whose nature was essentially shaped by wartime conditions, but as a political ideal of the New Reich.

Steven Spielberg's powerful and successful film, *Schindler's List*, and the controversy that followed its release, gives a second example. A small number of mostly Jewish critics who were disturbed by the film and by its reception raised the question whether, despite the declared intentions of its makers, the film undermined truthful perception of the Holocaust and, in so doing, the ground of our need to remember it. To my knowledge none of the critics denied the film's power. On the contrary, their acknowledgment of its power gave weight to their misgivings.

Many—perhaps most—Jews, including many survivors of the death camps, responded to the film with a euphoria that seemed to be the consequence of having many times suffered the nightmare that Primo Levi recounts—that he is freed from Auschwitz, that he tells of what he suffered and saw there, but no one believes him. More than anything, I suspect, that explains their intense irritation with the film's critics. They saw them as unable to see, and as spoiling, this unprecedented opportunity finally to stop that nightmare. They believed the world would see this film and weep over what they and the dead had suffered, and over the world's indifference to it.

Sadly, the euphoria expressed a loss of contact with reality. The degree of it showed in the fact that many people hoped that those who had been corrupted by Holocaust deniers to doubt that millions of Jews were murdered in the death camps would be persuaded to believe it by a film made by an internationally influential Hollywood Jew. As though *The Protocols of the Elders of Zion* had taught us nothing about the nature of anti-Semitism! Younger people who felt the power of the film sometimes believed themselves to be obliged, in fidelity to that very power, to apply, with no conceptual unease, what they took to be its lessons to the former Yugoslavia, to the settlement of Australia and, of course, to the conduct of Israeli soldiers on the West Bank. Nothing in the film substantially contradicts them. Nothing of dramatic power in it shows, or even suggests, that the crimes depicted in it are different in kind from those that were committed in the name of ethnic cleansing. Nothing even seriously contradicts the revisionists. (The scenes in Auschwitz have almost universally been regarded as a failure.) Yet the illusion that *Schindler's List* would finally plant the lessons of the Holocaust in the hearts of millions of people seemed unassailable.

Less than a year later it was shattered by the honours awarded to Helen Darville's book, *The Hand That Signed the Paper,* and by the subsequent argument over it. This is my third example. Many Jews perceived the book to be anti-Semitic and to degrade memory of the Holocaust. In many cases their pain went deeper than indignation or anger. Robert Manne wrote poignantly of how the affair had 'destabilised him', profoundly affecting his sense of his place in Australia, the country he loved and to which he had given so much of himself. Others felt the same. Their pain does not prove their reading of the book to be the right one, but if its tone had been heard the discussion would have been different.

It wasn't heard for a number of reasons. For the purposes of this discussion, the most important was the widespread irritation with Jews and with the place they accord, and ask others to accord, to the Holocaust in humanity's self-understanding. To what degree that irritation was a cause, and to what degree an effect of a failure to understand the nature of the Holocaust, is hard to say. Amongst other ways, the failure showed itself in the repeated suggestion that we could get a perspective on the alleged anti-Semitism of Darville's novel if we remember that many of the great writers of the past were anti-Semitic. As though anti-Semitic aspects in the novels of Dostoyevsky or of Dickens, for example, before the Holocaust could have the same significance as an anti-Semitic novel written after the Holocaust and whose anti-Semitism is directed at undermining the moral response to the Holocaust that had been common to Jews and non-Jews alike.

Darville vindicated Spielberg's critics, if not in their judgment of his film, then at least in their dismay at the impatient response to the important questions they had raised. The Darville affair was partly the result of the carelessness about the characterisation of the Holocaust that showed itself in that impatience—sometimes in the vehement hostility—directed at Spielberg's critics and at critics of the war crimes legislation. Sooner than anyone predicted, that impatience reaped what it had sown. Darville succeeded in convincing many people that the crimes of the Ukrainians involved in the Holocaust were no different in kind from those now committed by all the combatants in the former Yugoslavia. It is true that the Ukrainians were probably seldom motivated by considerations of the kind that define the Holocaust. They would, however, be charged with crimes against humanity rather than with war crimes by any court that distinguished them. Many of Darville's younger readers did not know there is such a distinction to be made, and many older readers did not think it important to tell them. For Jews who had placed their hopes in them, the trials and Spielberg's film could hardly have failed more completely to educate people about the meaning of the Holocaust.

Apart from the time of the Nuremberg trails, the most interesting and intense discussion of the distinctive character of the Nazi crimes occurred, in my judgment, during and immediately after the trial of Adolf Eichmann in 1961. Eichmann was charged with crimes against the Jewish people. In *Eichmann in Jerusalem* Hannah Arendt said that he should have been tried for crimes against humanity, perpetrated on the body of the Jewish people. Critical though she was of aspects of the trial, she credited the judges in Jerusalem with a clearer and more constant grasp of what was at issue than was possessed by the judges in Nuremberg, who, she said, tended to think of crimes against humanity 'as inhuman acts...as though the Nazis had simply been lacking in human kindness'. Alluding to the rhetoric of the prosecution she praised the judges in Jerusalem for refusing 'to let the basic character of the crime be swallowed up by a flood of atrocities'. She writes:

> It was the great advantage of a trial centred on the crime against the Jewish people that not only did the difference between war crimes, such as shooting of partisans and killing of hostages, and 'inhuman acts,' such as 'expulsion and annihilation' of native populations to permit colonization by an invader, emerge with sufficient clarity to become part of the future international penal code, but also that the difference between 'inhuman acts' (which were undertaken for some known, though criminal, purpose, such as expansion through colonization) and the 'crime against humanity,' whose intent and purpose were unprecedented, was clarified. At no point, however, either in the proceedings or in the judgment, did the Jerusalem trial ever mention even the possibility that extermination of whole ethnic groups—the Jews, or the Poles, or the Gypsies— might be more than a crime against the Jewish or the Polish or the Gypsy people, that the international order, and mankind in its entirety, might have been grievously hurt and endangered.

It is easy to be misled by Arendt's remark that 'mankind in its entirely might be grievously hurt and endangered'. One might, quite naturally, take her to mean that humankind was in danger of suffering what the Jews had suffered. It is true that other groups were marked for genocide, and it is true that in other works Arendt shows deep concern over the possibility that the Holocaust would be repeated, though not necessarily against Jews.

Such thoughts, however, are not the ones driving this passage. Arendt expresses herself better, I think, when she says that genocide should be seen as a crime against 'the order of mankind', just as the murder of an individual is an offence, a 'hurt', against a community even when it does not have the potential to encourage more crimes of the same kind. Arendt's praise of the French prosecutor at Nuremberg for calling crimes against humanity 'crimes against the human status' was motivated by the same thought. Elaborating on it, she suggests that we think of a crime against humanity as 'an attack upon human diversity as such, that is upon a characteristic of the "human status" without which the very words "mankind" or "humanity" would be devoid of meaning.'

Eichmann in Jerusalem provoked widespread anger and dismay. To many people it seemed too abstract, too cold. Arendt was often accused of heartlessness. Gershom Scholem wrote to her saying:

> Why, then, should your book leave one with so strong a sensation of bitterness and shame—not for the compilation, but for the compiler?...Insofar as I have an answer, it is one which, precisely out of my deep respect for you, I dare not suppress...It is that heartless, frequently almost sneering and malicious tone with which these matters, touching the very quick of our life, are treated in your book to which I take exception.

No one could sensibly have wanted the judgment of the Jerusalem court to have been distorted by a 'flood of atrocities', but often the atrocities recounted in the court appeared to be essential, not only to the evil of Eichmann's crimes, but also to an adequate understanding of their novelty. It seemed implausible that the death camps could be regarded merely as an aggravation upon a crime whose essence could be captured without reference to them. Yet to many that is how Arendt appeared to take them when she praised the judges in Jerusalem for refusing to let the basic character of the crime be swallowed up by a 'flood of atrocities' and even more when she declared the essence of that claim to be its attack on 'human diversity'.

She was misunderstood. Talk of the 'flood of atrocities' inevitably brings the death camps to mind. The name 'death camps' invites us to think of them as killing centres. And of course they were that. Films and photographs we have seen will ensure that our imaginations are assailed by terrible images of corpses piled high. Considered only as killing centres, however, even as horrifically brutal ones, the existence of the camps provides no reason to seek a new name for a new crime. Nothing in the images that assail us could give us that reason. Attention to the bureaucratic efficiency that facilitated the mass murder will not do it either, I think. Considered as a means to mass murder, the bureaucratically efficient 'industrialisation of death' was (perhaps) a new means to the achievement of an old end, but that does not imply that the new means was different in kind from older ones.

To put the point brutally: piles of corpses will look the same and horrify us in the same way whether they were produced for the sake of the ancient political end of eradicating opposition or to eliminate from the earth a people believed to be pollutants of it. Only the latter counts as genocide. If one thinks of the camps as essentially killing centres, as the locus of nightmarish atrocities, perhaps the most terrible that human beings have ever committed against one another, then stories from the camps, told in a court of law, are more likely to obscure than to reveal the nature of the criminal purpose which the camps served.

The matter becomes even clearer if one thinks, as I do, that reflecting on the forcible sterilisation of a people should incline one to think that genocide may be committed though not one person was murdered to achieve it. Even when they are considered as existing in the service of a genocidal end, the death camps are, therefore, as Arendt implied, an aggravation on a crime whose nature need not involve killing at all. Seen from that point of view, Arendt's fear that the essence of the crime for which Eichmann was charged would be obscured by 'a flood of atrocities' was not the expression of heartlessness.

Not heartlessness, but perhaps some degree of confusion. My defence of Arendt has so far assumed that the charge against Eichmann—that he was guilty of crimes against humanity—should be read as the charge of genocide. Many assumed, however, that the charge against him should distil the essence of the Holocaust, an assumption that was almost irresistible. Yet, on reflection, it is far from clear that genocide is the essence of the Holocaust, not if one keeps in mind the features of it that make people say it is unique, even that it is, and will forever be, mysterious. If there is reason to distinguish between genocide and the essence of the Holocaust, then there is reason to suspect we distort the significance of the death camps if we think of them merely as efficient killing centres serving a genocidal intent, even if we stress the terrible purity of the intent and the relentlessness of its execution.

Anyone who has read Primo Levi or Martin Gilbert will, I think, find it impossible to separate the death camps from whatever inclines them to say the Holocaust is unique, that it can never be explained, even when they separate the reasons why they say that from their understanding of genocide. The death camps made apparent something that was not evident even in the killings in the east. News of those killings, their massive and unrelenting scale, convinced many in the Polish ghettos that something different and more terrible in kind had begun than anything they had experienced in the ghettos. We naturally think the Holocaust includes the destruction of the ghettos, the killings in the east and the death camps. We are right to do so and it would be a mistake to think that the Holocaust proper began only with the institution of the death camps. But just as some of the Jews in the Warsaw ghetto sensed that they had glimpsed something terrifyingly different in kind from what they had suffered in the ghettos when they heard of the killings in the east, so, it seems to me, there is also a difference in kind between the killings in the east and the death camps.

Or perhaps the point can be put slightly differently this way. Some people realised what was really being done in the ghettos when they heard of the killings in the east. The death camps made others realise what was really being done in the east. In the east the Nazis' genocidal purpose became transparent. In the death camps it became clear that something even more terrible than genocide was being committed. The death camps are essential to our under-standing of the Holocaust, not because they were horrifically efficient killing centres, but because there occurred in them an assault on the preciousness of individual human beings of a kind never seen before. That, I think, is the truth in Avishai Margalit's claim that the Holocaust was unique because it combined mass murder with demonic efforts to humiliate those who were destined to be murdered.

Distinctions such as I have drawn are not likely to show themselves at all clearly in a courtroom where survivors from the Warsaw ghetto, survivors of the *Einsatzgruppen* and survivors from the camps tell their terrible stories. Again, floods of atrocities would obscure them. But, unlike the way they obscure the nature of genocide, some of those atrocities—those that occurred in the death camps—can take us to the essence of the Holocaust. Arendt was right to say that a flood of atrocities would have obscured the essence of the crime with which Eichmann should be charged, if we assume that he should have been charged with genocide. But if I have been right to draw the distinction I have, then it is also true that 'a flood of atrocities'—that is to say, atrocity piled upon atrocity irrespective of whether they were committed in the ghettos, in the east or in the camps—would also have obscured the distinctive evil of the Holocaust, an evil different from and worse than genocide and which cannot be understood apart from the camps. The camps are the purest and worst examples of genocide and something worse still.

It is not surprising that the distinctive evil of the Holocaust and the purity of the genocide perpetrated in it should not have been distinguished in Nuremberg or in Jerusalem. The relentless destruction of a people is the salient fact in both and both are probably unprecedented. If one tries to articulate the distinctive evil of the Holocaust by focusing on what is unprecedented in it, then one is almost bound to run together moral phenomena that should be kept distinct, and perhaps only one of which (genocide) is tractable to law. Only gradually has the difference emerged in the writings of survivors like Primo Levi. He does not articulate the difference, but one becomes aware when reading him that the camps represent an evil different from genocide in even its purest form. Like the concept of an atrocity, the concept of an unprecedented crime is unresponsive to the difference.

Marvellous though it is in its serious tone and sober judgment, Arendt's discussion is an example that reveals, in a fertile confusion, the tendency to conflate the distinctive evil of the Holocaust and the distinctive moral character of genocide. She assumed that the perpetrators of the Holocaust should be charged with a crime whose name would express its distinctive evil. That is why she ran together her reflections on the banality of evil, as these were informed by her sense of Eichmann's character, with her reflections on the nature of genocide. Her conclusions about that informed her discussion of the kind of crime he should be charged with. It is at least plausible that, when set against the terrible evil of his deeds, the banality of Eichmann's character would deepen our understanding of his crimes and so of the distinctive nature of the Holocaust. It is not plausible, however, that it would reveal the essence of genocide which can be committed by exactly the kind of monsters that Arendt, rightly or wrongly, denied Eichmann to be.

When the court in Jerusalem passed judgment on Eichmann and sentenced him to death, many were impressed by a sense of the unbridgeable distance between the evil he had done and what it was possible for the court to do. It seemed to many, in Jerusalem and on other occasions, that the crimes of the Holocaust mocked the instruments of justice which had never been fashioned, and could never be modified, to deal with them. Before Jerusalem and after, people have persistently expressed a sense of the incommensurability of the evil of the crimes that define the Holocaust, and the conditions of legal practice. It is as though the terrible and unique evil of these crimes reveals that the law, which of course is no stranger to the varieties of brutality and sadism, is founded on assumptions about our common humanity, our intelligibility to one another, which these crimes undermine.

I do not say such a response is clear let alone right to the extent that it can be stated clearly. But it has been expressed so often that it should be respected. It does not entail that there should not have been trials, nor that Eichmann should not have been hanged, even though Martin Buber (who as Arendt observes should have known better) claimed that to hang him would be to declare that there existed a punishment that would be appropriate to his deeds. Arendt has some sober and justifiably scathing words about this. But just as a sense of incommensurability, between the crimes committed by Eichmann and the conditions of legal practice, does not entail Buber's conclusion, rejection of his conclusion does not entail rejection of that sense of incommensurability.

Arendt is not always concerned enough to avoid misinterpretation on this point. She seems sometimes to imply that the sense of incommensurability is sustained by a failure adequately to distinguish between law and morality. 'The wrongdoer,' she writes:

> is brought to justice because his act has disturbed and gravely endangered the community as a whole, and not because, as in civil suits, damage has been done to individuals who are entitled to reparation...For just as a murderer is prosecuted because he has violated the law of the community, and not because he has deprived the Smith family of its husband, father, and breadwinner, so these modern, state-employed mass murderers must be prosecuted because they violated the order of mankind, and not because they killed millions of people.

True and important though Arendt's point is, one must be careful not to draw the wrong lesson from it. Despite the distinguished place, in some legal philosophies, of the view that law and morality are quite distinct, our practices often bring them together with a justified lack of anxiety. It is true that the moral wrong of, say, murder is an offence only against its victims, whereas the crime of murder is also an offence against the community. The difference shows itself in the fact that the law will insist on prosecuting attempted murderers even if their victims are ready to forgive them. Clearly, therefore, there exists an important difference between the criminality of murder and the moral wrong of it. That difference will not appear as radical as it otherwise might, if one remembers that the kind of community we are is partly constituted by our concerns for the *wrongs* suffered by its members when they are the victims of *crime*. The concept of a crime carries with it a richer concept of criminal and victim, and a richer concept of the community to which both belong, than anything that could be captured in a narrow legalism that radically separates law from morality. The legitimate desire to resist the reduction of a crime to moral categories should not lead us to obscure that.

The suspicion, therefore, that the crimes of the Holocaust cannot be captured in concepts sufficiently tractable to serve the purposes of law does not—certainly it need not—rest on the assumption that the law is concerned with the criminality of deeds rather than with their moral character. It is because of something peculiar to the Holocaust. The difficulty in understanding the nature of genocide is also a difficulty inseparable from understanding its distinctive moral nature—here morality and law are indivisible. But I doubt that the difficulties are of a kind that should make us fearful that genocide is beyond the conceptual reach of the law. That is partly because evil is not the concept that marks the inexpungeable moral dimension of the concept of genocide; it is not, I think, the concept that even partially explains why we have had such difficulty in trying to understand the experiences that we bring under the concept of genocide. Considered as a 'crime against humanity', 'against the human status', 'against human plurality', genocide can be committed even in its purest form, and its essence can be understood, by people who have no understanding of 'goodness beyond virtue and evil beyond vice'.

The combination of the belief that we *must* deal with the crimes of the Holocaust with the strong sense that we *cannot* has parallels elsewhere. Sara Horowitz noted that some of the survivors of the death camps were driven by the bitter imperative that they must tell others, but that others could not understand. It is the reason for the tone of despair which is for the most part absent from the writings from the Lodz and Warsaw ghettos. Chronicles were written in both ghettos which meticulously record the daily life in them—from the killings to the supply of potato peelings—with a confidence that they would be understood by those who read them after the war. The chroniclers conceived the evil they suffered to be no more than a terrible interruption in the movement of civilisation, for which there had been many historical precedents. It is true that for a considerable time life in the ghettos had some of the trappings of normality, but that is not why the chroniclers wrote with such confidence. Later, when that confidence was shaken, when a note of despair crept into some of their writings, it is not because the brutality had increased (although it had), or because they feared they would all be killed (although they did). The despair came when they heard of the killings in the east and began to understand the relentless determination of the Germans to hunt down Jews and to kill them in their thousands wherever they could find them. It deepened and seemed to take on a different character in 1942 when almost three thousand Jews were sent to Treblinka.

The dawning of the terrible realisation of what the Holocaust meant conditioned the tone of the despair. Horowitz writes: 'The Ghetto writers anticipate the outrage of a future reader—outrage based upon shared values and a common idea of civilisation. Generally they remain untroubled by the suspicions which plague survivor reflections that these values were killed by the Holocaust, or indeed brought it on.'

Survivors from the death camps tell us again and again that the essential dimension of their experience cannot be understood. Descriptions of subjective states, especially of traumatic ones, are of course inherently difficult, but that is not the reason why survivors cannot convey to us what they have experienced. The reason is that there is a critical element of their experience which is incomprehensible even to themselves.

To distinguish and characterise the many reasons why people have said that the Holocaust is unique has proved impossibly difficult. It is not unique in the sense of being unrepeatable. Indeed, often the very people who have insisted that the Holocaust is unique have expressed the fear that it will be repeated, if not against the Jews, then against others. More commonly, people will say that the Holocaust is historically unprecedented, and although that is true in more ways than one I do not believe that it captures what is most important in the impulse to say it is unique. Often those who were moved to speak of the Holocaust's uniqueness were not historians, and I suspect that those who were did not call it unique because they had an assured scholarly sense that there are no salient historical precedents. They spoke as they did because, when the facts of the Holocaust became known, they felt that the meaning of those facts could not be captured adequately by existing legal, moral or political categories.

Indeed some people thought that the facts subverted those categories. For them, as Horowitz brings out, the Holocaust did not merely crush the hopes of continuous human progress, the hopes of the enlightenment. It did so in ways that put in doubt our understanding of ourselves as moral and political beings. The fact that people responded that way to the Holocaust does not, of course, show that they were right to do so, that their responses were true to the facts. But those common responses to the Holocaust differ markedly, I think, from responses to genocide, even in its pure form as it occurred in the Holocaust, to the extent that they can be separated. And that provides reason for believing that we should distinguish the distinctive evil of the Holocaust from that of genocide, as that term is applicable, for example, to the massacres in Armenia, perhaps in Rwanda, or in Tasmania. Difficult though it may be adequately to capture the nature of genocide, our bafflement over it has not appeared to us radically to threaten the categories with which we understand ourselves.

If I am right, then the idea of a crime against humanity should be reserved to articulate the nature of genocide rather than the deeds that define the Holocaust. Argument about the nature of the Holocaust will continue, probably intractably. But just as the evil of genocide is not necessarily greater than other evils, so the evil of the Holocaust need not be the greatest evil. Nothing I have said entails that it is greater than, say, the evils committed by Stalin. If someone were to ask me which of these is greater I would have no idea how to answer or even how to think towards achieving an answer. Our sense of the distinctiveness of the Holocaust as something different from and worse than genocide, and our sense (if we have it) of it as deeply mysterious, depend on our sense of the evil that it manifests. But even if these, singly or together, justify the claim that the Holocaust is uniquely evil, it is yet a further, and I believe unjustified, step to say that therefore the evil of the Holocaust is the greatest evil we know.

What, then, distinguishes genocide from other, less serious, crimes against human plurality—crimes such as the destruction of a culture? What I am about to say towards an answer should not be taken as even a rough definition of genocide. But it will, I hope, identify something that is fundamental to genocide and also show why the absorption programs described in *Bringing Them Home* were sometimes genocidal in a sense which rightly attracts the obloquy the term has acquired through association with more terrible examples. A clue lies in the closing pages of Arendt's book when she outlines why she thinks Eichmann deserved the death penalty. In an imaginary address to Eichmann she says:

> And just as you supported and carried out a policy of not wanting to share the earth with the Jewish people and the people of a number of other nations—as though you and your superiors had any right to determine who should and who should not inhabit the world—we find that no one, that is, no member of the human race, can be expected to want to share the earth with you.

Leave aside whether that justifies Eichmann's execution. These words capture something essential about genocide, especially when we read them against what we know to be the spirit in which the Nazis killed the Jews.

The desire not to share the earth with a people because they are perceived to be unfit to inhabit it, the desire to rid the earth of them because they are seen to be pollutants of it—these desires and the intentions and actions they inspire can mean different things in different contexts. The words that describe them do not give us a clear and simple standard with which to measure the genocidal elements in crimes. The Holocaust is our paradigm for one kind of terrible application of them. They are not uniquely adequate words to capture what makes it a paradigm. None could be.

Still less could there be uniquely adequate words to capture the distinctive evil of the Holocaust. Elie Wiesel says that only those who were its victims can really understand it. He seems to suggest that this is for reasons that are distinctive to the Holocaust rather than to an understanding of the traumatic experiences of others—those who suffered in the Gulag, or who have been tortured, for example. Sometimes he appears to suggest that the reasons why it is impossible for anyone who did not suffer directly in the Holocaust to understand it are reasons why there is no serious point in trying to do it. Even if it were desirable not to try and to maintain pious silence, it is not possible. We are haunted by the Holocaust precisely because there is reason to say it is unique and we will continue to make what sense we can of it. The reason why we are obliged solemnly to remember it is the reason why we cannot stop trying to fathom it, and if we cannot fathom it to understand better why we can't.

The place occupied by the Holocaust in Western thought has sometimes justifiably been resented by other victims of terrible crimes and by others on their behalf. They have sometimes felt that their suffering has been denigrated by the pre-eminence accorded to the Holocaust in our concern with the atrocities of the twentieth century, and by the political exploitation of that concern. I take it for granted that the politically corrupt uses to which the Holocaust has been put—most often in the service of Israel or, perhaps more accurately, to the service of certain kinds of Zionist ideologists—need no labouring by me. And, as I have already argued, preoccupation with the mystery of the Holocaust, bound up as that is with its distinctive evil, does not entail, and should never lead to, the claim that all other evils are lesser than the evil of the Holocaust.

With less assurance I assume that the kind of 'Holocaust theology' that appears to find edification in the idea that the Holocaust has given a new dimension to the problem of evil—the problem, that is, of how, given the evil in the world, there could be a God who is omniscient, omnipotent and also good—is morally suspect. What kind of person would need the Holocaust to raise that problem for him? It would of course almost always be impertinent to question the religious or moral authenticity of those who actually did lose their faith in the camps and elsewhere. But there is something unsavoury in asking in a theoretical way whether the Holocaust should prove that God must lack at least one of the qualities generally attributed to him because the possession of all three looks to be inconsistent with the evil in the world. As though it requires the Holocaust to make the evil in the world sufficiently terrible to test the faith of a Jew or a Christian. None of these and other corruptions should incline one to think preoccupation with the Holocaust in our understanding of ourselves, in the West in the second half of the twentieth century, demeans the suffering of others, including other victims of genocide and mass murder.

Nor should the occurrence of the Holocaust be a reason for political pessimism. It is true that a belief in the inevitability of progress is unlikely to survive serious reflection of the nature of the Holocaust and its causes, but one doesn't need the Holocaust to put paid to that superstition. That being said, the Holocaust gives one no serious ground for predicting one kind of future rather than another. Contingently, things may get better. Contingently, they may get worse.

Optimism and pessimism are, anyhow, relatively trivial dispositions of personality. One can be a pessimist in the sense that one is disposed to take a gloomy view of prospects in most situations, seeing in them more reason to predict ill than good, and one can combine this with a temperamental melancholia, yet respond joyously to life as a gift. Deeper than the question of whether the Holocaust undermines grounds for optimism is whether the Holocaust has justifiably blighted faith in the kind of goodness I attributed to the nun, whether one could believe in such goodness only if one did not understand what the Holocaust meant. Many people lost their religious faith in the camps and many survivors could no longer respond to life as a gift and to the kind of goodness that is its source. Who would dare be critical of them? But just as the loss of religious faith is no basis for a generalised theology of the Holocaust, so, I think, a survivor's loss of faith in goodness cannot be the basis for generalised denial of its existence.

Consider this story from Primo Levi:

The night held ugly surprises.

· Lakmaker, in the bunk under mine, was a poor wreck of a man. He was (or had been) a Dutch Jew, seventeen years old, tall, thin and gentle. He had been in bed for three months; I have no idea how he had managed to survive the selections. He had had typhus and scarlet fever successively; at the same time a serious cardiac illness had shown itself, while he was smothered with bedsores, so much so that by now he could only lie on his stomach. Despite all this, he had a ferocious appetite. He only spoke Dutch, and none of us could understand him.

Perhaps the cause of it all was the cabbage and turnip soup, of which Lakmaker had wanted two helpings. In the middle of the night he groaned and then threw himself from his bed. He tried to reach the latrine, but was too weak and fell to the ground, crying and shouting loudly.

Charles lit the lamp...and we were able to ascertain the gravity of the incident. The boy's bed and the floor were filthy. The smell in the small area was rapidly becoming insupportable. We had but a minimum supply of water and neither blankets nor straw mattresses to spare. And the poor wretch, suffering from typhus, formed a terrible source of infection, while he could certainly not be left all night to groan and shiver in the cold in the middle of the filth.

Charles climbed down from his bed and dressed in silence. While I held the lamp, he cut all the dirty patches from the straw mattress and the blankets with a knife. He lifted Lakmaker from the ground with the tenderness of a mother, cleaned him as best as possible with straw taken from the mattress and lifted him into the remade bed in the only position in which the unfortunate fellow could lie. He scraped the floor with a scrap of tinplate, diluted a little chloramine and finally spread disinfectant over everything, including himself.

I judged his self-sacrifice by the tiredness which I would have had to overcome in myself to do what he had done.

As much as the nun's example, perhaps even more than her example, this is goodness to wonder at. No evil can diminish its beauty. And Levi's writings, one of the great spiritual achievements of humankind, inspire a similar wonder. It is impossible to describe their spirit without appealing to the concepts of goodness and truth. He achieves what Emmanuel Ringelblum, the founder of *Oneg Shabbes* (enjoyment of the Sabbath), the chronicle of the Warsaw ghetto, demanded of his journalists:

> We deliberately refrained from drawing professional journalists into our work, because we did not want it to be sensationalised. Our aim was that the sequence of events in each town, the experiences of each Jew—and during the current war each Jew is a world unto himself—should be conveyed as simply and as faithfully as possible. Every redundant word, every literary gilding or ornamentation grated upon our ears and provoked our anger. Jewish life in wartime is so full of tragedy that it is unnecessary to embellish it with one superfluous line.

Ringelblum was innocent of the kind of evil that came with the death camps, and to which Levi gave witness, when he wrote that passage. It shows in the fact that he spoke only of the tragedy of Jewish life in *wartime*.

Levi's reverence for each individual life whose fate he records directly or implicitly is expressed in the rigorous and unrelenting observance of an obligation to truthfulness and objectivity that informs his work. Iris Murdoch has observed that this kind of effort to see things as they are is an effort of love, justice and pity. There is despair in Levi's writings but it is never a form of numbness. It is a terrible mistake to believe that numbness could be an appropriate (as distinct from understandable) response to evil which could at the same time reveal to us its nature and reality. When he records the evil that he has seen and suffered, Levi reveals how it is a violation of the preciousness of each individual. A tradition, going back to Plato, has taught us that evil can be properly and clearly understood only in the light of the good. In the death camps only that light could illuminate each individual soul and reveal him or her to be infinitely precious.

If the concept of evil as one that marks a distinctive moral phenomenon becomes lost to us, then, I think, people will no longer respond to the Holocaust as to something mysterious. Its distinctive dimensions will be seen as those which make it a paradigm of genocide and no more. If that happens, then distinctions I have drawn in this chapter will appear obscure and unimportant—especially the distinction between the death camps as efficient centres to service a genocidal intent, and as institutions which realised an evil beyond the intention of those who conceived them, who administered them and who worked in them.

Though not all the perpetrators were banal in the way Eichmann was, and though one could not say that the genocidal intention expressed in the Final Solution was banal, I do not believe that the Holocaust gives us evidence to settle ancient disputes about whether evil can have depth. Our sense of the distinctive evil of the Holocaust is, I have tried to suggest, based on the way the death camps were an unprecedented assault on the preciousness of individuals, an assault that was partly self-conscious of its nature. That self-consciousness is what makes us think that the assault was demonic. But that, of course, may be an illusion. From the perspective on evil adopted by the tradition in which Arendt found herself, the 'demonic', like the sadistic to which it is closely allied, looks to be based on a false perception of that which it appears self-consciously to violate—the unconditional preciousness of each individual, or, to put it religiously, the sanctity of each individual.

The Holocaust offers no privileged perspective on this. Arendt may, therefore, have been right to think that Eichmann was emblematic of the Holocaust, affording us insight into its distinctive evil. To take him as emblematic of the distinctive evil of the Holocaust is not thereby to take him as the basis for an empirical generalisation about the kinds of people who were its perpetrators.

It would be foolish to do so because those perpetrators were of many kinds, ranging from Eichmann through Ivan the Terrible to Dr Mengele. But the brutes and the sadists do not give us reason to distinguish the Holocaust from the many barbarities throughout history. Reflection on the banality of Eichmann may therefore deepen our understanding of an essential aspect, if not the essence, of the Holocaust. The more general thesis that evil is always banal, that it never has depth, does little to deepen our understanding of the Holocaust, and the Holocaust does nothing, I think, to deepen our understanding of it.

A television program about Primo Levi has a particularly disturbing film clip. We are shown a large shed which is filled two-thirds to the roof with something we cannot at first identify. It looks like wool, or some other form of material. A man is standing on top of it—an ordinary man, middle aged, in a double-breasted dark suit. He looks like a salesman and talks enthusiastically, obviously proud of what he is showing his audience. His enthusiasm is evident when the voice-over allows us to hear him. The voice-over sounds for all the world like the voices in old newsreels, celebrating a national achievement—a good harvest, perhaps. We then learn what he is standing on. It is human hair.

As an image, it is I think more truly emblematic of the Holocaust than any of the images from the camps, even though many of them are in obvious ways more horrible. The camps are, of course, evoked for anyone who knows about them, by the hair, and the hair, perhaps even more than images of corpses, evokes a sense of an unrelenting assault on the preciousness of each of the Nazis' victims. Like Homer's references to the loved ones who will grieve for the dead warrior, the hair (of women I imagine) conjures moments of tenderness—hair brushed by a mother, caressed by a lover.

I have found this the most disturbing image I have seen of the Holocaust. When I reflected on why it should be so, I kept returning in my mind to Arendt's remarks about the banality of evil. She did not, as I have already remarked, intend them to diminish the evil of the Holocaust. On the contrary, her sense of the banality of evil frightened her more than her earlier sense of its radicalness had. Many people who were present at Eichmann's trial said that their imaginations were defeated by the effort to put together this man, so ordinary and unprepossessing behind the glass booth in the courtroom, with the crimes of which he was clearly guilty. But in the film clip I described, the grotesque sight of a man in civilian clothes standing on the 'harvest' and rejoicing in it, we have exactly what they could not put together: the banality and the evil, and the two together in a way that intensifies rather than diminishes our sense of the evil.

Forms of
the Unthinkable

David Irving is an intelligent, knowledgeable man whose historical writings on Churchill have earned him considerable respect.
He is also one of the more notorious people who deny that the
Third Reich made any serious attempt to exterminate the Jews,
attributing the common belief that it was so to the effectiveness of
Jewish propaganda. A number of countries including Germany
(which has special laws prohibiting the defilement of the memory
of the Holocaust), Canada and Australia have refused him entry or
the right to speak. Controversy is fierce whenever this happens.
He is often called a crank. But tempers do not flare because people
think he is a crank. They flare because many find what he says
deeply offensive. It is bad enough, some say, that he should publicly
deny the evil suffered by the Jews during the Holocaust. The
obscenity of it is compounded when his denials are treated as
though they deserve a reply. Irving is, therefore, a good example of

someone whose views are rejected by many people as beyond consideration, both morally and intellectually. That puts an interesting complexion on arguments offered in support of his right to articulate on public platforms his brand of Holocaust denial. What is interesting is not so much the arguments in support of his right to speak, for they are classically liberal arguments, but the fact that those who offer them are generally not struck by something strange.

The strange thing is this. Classical liberal arguments presuppose that unpopular, even hateful, beliefs should be allowed free expression in public discussions so that they might be assessed, and, if they really are hateful, shown to be so. Generally, the thought is that such discussions really are discussions, that the protagonists are open to having their minds changed, however unlikely they think that might be. And (this thought continues) if the protagonists in argument do not learn from one another, some who listen to them might. Behind the thought that Irving should be permitted to speak, there often lies such an assumption about the potentially open and unpredictable nature of argument with him. It would debase the noble ideal of free speech to think of it as a gift bestowed by those who wish to ridicule the opinions they expose to public debate.

The right to free speech conceived as a positive ideal, rather than as a necessity granted because one fears the consequences of refusing it, assumes a constituency in which real argument is possible. That constituency cannot, therefore, be composed of lunatics. Whatever right they have to speak is of a different kind. The reason is not that lunatics are rowdy, dogmatic and seldom prepared to listen. All that and more is often true of people who rightly belong to the constituency. Lunatics are, as we put it, 'out of touch with reality'. That protagonists in a discussion should be in touch with reality is a condition of something actually being a discussion rather than a parody of one.

Something similar is true of cranks and people who, like small children, are in need of extensive general education. They too are excluded from the constituency. As much as the right to free speech is assumed not to belong to a constituency of lunatics, so it presupposes that those with whom we argue are not radically in need of our education. We assume that, unlike children, when adults need to be 'educated', it is on some specialist topic. The idea that an adult might, like a child, be generally in need of an education before he or she can properly participate in political discussion, or be fully deserving of the right to free speech, is as Arendt observed a dangerous and illiberal one.

Could anyone believe Irving without being either an anti-Semite, a crank or someone radically in need of education—someone, for example, who did not even know that Irving's views conflict with those of nearly all the world's historians, that amongst historians his views on the Holocaust have the same status as flat-earth claims have amongst scientists? (One might be inclined to say anti-Semites are cranks just in virtue of being anti-Semites. Sadly that is not true.)

On the other side, could anyone prepared to argue with Irving seriously think there is a case to be answered rather than merely exposed without fearing for their judgment? I think not, which is probably why I have not heard one person give even the slightest indication that Irving might rightly persuade them. God forbid that one should even think it, they seem to imply. If I am correct, then the realisation of Irving's right to free speech would be a 'debate' between Irving, anti-Semites and cranks on the one side and those who have set out to expose them on the other. Expose them to whom? Presumably to an audience made up of the same kind of people as on the platform with the addition, perhaps, of people who are so ignorant of Irving's standing as an historian of the Holocaust, of what anyone who is not a crank rightly takes to be common knowledge about the Holocaust, that they are like children.

That is not the constituency assumed by the ideal of free

speech, a constituency in which people could profoundly—even violently—disagree, but who like Voltaire would 'fight to the death' for the right of each to persuade the other of their opinions. Behind that ideal was the vision nobly expressed by John Stuart Mill of a constituency of liberal minds who would be open to changing their minds even about beliefs they hold passionately. There, he argued, truth is likely to emerge. That could hardly be said of a constituency of cranks, anti-Semites, the radically ignorant and those who suffer from none of those maladies, but who know they would join the ranks of the cranks if they began even to suspect that Irving had a case.

'Cranks' is an interesting word. One tends to assume that it has no interesting place amongst the terms that mark our critical vocabulary, the vocabulary which we use to assess whether we or others are thinking well or badly. But it is not just a term of abuse. It refers to someone who has so radically lost his capacity for judgment that his views are not worth even considering. Like those who are severely mentally ill, the most interesting thing about cranks—about what makes someone a crank—does not show itself when they declaim what they believe. It does so when they do not rule certain things out of consideration. They suffer from something far more serious than ignorance. Knowledge and understanding—and therefore, all serious radical critique—depend upon the exercise of sound judgment about what counts as evidence, about when authorities can be relied upon, when they are justifiably discredited, and so on.

. Were I to discuss the Holocaust with Irving, I am sure that he would wipe the floor with me. There would be many occasions when I would have no answer to his aggressive challenges. Normally if I were so often forced to concede that I did not know how to answer the point, I would rightly be forced to acknowledge that I should at least reconsider my position and look more closely at the evidence. Ordinarily, on such a showing as I would put up against Irving, reason would require me to keep an open mind if I were justifiably to think of myself as a seriously reflective person who tries to be free of prejudice. Yet were I to do so after such a miserable performance against Irving I would fear that I was becoming a crank. I would fear that I had lost the very thing I most need to keep my wits about me, to think critically—something whose absence condemns the entire apparatus of thinking, the apparatus which gives sense to the distinction between a prejudiced and an unprejudiced mind, to a parody of itself.

Lack of judgment makes us vulnerable to gullibility, superstition and, perhaps, at the limit, insanity. Scepticism, or open-mindedness that is unrestrained by sober judgment, is one side of the coin whose other side is gullibility. To oversimplify a little: the concept of sound judgment—as it is expressed in the ways things are ruled out of consideration—is partly constitutive of the boundaries within which concepts like evidence, common knowledge and authority mean what they do to us. Without it open-mindedness degenerates into the parody of itself that is the butt of the joke, 'He had a mind so open that his brain fell through'.

I would fare no better with a flat-earther than with Irving. My appeal to ships appearing on the horizon, or to satellite photographs, would meet with his derision. Again, according to the ordinary critical standards that govern debate, I would have to acknowledge that I had been knocked out in the second round. When I recover, should I not rethink matters? What else are the lessons of my liberal upbringing? Was I not raised on stories that exposed scientific establishments which ridiculed as cranks those who dared oppose them and who often made the great discoveries in science? Was I not taught that if I am repeatedly and fairly beaten in argument, then I should at least reconsider what I had previously believed? Again, however, were any of this even to enter my head, I would fear for my judgment, and so for my ability to think critically. I would feel like someone who suspects he is losing his mind and who is still lucid enough to feel the full terror

of the realisation that he cannot trust his mind when it assures him
that it is not so.

Is this oversimplified? To some degree it is, for no serious
place has been accorded to the fact that we must all trust the
authority of others if we are rationally to believe anything. From
the beginning, as children, we must first believe if we are responsibly to doubt, that is to say, if reason is to support our doubts. It
has often been pointed out in philosophical discussions of scepticism that one needs reason to doubt as much as one needs reason
to believe. In a wonderful little book, *Meditations on First Philosophy*, which has informed much of the modern temper about
reason and scepticism, René Descartes says that because he has
been deceived he will not trust again. He will turn inwards and
through solitary meditation determine for himself what he can
know with certainty and what he cannot. But Descartes' response
(as he described it, though admittedly not very seriously) is not
that of a reasonable person. It is the response of someone who has
been panicked into a state of pathological suspicion which, were it
to persist, would count as a form of mental illness.

Descartes begins his meditations reflecting on the dogmatic
state of the sciences, disillusioned by the arrogance of even the
most celebrated scholars. The lesson of such dogmatism for us,
however, is not that we should be radically suspicious of all
authority in science and other forms of scholarship. Reason
cannot require that because it would then undermine the conditions in which its application enables us to maintain contact with
reality. That is why, in political and in another matters, one of the
most important parts of a person's education is an education in
judgment. Like everything else this has its failings and corruptions.
They are of the kind that sometimes made people shout 'Crank!
Rubbish! Humbug!' when great discoveries were made in science.
Stories about them are the monster stories of a liberal education.
The monsters are real enough. To think, however, that one could
maintain one's capacity to reason, one's capacity for serious

critique, while succumbing to a pathological distrust of authority, would mean that one had become like Chesterton's madman. 'The madman,' writes Chesterton, 'is not someone who has lost his reason; he is someone who has lost everything except his reason.'

Chesterton developed that epigram in ways I find uncongenial, emphasising the importance of imagination against, rather than as a partner to, reason. He was, I suspect, unsure whether he wanted to attack reason or a limited, scientistic, conception of it. It is a common confusion. Nonetheless, like all good epigrams, Chesterton's expresses a profound insight. Reflecting on it will take us some way to understanding our response to Irving and to flat-earthers.

Paranoia is probably the form of insanity that the epigram first brings to mind. A clever paranoid is a formidable opponent in argument for anyone foolish enough to engage him. Logic is seldom what fails him in the deployment of his seemingly boundless ingenuity. To this it is tempting to respond in something like the following way. His arguments may be sound but his premises are false and they are so often and so radically false that the ordinary causes of error cannot explain them. His radically false beliefs are caused by pathologies of the brain or the psyche, which the relevant experts—psychiatrists, analysts, psychologists—investigate. That is why we rightly say that he is mentally *ill*.

The trouble with such an account, I think, is that it makes madness seem too much like having radically false beliefs about, for example, an enemy because one is filled with hatred for him. Here too we explain false beliefs by reference to unusual psychological causes. What is wrong with that? The answer, I think, is that, insofar as we feel there to be a difference in kind, between someone who is mad (literally) and someone who has succumbed to many and sometimes radically false beliefs because his emotions overwhelm his reason, then we think the difference should show in their cognitive states, in how they see the world, rather than in the psychological (or physical) causes of those states. We capture this colloquially when we say that people who are insane are 'out of touch with reality', or that 'they have lost their wits'.

'Out of touch with reality' is an especially good expression. It does not direct us to the causes of a cognitive dysfunction, but instead marks its character in a way that is not captured merely by noting the contents of those beliefs which show a person to be out of touch with reality. Of course the content is what is most evident to us. A paranoid might believe that everyone is trying to poison him. Because that claims our attention so dramatically, we are prone to overlook the equally important fact that we are distinguished from the paranoid not just because we do not hold the beliefs that he does, but also because it never occurs to us to hold them. That is the aspect of madness that is captured in the expression 'out of touch with reality', and it is why an account of the psychological or physical causes of the paranoid's false beliefs will not capture the nature of his cognitive orientation. Not ruling things out of consideration is an aspect of how mad people see the world, and it is not reducible to elaboration of the contents of their beliefs or the emotional colouration of those beliefs, or both.

This is a fact which is, I suspect, of more interest to philosophers than to psychologists. The content of the mad person's beliefs determine medical accounts of the kind of illnesses he suffers from and their causes. Those who are interested in the concepts which determine what it is to think well or badly will be rewarded, however, if they turn their attention from the content of the mad person's beliefs to the fact that such beliefs even occur to him. They will discover deep and pervasive assumptions about some of the most important of our critical concepts.

One of those assumptions is to believe that if we are sane, it does not occur to us that the waiter is trying to poison us because our capacity to entertain this well grounded empirical assumption has not been undermined by illness. It is, of course, an important fact about human life that people do not usually try to poison us. The fact that it does not occur to us to think they will is related to this important general fact. The question is whether the relation is rightly represented as between that fact and an inductively well grounded belief.

If it is, then strictly speaking it is merely unlikely—no doubt highly unlikely—that waiters will not try to poison us. It is so unlikely that, for all intents and purposes, we can, indeed, rationally we ought, to regard it as certain that they won't. Though that may sound like the plainest commonsense, it really is not. It makes it seem as though if one were super-rational, if one's 'intents and purposes' did not drag to earth epistemic capacities suited to higher things than usually preoccupy embodied, practical creatures like us, one could always keep before one's mind that it is strictly true that the waiter might—just might—poison us. Presumably one could adjust the probability of it according to the circumstances.

Is that an edifying picture of how we would be if we were able to be truly rational, or is it the same parody of reason that lunatics display? The latter, surely. If it did seem to us to be possible, though highly improbable, that the waiter might try to poison us, we would have one leg in the psychiatric clinic. Insisting that the probabilities of it are really very small, but real nonetheless, would not enable us to get it out again. The reason is not because here on earth, in an epistemically fallen state, we are doomed to treat things as certain though they are merely probable. It is that, even in the best of worlds, the sane would be distinguished from the insane by the fact that they rule things out of consideration.

We can, of course, be mistaken. Suppose that one day the waiter actually does try to poison us. After that we are likely to look suspiciously at other waiters in other restaurants. We might do it for the remainder of our lives. But, if we do, it will not be because we have been jolted from our 'dogmatic slumbers' into a state of heightened rationality. On the contrary, because we were once poisoned our friends will excuse behaviour in us which in other circumstances would decisively prove we were mad. The lesson of madness is, I think, that reason is not what determines what it is to be 'in touch with reality'. Rather, being in touch with reality is a condition for the sober exercise of those critical concepts which mark our sense of what it is to think well or badly, concepts whose proper application is what we call the exercise of 'Reason'. That, as I understand it, is Chesterton's point.

If the problem lies, as I suggested, in treating the fact that characteristically it does not occur to us to think that the waiter is trying to poison us as the expression of our confidence in a well supported empirical assumption, then how else should we treat it?

Usually we are not poisoned when we go to restaurants. People usually tell us the truth when we ask their names. They do not normally spit in our faces when we ask for directions. And so on. Developing an aspect of Wittgenstein's thought in *On Certainty*, I suggest that these regularities condition the concepts used in our reasoning, rather than providing support for it. The fact that it generally does not occur to us that someone is trying to poison us is not merely a condition which enables us to keep a grip on concepts we use to assess whether or not a belief is well supported by the evidence. Something counts as assessing the evidence, carrying out an investigation, constructing a proof and so on, only within the ranks of the sane and the sober, amongst those who are 'in tune with reality'. In individual cases, of course, sanity and sobriety are rightly seen as conditions which enable a person properly to use the conceptual tools which enable what she does to count as marshalling and assessing evidence, for example. But the general fact that we rule things out of consideration in ways that paranoids and cranks do not determines what those conceptual tools mean for us. The sane and sober practice of the community which determines the public structure of our concepts is not an enabling condition for the rational deployment of conceptual tools whose nature can be characterised independently of that practice. Together with other ways of ruling things out of consideration, that practice partly conditions the very nature of those tools.

This difference between the two ways in which general facts

of human life are construed as relevant to an account of why we do not consider certain things, may look like a fine one, but it is fundamental to our understanding of our responses to people like Irving and therefore to our understanding of the ideal of free speech. An adequate discussion of it, however, takes one to the deepest problems of philosophy. The tendency in philosophy to idealise a conception of thinking—thinking as it would be in all possible worlds, its essential categories unconditioned by the lives of creatures living particular forms of life, goes deep in philosophy. Stanley Cavell called it philosophy's predilection for 'the denial of the human'.

The ideal of a thinker, free of human encumbrance, thinking from no particular perspective, seeing the world 'as from no place within it' (as the American philosopher Thomas Nagel puts it) is both a function and an expression of a long history of speculation about which intellectual properties it is intelligible to ascribe to an omniscient God—the God of the philosophers, that is. One need not believe in God to see the point of such speculation. The question that inspires it is not, which properties does God actually have?, but which ones does it make sense to ascribe to him? The idea of such a God, and the abstraction from it of an ideal of seeing the world as He would see it, inclines us to think that our need to trust authorities, to develop sound judgment and so on reflects only the contingencies of the life we lead. We need to trust, we need sound judgment, we need commonsense and other forms of sobriety (this thought continues), rather as we need literally to be sober, to have a clear head, or as we need to overcome laziness and a tendency to favour evidence that supports our theses and so on. God of course needs none of this. He does not need to struggle against laziness or hangovers, nor does he need to educate Himself in the forms of sound judgment so that He knows which authorities to trust.

The picture is almost irresistibly compelling. Its finest representation outside theology is again in Descartes' *Meditations*. He concluded in his second meditation that, though he may doubt everything, that he has a body, that there exists a world outside his thoughts, he cannot doubt that he is thinking. That untroubled certainty expresses the picture I drew above. It seems not to occur to Descartes that there might be a conceptual obstacle to his supposing that there could be such a thing as reason and its exercise completely divorced from the circumstances of a particular way of life which partially conditions the concepts which enable us to distinguish sober from frivolous forms of scepticism. Descartes imagines himself progressively to disengage from the conditions of living a human life—a life of any kind—without ever wondering whether in doing so he is sawing away the conceptual branch on which he is sitting. It never occurs to him that he might be depriving himself of the conditions under which he can meaningfully pose, let alone answer, the question he repeatedly asks himself: can I be serious? God could not ask himself such a question. (That is not an empirical or metaphysical claim about God, but one about our concept of God.) Descartes imagines, however, that he still possesses the concepts that enable such a question to mean something. Having asked the question, he reassures himself: 'I am forced to admit that there are none of the things I used to think were true which may not possibly be doubted, but for sound and well considered reasons.'

Suppose that someone writes on a blackboard an argument which leads to the conclusion that he may, at that very time, be dreaming. Amused, he goes over the argument to discover what is wrong with it. As he did the first time, he finds its conclusion inescapable. Again and again he goes over the argument, but can find no fault in it, not in its premises and not in the reasoning from them to the conclusion. He cannot accept the conclusion, but he cannot deny that the argument compels him to it. How can he, he asks himself, committed as he is to reason, reject a conclusion he finds inescapable, however unpalatable or even lunatic it might seem to be?

The philosophical tradition has provided a classic solution to his dilemma, one found in different forms in Descartes, Hume and in most philosophers who have been driven to doubts which would be regarded as absurd outside of philosophy. The solution tells us that the notion of professing a conclusion in all seriousness is an ambiguous one. G. E. Moore, one of the most influential English philosophers in the first half of the century, expressed it most clearly when he said that we can seriously find something doubtful yet be unable to doubt it. The person in my example can seriously put a question mark next to the proposition that he is dreaming, but he cannot as a human being get fully behind that question mark. Intellectually it is possible to doubt things that psychologically we are unable to.

Descartes puts it more dramatically. He tells us that:

> the meditation of yesterday filled my mind with so many doubts that it is no longer in my power to forget them. And yet I do not see in what manner I can resolve them; and just as if I had all of a sudden fallen into very deep water, I am disconcerted that I can neither make certain of setting my feet on the bottom, nor can I swim and support myself on the surface.

Repeatedly, however, and 'insensibly, a certain lassitude leads [him] into the course of ordinary life'. The more urbane Hume tells us that the doubts that reason forces on him disappear when he enjoys convivial company, especially when he plays backgammon. The basic idea is always the same.

What is it, then, for the person in my example—the person who writes at the end of the argument on the blackboard that he may be dreaming—actually to conclude that? What makes that seriously his conclusion rather than merely a 'blackboard conclusion', a conclusion that the rules of inference compel him to write after the 'therefore' sign, but which he cannot unequivocally profess as his. He is quite sincere in his profession that he is compelled to the conclusion because he must write it at the end of the argument. But a sincere profession of something can, after all, be 'mere words'. Where does the distinction between a serious conclusion and mere words, sincerely spoken, get purchase in his case?

It seems the answer is that it gets purchase at that point where we can see how the profession of a belief or doubt shows in a person's life. But how can the belief that one might be dreaming in circumstances such as those of the person in my example show itself in someone's behaviour? Are they inclined to go to bed? The supposition is absurd and so would any others be. There is nothing in a person's behaviour that could convince us that he seriously believes he might be dreaming, nothing that could convince us even that he seriously believes it might be so but that because the likelihood is so small he can confidently go about his affairs as though he is awake. We don't even know what it would look like for anyone to behave as though they believed they might be dreaming, in circumstances of the kind described in my example and envisaged by Descartes. How, for example, would an actor portray it?

Of course we have no idea. Would we conclude that anyone who seriously believed they were dreaming was a lunatic? No, because as I remarked earlier there is no form of mental illness which has as its chief symptom, or even as one of its symptoms, the serious belief that one might be dreaming. If you seriously believe that someone is trying to poison you, then you are likely to attract the attention of someone professionally concerned with mental health. If, in ordinary circumstances, you claim seriously to believe that you may be dreaming, you can be sure it will occur to no one that you should seek psychiatric help. The reason is not flattering to philosophy. It is not because people know that you will refrain from acting on the belief and disturbing the peace. It is because it is impossible to take such a belief seriously.

The thinness of the conception available to Descartes and to others in the sceptical tradition of what it is seriously to doubt, to believe, to be open to the possibility that something is so, must at least raise the question whether it can be at all adequate. Can repeatedly and carefully examining an argument and finding oneself compelled to a conclusion be, even in a very restricted domain of inquiry, a serious conception of professing a conclusion? Or is the acknowledgment that that is all that is left to one an admission that the conditions that give sense to the idea of seriously professing a conclusion have been artificially set aside and then forgotten?

If one takes the latter view, as I have been suggesting one should, then nothing counts as the serious profession of the kinds of doubts Descartes—or more strictly and perhaps revealingly, the persona of the first meditation—proposes in *Meditations*. The deepest lesson of scepticism would then be that a seriously professed conclusion must be someone's conclusion in a sense more substantial than can be conveyed by the idea of a thinker abstracted from an actual thinker living a form of life that conditions the concepts with which we mark the forms of sober judgment. That would be an anti-transcendental moral whose implications reach far beyond the concerns of philosophical scepticism. We cannot imagine our thoughts to be those of a mere thinking thing living no particular form of life while retaining the concepts necessary for the exercise of sober judgment. Descartes says, 'I am forced to admit that there are none of the things I used to think were true which may not possibly be doubted, and not because of carelessness or frivolity, but for sound and well considered reasons.' Another translation has him saying, '...for reasons which are very powerful and maturely considered'. I think that the gravity he intends to convey, and which supports the thought that he is 'forced to admit' that he must doubt, or the thought that the reasons he has reviewed 'are very powerful' cannot be sustained on the very thin conception of reason he leaves himself with when he imagines himself to be nothing more than a mere thinking thing.

One way, therefore, of characterising what has gone wrong is this. Reason seems to compel Descartes and the person in my example to a conclusion which they cannot seriously conclude. The person in my example believes that he must conclude that he may be dreaming only because the rules of inference require him to put the sentence that expresses it after the therefore sign. But a conclusion which no one can conclude, in the sense of seriously professing it as their belief, is a conclusion in inverted commas only, a blackboard conclusion. It is a sentence with no serious place in speech or thought. What we call reasoning, inferring, concluding, reviewing an argument and so on, stand in non-accidental relations to the possibility of seriously professing a conclusion as one's belief. The interrelated concepts of a consideration, of a reason, of an argument, of a proof, of a conclusion—all seem to lose their substance when applied to the sceptical professions of the first meditation. They look like shadows cast by the substantial applications of those concepts. If that is true, then the person in my example and the persona of the *Meditations* are not exemplars of the exercise of an intelligence purified of the dross of human existence, seeking the truth however strange it may turn out to be. They are false semblances of a radical, critical intelligence.

If we take seriously the human conditioning of what it means soberly to judge something to be possible or impossible, of the forms of serious judgment in even the most radical philosophical inquiries, then we will have a better understanding of the concepts which mark the way we rule things out of consideration. We will secure a more fertile critical distance from the thought we find so natural and so edifying, namely that if we were perfectly rational, then there is nothing we would fear to think. Or, perhaps more accurately, concepts we naturally deploy would be less exposed to distortion by a false conception of the constitutive categories of reason. We would be more ready to entertain the possibility that the certainty expressed in the claim that something is beyond consideration—that only someone who is a crank, or insane, or radically wicked, would consider it—is neither a psychological state nor something we could adequately account for by elaboration on the idea of a rationally supported belief.

The certainty expressed when we rule things out of consideration is cognitively more interesting than a psychological state and more basic than a rationally supported belief. As we have seen, without the concept of sober judgment which is interdependent with our practice of ruling some things out of consideration, we can give only very thin meaning, if we can give meaning at all, to the idea of the serious profession of a belief that is claimed to be rationally justified because it has survived the most radical kind of scepticism. An actual deficiency in one's capacity for sober judgment undermines one's ability to apply properly the very concepts which give substance to the idea of a rationally supported belief: in the absence of judgment the application of these concepts will take us *away from* rather than *to* reality. The fate of the concept of evidence in the hands of a paranoiac is an extreme, but instructive, example.

Distortion of the notion of commonsense is one of the unfortunate legacies of philosophy's preoccupation with scepticism. We normally think that commonsense is possessed by someone who declines to believe that Elvis Presley might be alive and well, that one can read one's future in the stars, that one can bend spoons with one's mind—and, of course, that the Holocaust is a fiction invented and sustained by Zionist plotters. Outside of philosophy commonsense is generally thought to be a virtue. Within philosophy it is often treated with suspicion, because the philosophical tradition made it seem so close to mere prejudice. In philosophy, commonsense is said to be possessed by someone who doesn't for a minute entertain the thought that he might be dreaming. Moore became its champion when, in a famous lecture to the Aristotelian Society, he held up two hands and said that he knew that he had two hands and that therefore he knew there were at least two things in the external world.

It sounds like a parody, I know, and I would not wish my tone in describing it to be mistaken for one that implies that philosophy's concern over such matters is of no serious interest. To the contrary, I belive it takes us to some of the deepest things we can think about. If, however, my tone had a note of parody in it just then, it is because it *is* comical to suggest that the belief that there is an external world with other minds in it is an expression of commonsense. That suggestion is both cause and effect of the fact that the notion of commonsense has not seriously been examined. It has almost always been taken as a body of beliefs which may legitimately be subject to critical examination in an inquiry whose fundamental critical canons can be specified without reference to the ways we rule things out of consideration and, therefore, without the conceptual resources to yield a substantial concept of sober judgment.

We would distort things as badly if we thought that someone could entertain doubts about the external world or other minds only if he were mad. (Descartes raises the question of whether he is mad, but interestingly, he thinks he can answer in the negative because he can produce good arguments to support his scepticism.) There is no form of madness which is to doubt that there is an external world or that there are other minds, and the reason, I have suggested, is that no one can seriously doubt such things. It is essential to madness that the mad person seriously doubts and believes what he says he does.

And just as the sceptical philosopher is not mad, so flatearthers and Holocaust deniers are not mad either. Nonetheless, I hope that I have given some reason for believing that the fact that the crank and the mad person do not rule certain things out of consideration is at least as revealing about the nature of their cognitive orientation as their manifest errors are. More than any other part of our intellectual tradition, the epistemological tradition that has its purest expression in philosophical scepticism has, I believe, encouraged us to misconstrue the significance of the various ways we rule things out of consideration. Though very different from one another, these ways condition rather than rely upon the concepts we use to characterise a well supported belief. The significance of the fact that we must trust if we are to believe will strike one differently according to whether one favours the account I have been offering or the traditional one I have been criticising.

Who then is to judge who is a crank and what is common-sense? The answer, I am sure, is roughly the people who now do so. Scientists tell us that flat-earthers are cranks. Historians tell us that Irving is one. Often, of course, the telling is indirect. It is our immersion in a scientific culture that enables us to know that it is not an intellectual virtue to keep an open mind over whether Elvis Presley is alive and working for the CIA, that Uri Geller can bend spoons with his mind, that one can read the future in the stars. That, say the cranks, is exactly the point. We are dupes of a dogmatic scientific culture. Every so often the cranks will have the last laugh. But that is no reason to abandon the idea of judgment, no reason to erode a robust notion of gullibility. In our culture it is gullibility rather than justified scepticism that often shows itself in the attacks on science, truth and objectivity. That is why our culture is marked both by the ubiquitous profession of scepticism and the uncritical certainties of political correctness.

Who is to judge is a question whose rhetorical intent often goes in two directions. Scepticism aims at radical critique, but radical critique needs sobriety and judgment as much as do arguments which support the status quo. Difficulties intrinsic to judgment cannot give good cause to abandon it. Still less can they give us good cause to undermine the very concept of it, or rather, the concepts that identify its applications in the way we rule things out of consideration.

The political realm is the other direction in which the question points. There it means, who can we trust? One part of the answer I have already given. One must trust the scholars. To be able to do that with confidence, however, one must maintain high standards of research and teaching, maintain the conditions under which free, radical and critical inquiry flourishes and maintain the conditions under which scholars, who are certainly no braver than other people, may be protected from the baleful consequences of their cowardice. The mendacity which now poisons university life, as universities try to hide what they have compromised in efforts to accommodate the pressures on them, is a consequence of our failure to maintain those conditions. When truthfulness seems to have little value, it is not surprising that philosophies should flourish which debunk even the desire for truth or objectivity, declaring the celebration of both to be attempts to disguise the exercise of power.

Nothing I have said in support of a robust conception of sober judgment, or about the constituency presupposed in the positive ideal of free speech, entails, or even supports, the demand that someone like Irving be denied a public platform on which to defile the memory of those who were murdered in the Holocaust. My claim is only that, when undoubted cranks are given such platforms, we should not celebrate that to be a dramatic and edifying example of our commitment to free speech as a positive ideal. One may think, however, as I do, that it would be politically dangerous to deny Irving and other cranks a platform. The reasons are of a familiar kind and are all a variation on the fear that to do so would play into the hands of authoritarians. That fear is of course what drives many people to ask, who is to judge who is a crank?

Flat-earthers are not denied entry into countries and prohibited from publicly arguing their position. Nor was Irving banned from entering Australia and other countries because he is a crank. He was denied entry because many find his claims about the Holocaust morally offensive. To deny someone a platform because one finds his view morally offensive is, many people say, a serious danger to free speech. Moral arguments inflame our passions in the way that arguments about whether Elvis is alive and well do not.

That is why (this thought continues) the notion of the morally unthinkable is far more dangerous than the notion of a crank.

And not only more dangerous, but inherently much more suspect. Astronomy shows up astrology, but what shows up the morally unthinkable? There appear not to exist moral authorities who play the same role in the formation of moral judgment as scientific and other scholarly authorities do in relation to matters related to their disciplines. Did I not myself earlier present cases in which people find unthinkable what they should not? M and Isdell, for example, found it unthinkable that blacks could be wronged as whites can be. And there are Australians who find it unthinkable that those who are guilty of genocide and some other crimes against the stolen children should be brought to trial.

Examples of the morally unthinkable that naturally come to mind do not seem to play the same role in our understanding about how we think as does the concept of a crank. Irving is not a moral crank. Nor was Isdell, nor was M. The idea of the morally unthinkable is not the idea of an intellectual impairment of the kind suffered by someone who is radically bereft of judgment. The concept of the morally unthinkable is, therefore, in important respects different from the concepts with which we mark many of the other ways we rule things out of consideration. But the difference is not that the concept of the morally unthinkable expresses only extreme, deeply entrenched beliefs whereas the concept of a crank, for example, arguably belongs to our understanding of the very nature of critical judgment. To think that would be to distort the cultural role played by the idea of the morally unthinkable and its role in individual moral thinking.

An example will, I hope, make clear why. In the early nineties a man in London, brandishing a knife, demanded money of a young mother who was wheeling her baby. He threatened to mutilate the baby if she refused. She gave him her purse and her jewellery. He then slashed the baby's face and body and ran off. The baby died in hospital. Its mother was admitted to a psychiatric hospital.

I sometimes told that story to students who profess to be sceptical of the reality of evil as students almost always do in first-year moral philosophy tutorials. I ask them to put aside, for the moment, worries about freedom of the will, about cultural conditioning, about who has the right to judge, and other worries of that kind which inform their scepticism. I ask that, for the moment, they do not argue as devil's advocates, nor argue what someone might say or others have said. My wish is for them to say only what they can say in reflective, considered seriousness in response to these questions: will they deny or even express the doubt that the man did evil to the mother and her baby? Will they say that perhaps there is no such thing as evil, or that it is a concept for which we have no real use, or that it is an illusion generated as an instrument of social control, and so on? Sadly, there is no shortage of examples to use for such purposes and I have been asking my students such questions for over twenty years. Only one has expressed a moral scepticism that was both sincere and serious, but it was quite clear that it had no intellectual origins. It would not be much of an exaggeration, if an exaggeration at all, to say that in each tutorial in those twenty years and more most students professed a form of moral scepticism.

Agreement that what the baby slasher did is evil is not just agreement about how to use a word, nor merely agreement on certain paradigms of judgment whose acceptance is a condition of other, more controversial or speculative judgments. Such agreements are, of course, important, but the realisation—common to the students and to me—that we could not deny or doubt the evil of what the baby's murderer did was a realisation that much more than error or muddle or even incoherence was at stake. The fear of thinking that perhaps there is no such thing as evil is not, as is the fear of thinking the earth might be flat, a fear that one is losing one's capacity for sound judgment. It is the moral fear of becoming the kind of person who seriously doubts the reality of evil. At stake is nothing less than one's moral being.

To be morally serious, the students soon discovered, is to fear to doubt the reality of evil because that fear is inseparable from understanding what evil is. If that is so, then the fear of doubting the reality of evil is quite different from the fear of having one's pet theories, cherished assumptions, or entrenched prejudices overturned, yet it is almost always assimilated to them. Those latter fears, like all fears of facing painful truths, do not belong to the nature of the conceptual content of such theories, assumptions or prejudices. But, the fear of doubting the reality of evil is inseparable from an understanding of the very nature of evil because it is central to our understanding of the *kind of seriousness* that we attribute to any morality informed by a sense of evil. Kierkegaard expressed the point when he said that just as the logician most fears a fallacy, the ethical thinker most fears to fall away from the ethical. There can be no more dramatic way of falling away from the ethical than seriously to doubt its reality. That is critical to understanding the *kind* of certainty the students expressed when—after having been called to sobriety—they confessed that they could not doubt the evil the baby slasher had done.

Once they saw that, the students were no longer inclined to say that the certainty we have about such examples is merely the psychological consequence of effective social conditioning—the expression of taboos so deeply internalised that we cannot even contemplate their critical examination. To acknowledge that our beliefs are socially conditioned or that our certainty is merely a psychological phenomenon is to acknowledge that we should at least try to step back from those beliefs in order to reassess them. That is, of course, likely to be difficult. When they are deeply entrenched it may prove psychologically impossible. One cannot know that it is impossible, however, unless one seriously tries and fails to step back from them. But when one realises that the fear of doubting the reality of evil is inseparable from a serious understanding of it, and that one cannot even try, then one also realises that the impossibility of adopting a sceptical stance is of a different kind from those impossibilities whose nature can be explained by elaboration of the power of social and psychological forces.

Did I get such a response over so many years because I bullied my students with a catalogue of horrors? Given the nature of nihilistic scepticism (for that is what the radical denial of the reality of the ethical comes to) it is natural to voice that suspicion. The responses of my students are in keeping, however, with an astonishing fact about our philosophical tradition. Although professions of nihilism haunt it, as they do contemporary intellectual culture, there is virtually no philosopher in the mainstream— and I do not exclude Nietzsche—who has seriously professed such scepticism in the first person. It is usually attributed to someone else 'for the sake of the argument' or, as in Plato's dialogues, to characters whose intellectual seriousness and stamina are inadequate to the rigours of argument. They sulk and run off as soon as the going gets tough.

There has, to be sure, been serious scepticism of whether moral judgments can, in some substantial sense, be true or false, and of whether there can be something properly called moral knowledge. But philosophers who have professed that kind of scepticism have almost always insisted that it has no serious consequences for our moral life. The reason is not because we are such tawdry creatures that we will continue to live lies at any cost. It is because a clear-sighted acknowledgment that, strictly speaking, there is no moral truth and no moral knowledge, need have no nihilistic consequences. Professions of nihilism on intellectual grounds are a mixture of confusion and posturing radicalism. As the English philosopher R. F. Holland put it, the intellectual variety of nihilism invariably seems a 'trumped up affair'.

My reply therefore to someone who suspects I morally bullied my students and betrayed my role as one who should teach them to follow reason wherever it leads them, would go like this. I wished to teach them what it is seriously to follow an argument to a painful conclusion. I wished to teach them that the conclusion of an argument is something one must seriously be able to *conclude*, that is, to profess seriously in the first person. As in my discussion of Descartes, I intend that as a conceptual remark on what it is for something to *be* a conclusion and on what it is seriously to follow an argument wherever it takes one. The lesson was, therefore, about the nature of sobriety in discussion. But not about sober judgment as that is necessary if one is not to be a crank. The fear of becoming the kind of person who doubts the reality of evil is first a moral fear and only secondly a fear of confusion. It is important to remember, however, that because it is a fear internal to an understanding of evil, it is not to be contrasted with an effort to understand things as they are, independently of distorting fears and anxieties.

Cultures are partly defined and distinguished by what is unthinkable in them—unthinkable not in the sense that no one ever thinks them, but in the sense that they are beyond argument; they are 'indefensible' because any serious attempt to defend them would show one to lack the judgment necessary for the proper exercise of reason on the matters in question. Or, in the case of moral matters, because it is wicked even to contemplate them. It is, for example, unthinkable that we should eat our dead or can them for pet food in order to reduce the slaughter of animals. Any argument that led to such a conclusion would have found its *reductio ad absurdum*. It is also in the same sense unthinkable that we should consider murder as a means of political advancement. We have not considered this as an option in political life and rejected it on moral or other grounds. It is not up for serious consideration. That distinguishes us fundamentally from some other cultures, in which political murder is practised or—more importantly for the point I am making—considered an option amongst others and then rejected for fear of its consequences. What is unthinkable is different for different cultures and changes from time to time. Sometimes the change is for the good. It used to be unthinkable that black people should have the full rights of citizenship. Sometimes it is not. It used to be unthinkable that we should kill children three weeks old or less merely because we don't want them. Peter Singer believes that we would not seriously wrong the children if we did it. That belief is undisguised in his book, *Practical Ethics,* and he is right to believe that the extent to which people are now seriously prepared to consider his reasons for it marks a shift in the moral boundaries which partially define our culture.

For that reason the reception of Singer's views is an interesting case for anyone who is interested in the concept of the morally unthinkable. He argues quite openly that you would not wrong a three-week-old child if you killed it for frivolous reasons. You might, for example, have been offered the job you had always desired and your newly born child stands in the way of accepting it. Or, you might have won a holiday to Tuscany and you think the baby would spoil it. Rather than pass up such opportunities you could kill the baby—kill it, that is, without wronging it. Singer does not think that because you would not wrong the baby you are therefore morally free actually to kill it. Other reasons which don't focus on the child would almost certainly sustain a prohibition against it. You could, perhaps should, give it up for adoption, thereby giving pleasure to a childless couple. Or you might set a bad precedent if you killed it just because it stood in the way of your career prospects. Some people take comfort in those qualifications. Others find they compound the horror. Whichever camp one falls into, it would be hard to deny that the claim that you would not wrong the child is startling. It is therefore interesting that the intelligentsia generally accords Singer untroubled esteem. Of course Singer is not esteemed so generally because of that view. He is esteemed because of what he says about animals, and because his views on other forms of infanticide, of very sick or disabled children and on euthanasia more generally, are thought to be views that anyone should take morally seriously.

It is often said that Singer, and others who think like him

about when we would wrong children if we killed them, have followed their arguments wherever they go, however unpalatable the conclusions of those arguments may be. Maybe they did, but they did not reach their conclusions gritting their teeth as reason relentlessly compelled them to go somewhere they desperately did not want to go. Nobody is in that way compelled by arguments about anything remotely interesting in ethics. Firstly, because all the arguments in ethics have so many unclarities and depend on so many controversial premises, only someone unusually lacking in imagination and intelligence could fail to find loopholes through which to escape with a perfectly clear intellectual conscience. And secondly, all arguments in ethics (and elsewhere) depend for their persuasiveness on the fact that their conclusions are not taken as reducing to absurdity the steps that led to them. An argument, for example, that now led to the conclusion that it is permissible forcibly to take Aboriginal children from their parents so that in a hundred years we would have forgotten there ever were Aboriginal peoples in Australia, would no longer even be entertained. If Singer's arguments for infanticide are now accepted as deserving of serious consideration it is not just because of their logical power. It is because changes in the culture have disposed us to accept a conclusion that only thirty years ago discredited any argument that led to it, however logically powerful the argument might have appeared.

Examples such as these show that, in the cultural realm, the unthinkable, even what is morally unthinkable, is a barrier whose breach is not always dramatic. Singer breached it without much protest that some of his conclusions are morally repugnant. Anyone who argues that the repugnant nature of the conclusion that one would not wrong a healthy three-week-old baby if one killed it merely because one did not want it is more striking than the arbitrariness of a three-week cut-off point is likely to be treated with urbane condescension.

One would, therefore, seriously misunderstand what it means

to treat things as beyond argument in the way I have been discussing if one construes it as a deeply internalised form of self-censorship. Self-censorship is of what we think, but believe we ought not to think or say. In a similar way, political correctness is directed against what many of us think and say. Oversimplifying a little, the distinction can be put like this: self-censorship and the censorious pressures of political correctness occur *within* the boundaries of what is thinkable in a culture; our sense of what is unthinkable is partly *constitutive* of those boundaries. To believe, but not to say (or to believe, but to wish not to believe), because we judge that we ought not to, any of the following would be an example of self-censorship: that the Jews are too influential; that they played a significant part in the oppression of some European peoples who sought their revenge in the Holocaust; that the Jews have misused the Holocaust for their cultural and political purposes; that blacks have lower IQs than whites; that Aboriginal culture may be inferior to European culture. To think, however, that the Jews deserved, or even partly deserved, the evil done to them in the Holocaust is different, not only in degree, but also in kind. The former are conceptually appropriate targets for political correctness. The latter is not.

Social theorists have long argued that philosophers, especially in the analytical tradition, need to be more reflective about the social causes that give rise to philosophical schools and fashions. They are right, I think. But if that reflection is not to become reductionist, then together with an account of why philosophers attribute to reason and to argument cultural changes that really should be explained by other causes, we also need a better account than is on offer of what it means to be compelled by argument, and of the distinction between legitimate and illegitimate persuasion.

Nihilistic strands in postmodernism have exploited the absence of such an account, rightly seeing the naivete of much of what is on offer (at least in the mainstream), but wrongly construing the necessities and impossibilities which must be invoked in any account of argument and persuasion, as modalities of power. As though someone who says she must conclude that Socrates is mortal after she affirmed that all men are mortal and Socrates is a man, betrayed her deeply inculcated servility. In opposition to that I have suggested that we need an adequate philosophy of the unthinkable, of what is beyond argument, that construes it, not as the expression of psychological or social forces, external to the conceptual grammar of argument, but as part of any adequate conception of reason and argument. And because cultures are partly defined and distinguished by what they treat as unthinkable, that account will also be an indispensable part of the philosophy of culture. The concept of the unthinkable is at the intersection of philosophy (logic) and social theory. To treat it as belonging only to one or the other is to invite either naivete or reductionism.

I have been detailing the kind of naivete in question on the part of philosophers. In the case of the social sciences it shows itself in the idea that the unthinkable refers merely to deeply entrenched taboos, or at any rate to beliefs which in one way or another are treated as fundamental to a society, and which are therefore enforced in ways that permit no dissent. That is why the concept of the unthinkable, as I am invoking it, is not that of a taboo that has been so deeply internalised that it is psychologically impossible for us even to contemplate its critical examination. The concept of a taboo fails to distinguish, for example, between the thought that the Jews have *misused* the Holocaust and the thought that they *deserved* it. Collapsing the unthinkable into a species of the very offensive or the radically unsettling encourages the illusion that a genuinely critical and free intelligence will not be afraid to question anything.

I have many times acknowledged the dangers of declaring things to be beyond consideration. I have also emphasised the dangers that threaten when one is panicked by the risks of judgment, and the even greater dangers that would attend the destruction of any substantial notion of judgment.

Many people are afflicted by an anxiety—some by a sense of desperation—that the concepts which are fundamental to sober political judgment have come under attack. These are the concepts of commonsense and of common knowledge. Concerning many public issues—education, the raising of children, censorship, unions, the courts—anecdotes abound which are intended to illustrate a radical loss of commonsense or a denial of something which is common knowledge. In itself that might occasion no more than amused condescension amongst people who have different ideas about which beliefs express commonsense. But whichever beliefs one takes to be expressive of it, everyone has reason to fear the destruction of the concept of commonsense, for the concept of sober judgment will be destroyed along with it. Far from being radically critical, we will then be prepared to believe anything. The political dangers of that are illustrated in hair-raising detail by Solzhenitsyn in *The Gulag Archipelago* and by Hannah Arendt in *The Origins of Totalitarianism*.

Truth & the Responsibility of Intellectuals

George Orwell writes in his essay 'Looking Back on the Spanish War':

> Early in life I had noticed that no event is ever correctly reported in a newspaper, but in Spain, for the first time, I saw newspaper reports which did not bear any relation to the facts, not even the relationship which is implied in an ordinary lie. I saw great battles reported where there had been no fighting, and complete silence where hundreds of men had been killed. I saw troops who had fought bravely denounced as cowards and traitors, and others who had never seen a shot fired hailed as the heroes of imaginary victories, and I saw newspapers in London retailing these lies and eager intellectuals building emotional superstructures over events that had never happened...
>
> This kind of thing is frightening to me, because it often

gives me the feeling that the very concept of objective truth is fading out of the world…

I know it is the fashion to say that most of recorded history is lies anyway. I am willing to believe that history is for the most part inaccurate and biased, but what is peculiar to our own age is the abandonment of the idea that history *could* be truthfully written…The implied objective of this line of thought is a nightmare world in which the Leader, or some ruling clique, controls not only the future but *the past*. If the Leader says of such and such an event, 'It never happened'—well, it never happened. If he says that two and two are five—well, two and two are five. This prospect frightens me much more than bombs—and after our experiences of the last few years that is not a frivolous statement.

It can hardly be doubted that the practical consequences would be fearful if the very idea of objective truth were seriously undermined (can we seriously conceive of it being destroyed?). Orwell warns of them in many of his writings. In this passage, however, it is not those consequences that frighten him. What frightens him is just that if the leader says that 'two and two are five—well, two and two are five'.

'Looking Back on the Spanish War' is a form of witness as, in different ways, are the works of Alexander Solzhenitsyn and Primo Levi. Truth has important instrumental value in politics just as its suppression has. But truth also has a value for us which is not instrumental. Often that value drives those who feel obliged to be political witnesses. The destruction of a people's past, for example, is a crime against their integrity as a people. Much of Solzhenitsyn's work was in response to that fact. Lies can destroy the integrity of national life only because we value truthfulness in ways not reducible to the practical benefits it may bring. People find it terrible to live a national lie just as they do to live a lie in their personal lives. In neither case is truthfulness merely a means to something whose value we could understand without appreciating the need we have of truth, for its own sake, as we sometimes say.

It shows in the language we use. In *The Periodic Table* Primo Levi spoke of his disgust and his despair at the degree to which the fascists polluted the political life of Italy with their lies during World War II. 'Polluted' is his word. We speak naturally of the ways lies may pollute, poison, defile or degrade things which are precious to us—relationships, institutions such as universities or the press, and, sometimes, the entire political life of a nation. In such ways of speaking we show something about the way truth may matter to us. Simone Weil writes:

> The need of truth is more sacred than any other need. Yet it is never mentioned. One feels afraid to read when once one has realized the quantity and the monstrousness of the material falsehoods shamelessly paraded, even in the books of the most reputable authors. Thereafter one reads as though one were drinking from a contaminated well.

Levi was a chemist and he found in chemistry consolation, a healing spirit of truthfulness and a disinterested concern with truth which could nourish his need of it. If it sounds paradoxical to speak of a disinterested concern for truth when that concern satisfies a need, then one should remember that the need is for truth for its own sake. 'For its own sake', or 'for its intrinsic value' can be misleading expressions, I think, partly because they plug one into certain conflicts I wish to have no part of. I prefer to say that we value truth in ways not reducible to, or ways entirely explicable in terms of, the practical value it may have for us. It is more cumbersome, but that way of putting it suggests that when we value truth in ways not reducible to its practical value, its practical value may be part of a full account of how it is valued even then. For the same reason, that way of putting it may alert one to the fact that the non-instrumental value of truth is revealed to us only in examples which show the place it can have in a human life. The distinction between instrumental and 'intrinsic value' often tempts one to believe that such placing is a concession to the insistence that instrumental value is the only value truth can have.

Levi's lament reminds us of what people mean when they speak of truth as 'food for the soul'. He did not turn to chemistry to find truths—to increase the number of his true beliefs. He could have done that by counting the chairs in his room, the buttons on his shirt or the hairs on his arms. He turned to chemistry because it is a discipline whose tradition reveals what it may be to love truth, to serve it and be faithful to it. Because it is possible to love truth and to be faithful to it, it is also possible for lies to pollute and to defile those things which are precious to us and whose value is partly conditioned by our need for truth.

As much as Levi may have found solace in chemistry for his pain at the defilement of the political realm, a private good is no remedy for a public wrong. We need truth in politics just as I argued we need justice. Like justice truth is a good *sui generis*, even in politics. The language we use to express our sense of loss when lies pervade the public realm shows that. None of which means that a certain amount of lying is not to be expected and necessary in politics. Orwell, Solzhenitsyn, Levi, Weil—none of them was naive about that.

Weil who wrote with hard-headed insight on this theme was nonetheless mistaken when she said that part of the soul that says 'we' is always a threat to truth. There are many ways of saying 'we' and perhaps most of them are dangerous. But when it is the expression of a desire for community, it may also be a desire to celebrate the distinctive goods of political communality. It was not as an individual but as an Italian national that Levi deplored the lies that had polluted Italy. Justice is one of those goods. Truth is another. Often they go together. Sometimes they appear to be in tension, as was revealed in the need to establish a Truth and Reconciliation Commission in South Africa. Reports about the Commission's proceedings suggest that it harvested no more truth than would otherwise have been obtained by cross-examination at conventional trials and by a diligent media. Those same reports suggest that the harvest for reconciliation was even smaller. Even if such failures were, as some critics claim, inevitable, the national perception that truthfulness about the past was a condition of national life expressed a genuine political need. And again truthfulness about the past was not sought merely as a *means* to a decent national life. The need for truth was recognised to be an integral part of it.

Throughout his life Orwell lamented the fact that intellectuals—academics, writers, journalists and so on—are so often dishonest in their support of political causes. He appeared to believe that intellectuals who lie, suppress or distort the truth for the sake of a political cause do something significantly different and significantly worse than plumbers who lie for the same reason. The nature of the difference has proved hard to state clearly, but those who have tried to do it elaborate the reasons why they believe that intellectuals have an obligation to strict truthfulness just because they are intellectuals. Lying and the suppression of truth are the more dramatic instances of a failure to honour that obligation. Embattled intellectuals, who distort and oversimplify what they defend and oppose for the sake, for example, of retaining a united front against their political or cultural enemies, are often guilty of the same offence. Like lying politicians, the Orwellian thought continues, such intellectuals deny people the truth they need, but intellectuals compound the wrong by betraying their vocation and the trust they enjoy because of their vocation.

Such a view as I have attributed to Orwell represents one important strand in the long-standing argument about the political responsibilities of intellectuals. Some people also believe that a proper account of the reasons why intellectuals have, even in politics, a strict obligation to truthfulness will reveal why some of them feel obliged to enter political life. Intellectuals (this thought continues) become involved in politics for many reasons but, insofar as they feel obliged to, they will do so for one of two distinctive kinds of reason. The first is that they perceive a need which they believe they are particularly suited to satisfy. An historian, for example, may feel obliged to expose historical falsehoods because she believes that she is particularly well placed to do so. A plumber, a carpenter, a nurse, a doctor might offer their services in a national emergency in the same spirit. The second reason has to do with obligations intellectuals believe to be internal to their vocation.

To explore what is at issue here I want to begin with a personal anecdote upon which I have often reflected. It is about intellectual life at the University of Melbourne in the 1960s. It was then a fine university with some extraordinary teachers, among them Vincent Buckley, Frank Knöpfelmacher and Geoff Sharp. For a smaller group of students, there was Sibnarayan Ray, head of Indian Studies. There were, of course, others, but the ones I have mentioned had profound influence beyond their disciplines.

They were passionate, intellectually and morally in ways impossible finally to separate, and this attracted students to them. In classes, in the cafeteria and many times in their homes, they gave generously of their time. Inevitably this combination of passion and generous but demanding attentiveness made disciples of some of their students. Ungenerous observers said these men wanted disciples to flatter their vanity and to serve their political ends. My anecdote suggests a perspective on this.

Geoff Sharp was co-editor of *Arena* which described itself as 'a Marxist journal of criticism and discussion'. He was soon to become one of the most influential figures on the radical intellectual left. At the time he was almost forty, teaching in the Social Studies department at Melbourne University, and I was eighteen. It was then possible to buy a Citröen Light 15 for sixty dollars. One that actually ran cost an extra fifty dollars or so. With the hope that I could make one go and have spare parts besides, I bought two. Driving his battered old Rover, Sharp towed them to his farm in Plenty. Occasionally I went there and worked on the cars, repairing and painting them.

When the work was done, Sharp and his wife Nonie often invited me and whoever accompanied me to dinner. After dinner we continued to talk until close to midnight. In winter we sat in front of a wonderful fire into which one could feed a small tree from a hole in the side of the house. We talked about philosophy, psychology and sociology. Although all our conversations were indirectly shaped by the political interests we shared, we seldom talked directly about politics. Sharp's way of living and thinking inspired me.

The battles of the Cold War dominated intellectual politics at the time, the eve of the university's transformation by the war in Vietnam. Four years or so before I met Sharp, Frank Knöpfelmacher had been warning of the dangers posed to universities by communists and those sympathetic to them. Also around forty, he was passionate, courageous, shrewd and possessed a mind that was insightful and sharp but unreliable in its attachment to reality. Knöpfelmacher was Australia's most notorious anti-communist intellectual. Asked to produce evidence for his fears, he accused Sharp of planning a communist takeover of the Social Studies department. In collusion with others he did what he could to have Sharp thrown out of the university.

Knöpfelmacher spent hours talking to and encouraging students, often in the cafeteria. He was kind to me and directed me towards my choice of vocation. We became friends. Gratitude and admiration ensured my loyalty, though not my support, even when I thought he had acted badly. It is one of the glories of intellectual life that such friendships are possible between people separated by twenty or more years.

During the four or five years when as a student I knew Sharp and Knöpfelmacher, only once did Knöpfelmacher criticise Sharp in my presence, though he knew of my friendship with him. I told him that I didn't want to hear, that Sharp was my friend and that I could not, would not, credit his accusations. I waited for his scornful reply. Knöpfelmacher was not someone to indulge those whom he believed to be naive about communism or communists. I expected him to ridicule my trust in Sharp. Instead, he looked at me for a moment or two and said, 'All right. I understand. Let it be that way.'

Knöpfelmacher never again spoke to me against Sharp. Nor did Sharp ever say a word to me against Knöpfelmacher, although he had reason to be bitter. For some years, Knöpfelmacher's attacks on him made Sharp a pariah in the university. When the president of the university Labour Club asked him to deliver a lunchtime lecture, it was the first time a student had spoken informally to him for three years.

Looking back, I marvel at the sense of a teaching vocation possessed by these remarkable men. Their generous, hospitable attention as I enjoyed it was never marred by condescension, flattery or the desire on my part or theirs for uncritical discipleship. Despite the difference in our ages, that attention flowered into friendship because of the way we lived, together, the life of the mind, in a shared adventure of thinking and seeking for understanding. Both men reflected about the nature of their disciplines, and on what a life of the mind could humanly mean, awakening and nourishing that same reflection—indeed, a sense of obligation to it—in many of the students they befriended.

In later years I read and came to love Plato. In his dialogue *Gorgias*, Socrates tells us that the difference between legitimate and illegitimate forms of persuasion is at the heart of the difference between the love of wisdom and its spurious semblances. He also says that it is a presupposition of friendship which, no less than the pursuit of wisdom, depends on strict observance of the distinction between conversation and forms of speech which are corrupted by the desire for power. Plato dramatised powerfully the thought that intellectual friendship neither 'proceeds by force nor submits to force', including the force of a charismatic personality. This was the unspoken assumption of the friendships I was privileged to enjoy with Knöpfelmacher and Sharp.

Passionate though they were, in their dealings with me and with others, they respected our need for independence of mind. The respect for it, shown dramatically by Knöpfelmacher in the incident I recalled earlier and with quiet delicacy by Sharp on many days and nights at his farm, was inseparable from a sense that our lives were shaped by a shared need of truth and objectivity. Not truth with a capital T or objectivity with a capital O, but as we understand those notions through disciplined application of the concepts with which we distinguish the varieties of good from bad thinking and, together with that, legitimate from illegitimate persuasion. Their example gave authority to what they said and to what many of us read about the life of the mind. From them (though of course not only from them) we learned how to distinguish the genuinely collaborative search for understanding from its betrayal in the many seductive forms of counterfeit intellectual friendship.

Given the bitter hostility between them, that was exemplary moral restraint. The fact that I was a student—or to put it another way the fact that the relationship between the three of us was mediated by a particular understanding of the life of the mind—is essential to any full characterisation of that restraint. It gave the tone to the way they respected my freedom to be a friend to both. That is why I say that one could not characterise that respect without reference to their concern with truth and their sense of its value. Discipleship often caricatures that respect in its violation of it.

Only something like the concept of a vocation, I think, will enable one adequately to characterise the kind of obligations acknowledged in that respect and in the nature of their commitment to their students and to the life of the mind. It showed in the way a commitment to truth and truthfulness shaped their lives. The concept of a profession and its associated responsibilities and commitment will not capture it. It would divide their work from their life in the wrong kind of way and it would do so because it would make their passion into a contingent psychological attribute, external to the obligations they acknowledged when they reflected on what it meant to be a university teacher. By their example they disclosed values different from and deeper than any found in the most rigorous professionalism.

The concept of a profession in my judgment tends to betray into mediocrity practices that often have traditions with the potential to yield a much deeper understanding of their nature, of their deepest good and of the joys and obligations that define them. The almost universal tendency to rely on the concept of a profession to define the standards constitutive of academic practice and which are fundamental to the kind of worth they may have, has been one of the reasons why we have become estranged from a deeper sense of their intrinsic worth. In its contemporary usage the concept of a vocation means little more than a job, rather than something that non-accidentally fills a life and worthily fills it. It is not accidental that vocations are characteristically for a lifetime. We could not imagine a Socrates or a Wittgenstein taking early retirement (although Wittgenstein tried) and the fact that we could not derives from a sense of what they did, the nature of it, and of their vocation to it. It does not, I think, express merely a psychological fact about them which would explain how they approached something that others might approach quite differently. That, however, is how it must appear if we conceive of what they did under the concepts that define professional commitment. It is accidental how many professions one may have in a lifetime.

What is it to be a teacher or a student of philosophy, or of history, or of physics? This is a question whose answers may deepen without limit. And the obligations which partly define vocations cannot, as can the ethics of a profession, be decided by a committee. That is why we can say without absurdity (even if we say it falsely) that an entire age has lost an understanding of what it means to be a teacher, a doctor or a nurse. But that means also that an entire age has lost an understanding of what it means to have a vocation to teach, or to heal. Often that is obscured by the fact that most, if not all, professions may also be vocations. Reflection about their nature and the obligations which partly define them is therefore often unknowingly structured by the concept of a vocation.

At a certain point in our recent history the concept of a vocation became as anachronistic as the concept of virtue. When that happened our sense of the value of truth and its place in the characterisation of academic life changed. What one makes of talk of the love of truth, of truth as a need of the soul, of the need to be concerned with truth over vanity, wealth, status and so on, will be different according to whether one's conception of academic life and its responsibilities is structured by the concept of a vocation or by that of a profession.

Academics may have a very stern sense of their obligations towards truth without thinking of them, either explicitly or implicitly, under the concept of a vocation. The concept of love, for example, need never figure in any serious sense in their thoughts about the nature of their professional duties or in their thoughts about the nature of their concern for truth. If they are serious about their professional duties and the pursuit of their intellectual ambitions, they will need to develop virtues of character. They will need, for example, courage, truthfulness and humility. These, however, are names of virtues which are in substance quite different when they are connected with a serious conception of the love of truth.

The idea that one might be a professional lover of truth is a joke. But it is not a joke to say that the love of truth is an obligation fundamental to an intellectual or academic vocation—which is one reason why we (often, though not always) tend to think that the abandonment of such a vocation is either a sign that the person did not have one, no matter how brilliant her accomplishments may have been, or that it is a kind of infidelity. In his notebooks Wittgenstein agonises over whether his work is infected by a dishonesty born of vanity. Seen in the light of the concept of an academic vocation that is no more than should be expected of one who is lucidly mindful of its requirements. In the light of the concept of a career or a profession it is likely to appear neurotic or precious.

I would not claim that such thoughts about the notion of a vocation were shared by Sharp or Knöpfelmacher. Nonetheless those thoughts and others like them were part of the common understanding within which Sharp and Knöpfelmacher thought and worked and in whose light students were privileged to learn from them. The concept of a university as an institution distinguished from many other high-powered tertiary institutions was a central element of that common understanding and necessary to understanding their sense of vocation. They were not just teachers. Nor were they just what we now call researchers. They were both, but in a way that was informed by their sense of what it means to be both of these things in a university. And that, I am sure, grounded the respect they had for their students' independence. They were university teachers and we were their students. The many distinctions implicit in that fact—between teachers and students, between universities and other institutions of higher education, between universities and other political institutions—informed their sense of the difference between legitimate and illegitimate forms of persuasion as it applies to the relations between students and their teachers.

In those days there was much discussion about the nature of the university, of what is a real university and what is a false semblance of it. Such discussion can be barren, for not all concepts that invite reflection on real and false instances of them are fertile. But the concept of a university was not, then, barren. It yielded an historically deep and rich conception of one form of the life of the mind—the academic form. There was argument, of course, about what was best in that yield and what could still speak authoritatively to us in modern times, but it was agreed that an institution which does not require its members to reflect seriously on the meaning and place of intellectual activity in a human life is not a university, no matter how disinterested its pursuit of learning, and no matter how distinguished its contribution to it. That is one of the things that distinguishes a university from higher research institutes, even when the latter enrol students. In any university there will be many fine scholars and teachers who feel no such obligation. But their institution would not be a university if their practice determined its character. The difference between them and their colleagues is not, therefore, merely a matter of personality. For the latter the vocation to the teaching and scholarly life is transformed by a sense of necessities and possibilities that drive and are derived from their reflection on what it means to live that life in a university.

The idea of a university as an institution that requires its members to reflect on the life of the mind creates a conversational space within the university that provides a model for a similar space outside of it. It connects the vocations of an academic and that of a particular kind of public intellectual. Each of the teachers I referred to earlier transcended their discipline, but the notion of an interdisciplinary engagement will not adequately convey how. That notion is of a form of interaction between disciplines that is conditioned by the fact that participants wear their disciplinary hats. The philosopher speaks as a philosopher to the historian who responds as an historian, and although that is only the beginning of their conversation it is a beginning that colours the nature of the way they overcome the limits of disciplinary insularity. But the character of intellectual life at Melbourne University at lunchtime in the public lecture theatre, for example, was formed by people who wore no disciplinary hats, although what they said, the way they said it and the nature of their discussion showed, sometimes for good and sometimes for ill, that the temper of their minds had been formed by their mastery of a discipline. The difference is critical to understanding the nature of the kind of public commitment that I am describing.

In these discussions, in the public lecture theatre at lunchtime or in the evenings, a distinction was observed concerning what was permitted there and what was permitted in the classroom. Max Weber elaborates the distinction in his essay 'Science As a Vocation' and his name was often invoked in support of it. Rhetoric and a far less stringent regard for objectivity were permitted in the public lecture theatre. Nonetheless, the liberties permitted in the public lecture theatre at lunchtime were not nearly as extensive as those permitted in the town hall, a requirement which politicians who addressed audiences in universities were expected to honour as were students who sometimes disrupted their lectures. My point here is not a general one about the courtesies that should be observed between speakers and audience, nor is it one about freedom of speech considered as a democratic ideal. The town hall rightly tolerates degrees of rhetoric, evasion and even dishonesty from politicians, and wise politicians tolerate a degree of heckling and a few tomatoes thrown at them as par for the course. Democracy is not threatened by such things. In fact, a robust democracy might glory in them. A university could be destroyed by them.

Not that freedom of expression is necessarily greater in the universities than in the political domain. Our understanding of academic freedom—what we have historically taken it to be—has been shaped by the assumption that it is freedom in a university. Freedom claimed by a university might be different from those claimed by other institutions of higher learning, from say, a religious seminary, or from a research institute. Thinking about the life of the mind, of its place and value in a human life, is in a broad sense an ethical concern. If it is done passionately in response to a sense that it is an obligation intrinsic to an academic vocation, it will be an example of the Socratic claim that to inquire about how to live is amongst the most important things a human being can do. Not to do it, he said at his famous trial, was to live a life unworthy of a human being. That ethical requirement, intrinsic to the nature of a university, but not necessarily to that of a high-flying research institute, occupied with most of the same disciplines as a university, explains why universities may be more restrictive of the expression of opinion than such an institute, and more restrictive even than the political domain. Sometimes, of course, ethically motivated restrictions are merely the expression of the pressures of political correctness. The interesting thing about political correctness as it affects universities, however, is that even when it is illegitimately censorious, it is sometimes the corruption of an idea of the connection between the life of learning and the moral life which is at the heart of the university.

No one would agree to the appointment to a chair of medicine of someone whose ground-breaking discoveries were made when he experimented on prisoners in the Nazi death camps. I doubt that anyone would now agree to the appointment to a chair of anthropology someone who argued that Aborigines were savages from whom children of mixed blood needed to be rescued, for their own good and so that, as A. O. Neville put it, no one would remember there had been Aborigines in Australia. I doubt that anyone would agree to the appointment to a chair of moral philosophy someone who said that homosexuals are disgusting, that their behaviour should again be a criminal offence, and that those who offended repeatedly should be castrated. One can give many more examples. In many cases, at least, the person who is rightly denied an appointment on the grounds of his or her opinions should be allowed to profess those opinions in the political realm. To silence them would be a serious infringement of their rights as citizens to free speech.

Even in its quasi-political aspect then, the university should remain an ivory tower. The values of the outside political and professional worlds are often dangerous to it. It rightly remains unworldly. Strange though it may sound, that is its public duty. When a university provides students with a space that protects them from the pressures of the world—from worldliness in one of the many senses of that word—and from the pressures which conspire to make them children of their times, then it meets its primary public obligation. In that space students may form new desires and ideals in the light of values that they had probably not dreamed of and certainly never before fully understood. The unworldly expression 'a community of scholars' should not be a source of embarrassment. It should be celebrated as speaking to the essence of a university and its public duty.

The values of the university, as I have sketched them, can inform public intellectual life more generally. For the teachers who inspired me and many of my contemporaries, a sense of obligation to public intellectual life was all of a piece with their sense of what it meant to be a university teacher and scholar. The public space that used to be defined by the small magazines—*Arena, Meanjin, Quadrant* and others—was where it showed itself best. Untruthfulness seldom manifested itself there in such a direct form as lying, and no one justified it when it did. It showed itself most typically when understanding was sacrificed to cultural combat. The pressure to that kind of untruthfulness is inevitable because the small magazines look in two directions at once—they look to the standards that define university life and to the standards that prevail in ordinary political life where it is acknowledged that politicians will and perhaps must lie, and that they may pollute the political realm when they do. When politicians lie to parliament, for example, they damage not only that institution with its noble history, but also the democratic nation defined by it.

In speaking this way about the small magazines, I do not mean to suggest that they had no serious faults, or that public intellectual life could not be far more extensive than the readership secured by those magazines. Nor do I want to deny the many and unforeseen possibilities offered by the internet. By referring to them, I want to draw attention to an intellectual space which mediates between the universities, and radio, television and the quality press. That space is one in which, for example, serious but not technical discussion of the nature of truth should occur—a discussion we cannot avoid because of the place which scepticism about truth now occupies in our culture. It would be naive, however, to hope that the number of people who are prepared to think as hard as such discussion requires would ever be sufficiently large for the mass media to take a responsible interest in it.

Sadly, the universities no longer stand for an ideal of truthfulness that could inspire a public intellectual space outside them. The concept of a vocation is now anachronistic. So is any concept of a university that refers to more than a high-flying tertiary institution whose members are obliged to attract research grants. There is widespread scepticism about truth or, at any rate, the widespread profession of such scepticism. The institutions which are called universities are compromised by mendacity, by a pervasive untruthfulness in their descriptions of how they have changed to accommodate the political pressures of recent years. Academics tend to deny the extent of the untruthfulness, but everybody knows that it is now widespread and that knowledge generates a debilitating cynicism about the higher ideals of the university. For so long as this is so, universities cannot generate within themselves a conversational space of the kind I described earlier—a conversational space marked by a need and respect for truthfulness. It remains to be seen what that means for the nature of public intellectual life.

It is, I assume, clear that academics are obliged to try to recreate in their own institutions that public space in which there can be reflection on what it means to live the life of the mind. That obligation flows from the nature of their vocations. Are they obliged to do it so there may also be such a space in the public realm? That is not the same question, but it is related to another question: are academics obliged to be public intellectuals? The answer to both is, I believe, No.

Reflection on what it means to be a university academic yields no such obligation. I mean that it yields no obligation of the kind that arises from the very nature of being an academic. No such obligation is derivable from the one that I claim does fall on academics—to reflect, together with their students, on the worth of the life of the mind.

There are, of course, external reasons that might support a claim that academics should write, speak and advise outside their institutions—perhaps because they owe it to the society that pays their salaries, because they owe it as citizens to their fellow citizens, and so on. On such external reasons I offer no comment beyond two observations. First that they are external reasons, quite different in kind from those that derive from reflection on how properly to fulfil the obligations of an academic vocation. Secondly, that if too many academics became public intellectuals of that kind, if too many of them offered their expertise to other public and political institutions, or became involved too much in other ways in the political realm, then the unworldliness of their institutions would almost certainly be threatened. In the last fifteen years or so, exactly that has happened. It explains why vice chancellors can now dismiss academics who are critical of their universities, without so much as suspecting that it may sometimes be the duty of academics (let alone their right) to criticise their institutions—a duty that derives from reflection on the very nature of their vocation.

The academic form of the life of the mind generates an obligation to truthfulness. Might not reflection on the concept of a public intellectual generate a similar obligation to truthfulness and therefore answer pressing questions about the responsibilities of intellectuals in politics? Even to put the question that way leads one to see immediately, I think, that the answer is likely to be No.

Can one ask with a completely straight face what it means to be an intellectual? I think not. Unlike the concepts which mark the vocations, for example, a teacher or a doctor or a nurse, nothing of consequence emerges from reflection on what it is to be an intellectual. It is a mediocre concept whose only real virtue is to mark out a variety of ways in which one can live a life of the mind beyond the academic one, beyond expertise, and short of being an apparatchik. But the kind of concern with truth expressed by Levi and Weil is not derivable from it.

An academic who lies to his students for political purposes betrays them. I have suggested that the concept of a vocation and its obligations rather than the concept of a profession will yield the deepest sense of that betrayal. But if that same academic enters public discussion and lies for the sake of a political party, then I think he does nothing different in kind from the plumber who does the same. He might of course have psychological difficulties in maintaining his two personas, one as a strictly truthful academic, the other as a lying public intellectual, but that is another matter. His lies and those of the plumber who happens to be propaganda officer for the party may contribute to the pollution of the public realm. If that happens they will rightly be accused—as citizens by their fellow citizens—of betraying a trust implicit in the nature of our public need of truth. But they are guilty in the same way. There is no concept of an intellectual that will reveal that the intellectual does something interestingly different in kind and worse than the plumber.

Lying in politics is up to a point consistent with our need of truth as food for the soul, a need that can be satisfied only when truth is valued for its own sake. And in certain circumstances academics can lie for the sake of political ends without betraying their vocation, and without being answerable for it under concepts that significantly distinguish them from people whom no one would dream of calling intellectuals. Does that suggest that the difficulties I have expressed over the political and public responsibilities of intellectuals are illusory?

The answer, I think, is Yes and No. Yes, insofar as the question presupposes that reflection on the concept of an intellectual might generate obligations to truthfulness that generate in turn difficulties for any intellectual seriously committed to politics. No, insofar as there has in fact been a space outside universities where the obligation to truthfulness existed more or less as it does within the conversational space in which academics reflect on what it means to live the life of the mind. Political discussion within the university occurs within that space. I suggested earlier that, outside the university, the small magazines defined a similar space of discussion with similar requirements to truthfulness. But that space outside the university is, I think, parasitic on the one inside it. The obligations that define it cannot be derived simply by reflection on what it is to be an intellectual, on what it means in the most general sense to live the life of the mind.

Are there not other institutions—those of the media, for example—with traditions which would instil in those who serve in them the kind of commitment to truthfulness that is classically thought to cause trouble for politically committed intellectuals? None, I think, which do so as stringently as should the universities. Journalists have of course fine traditions of truth-telling to look back to, but, as everyone knows, they have contrary traditions to contend with. The point is not so much about practices as it is about the conventions, the standards in whose light one describes and judges practices. Long before postmodernism gained a stronghold in universities, journalists were asking, what is truth?, in tones that would have made strict concern for it impossible.

To take an example relevant to Orwell's concerns in the passage I quoted at the beginning of this chapter. While reporting the war in the Falklands the English journalist Max Hastings proudly announced a new-found patriotism and his readiness to lie for the sake of it. His boast that he was prepared to lie for his country was partly a foolish and naive reaction to his discovery that patriotism need not be jingoism, and partly an expression of the degree to which he was moved by the courage and by the suffering of the soldiers with whom he lived on the islands. But in what appeared to be his quite untroubled readiness to lie for their sake and for his country, Hastings showed no understanding of how terrible it is for a soldier bravely to sacrifice his life while being seriously deceived about what he is doing. The hair-raising extent to which politicians and the media may be unconcerned by this is what troubled Orwell so deeply. The pathos which despoils the acts of soldiers who die bravely while in a cloud-cuckoo land created by politicians and the media is often revealed in the bitterness which compounds the grief of those who love them, when they discover that much of the war propaganda, which otherwise might have consoled them, was 'lies, all bloody lies'.

Hastings should have known that. The knowledge of it should have been an essential part of his respect for the soldiers whose bravery inspired his enthusiasm. In fact the ease with which he seemed prepared to lie expressed his lack of respect for the very men he wished to praise and revealed that he did not, after all, know the difference between patriotism and jingoism. None of this stood in the way of his becoming editor of the *Daily Telegraph* and joint-editor of the *Sunday Telegraph*.

I have often appealed to the metaphor of conversation. Probably it is Michael Oakeshott who is responsible for its recent popularity in politics and elsewhere. It has been particularly resonant in characterising the ideals of public intellectual life. Oakeshott himself used it to characterise the ideals of liberal education as well as an ideal of civilised politics. He wrote:

> In a conversation the participants are not engaged in an inquiry or a debate; there is no 'truth' to be discovered, no proposition to be proved, no conclusion sought. They are not concerned to inform, to persuade, or to refute one another, and therefore the cogency of their utterances does not depend upon their all speaking in the same idiom; they may differ without disagreeing. Of course, a conversation may have passages of argument and a speaker is not forbidden to be demonstrative; but reasoning is neither sovereign nor alone…A girl, in order to escape a

conclusion, may utter what appears to be an outrageously irrelevant remark, but what in fact she is doing is turning an argument she finds tiresome into a conversation she is more at home in. In conversation, 'facts' appear only to be resolved once more into the possibilities from which they were made; 'certainties' are shown to be combustible, not by being brought into contact with other 'certainties' or with doubts, but by being kindled by the presence of ideas of another order...Conversation is not an enterprise designed to yield an extrinsic profit, a contest where a winner gets a prize, nor is it an activity of exegesis; it is an unrehearsed intellectual adventure.

It's a charming picture but it leaves one perplexed as to how to respond to the strident, non-conversational voices in our tradition—Nietzsche, Plato, Kierkegaard, Schopenhauer and many others. I am reminded of Arendt's remark in her essay 'The Crisis in Culture', that if we confuse a respect for the past with tradition we may, in the name of tradition and the respect we believe we owe it, deprive voices from the past of their power to shake us. Something similar may be true of Oakeshott's understanding of conversation, a suspicion reinforced by his more than half-serious remark that the delicate balance of voices in a conversation should not be upset by anything so vulgar as the imposition on them of a quest for truth.

Socrates goes deeper, I think. He first explored the connection between power, politics, truth and conversation and was often accused by his more urbane interlocutors of showing a vulgar streak because he returned again and again to the same themes, pressing on conversation the rigours of the dialectic. In *Gorgias*, a dialogue whose bitter political tone has often been noted, Socrates begins by distinguishing philosophers from orators. In characteristic fashion he asks the enthusiasts for oratory to give an account (in both senses of the word, it soon transpires) of what they do. Quickly a young aspiring orator, Polus, comes to the point.

Oratory, he tells Socrates, is an art that gives great power to those who master it, because it enables them to persuade others to do their bidding.

Plato shows the reader—though Socrates fails to do the same for his interlocutors—that far from being empowered by oratory, orators are enslaved by it to the fickle whims of the mobs they must flatter. En route to this conclusion, he makes a point central to our concerns. When Polus boasts shamelessly of the power he imagines orators to possess, Socrates tells him that he has forgotten his geometry. It seems a strange thing to say, but he means that Polus has forgotten that there are limits other than those of force. It is a point I have developed more than once in this book. 'You can't square the circle' expresses a limit quite different from the one expressed in 'You can't get your way, he's stronger than you', or in 'You can't get your way, he's quite resistant to your flattery'. Socrates means, I think, that other human beings constitute a unique kind of limit to one's will—the kind we express when we say, for example, 'He is susceptible to your flattery, but morally you can't exploit that fact. You can't treat him as a means to your ends.' Though we owe that last way of putting the point to Kant, in its everyday usage, it captures what Socrates meant.

So much is not radical. Important though it may be, it does not promise a deep grounding for the hope that public intellectuals have a strict obligation to truthfulness. Yet Socrates is aiming at something which might satisfy that hope. To reach it he relies on his famous distinction between knowledge and belief. The details of that distinction are controversial, but one can perhaps express the basic idea this way. When a person believes something (it doesn't matter what) she believes that her belief is true. Sometimes we express our uncertainty about something by saying that we merely believe it, that we are not sure, that we could be wrong. Characteristically, however, belief is contrasted with doubt and everyone recognises the conceptual strangeness of saying that one believes such and such, but it is not true. (There may be special cases, of interest to psychoanalysts where one does say something like this, but they are exceptions that prove the rule.)

In addition to believing one's beliefs to be true, one also believes (this is part of the concept of belief, not a generalisation about human beings) oneself to be rightly related to what makes it true. It has proved notoriously difficult to explain positively what counts as the right relation to what makes one's beliefs true, but that there is such a relationship, and must be if there is to be such a thing at all as belief, appears to be shown by the fact that there are clearly wrong ways of coming to a belief, even a true belief. Being indoctrinated is an obvious example. Being lied to is another. Wishing to believe something merely because one wants to, because for example it is too painful to believe otherwise, is another. Being seduced by flattery is yet another. If we come to realise that we believe something only because we want to or because we have been indoctrinated, or lied to, or because our sentimentality has been exploited, then we can no longer rationally hold onto that belief. Of course desire or indoctrination may be so strong or sentimentality may go so deep that it is difficult to give up the belief even though we know in our hearts that we hold it for reasons that have nothing to do with its truth. In the absence of such psychological factors, however, a belief which we acknowledge to hold for those reasons and only for those reasons would simply be extinguished by that acknowledgment.

Lucid possession of the right reason for belief would, if the belief were true, constitute knowledge, Socrates thought. He sought a general account of what it is to come to one's beliefs in the right way. I do not believe that anything interesting, positive and general can be said about that. What it means to come to a belief in the right way will be shown, for particular kinds of beliefs, by the critical terms which show—for that kind of belief, for that realm of inquiry and thought—what the distinction between legitimate and illegitimate persuasion comes to. If

Socrates was wrong about this point, however, it does not affect the value of the main thrust of his argument.

Socrates said to Polus that he (Polus) was good at oratory but not at all good at conversation. He meant that conversation respected our need to be rightly related to our beliefs, to what makes them true. Oratory abused and exploited that need. A good orator will, must, always generate the illusion in his audience that they have been rightly persuaded, rightly related to whatever makes their beliefs true. His capacity to do that will be the central element of his art. (Socrates refuses to call oratory an art; he calls it a mere 'knack'.) In that way, orators manipulate people to believe whatever they want them to, to suit their purposes. When they do this, they abuse a trust implicit in conversation, namely the trust that the person with whom one is conversing will respect one's need to be persuaded legitimately rather than illegitimately. To put it in Socrates' terms, one trusts that the person with whom one is conversing, or the orators to whom one is listening, will respect our need for knowledge rather than merely belief, even true belief. Conversation requires renunciation, the renunciation of the power to persuade someone by illegitimate means. Sharp and Knöpfelmacher honoured that trust, renounced the power they had to attract uncritical disciples, when they respected their students' need to think independently. Such respect and renunciation are at the heart of the conversational space that defines the university as a community of scholars.

Whereas philosophy is food for the soul, oratory, Socrates said, panders to the soul in the way that pastrycooks pander to the body. (That is his simile.) In this idea, that oratory is the false semblance of philosophy, lies the seed of Socrates' most ambitious attempt to place philosophy and ethics on a foundation so basic that no one could resist their claims. Such hopes have survived in philosophy to the present day. One finds them, for example, in the work of the influential German philosopher Jürgen Habermas.

Socrates appeared to believe that conversation and the trust necessary to it are actually a condition of speech itself. If that is true, and if the honouring of that trust is the recognition of the kind of limit expressed in the acknowledgment that one cannot treat another human being merely as a means to one's ends, then it would appear that the very existence of language presupposes acknowledgment of the ethical. One can see, then, why Socrates argued that oratory is not a morally neutral skill which can be used for good ends or bad according to the type of person who uses it. He thought it rotten through and through because, even when it is used for good ends, it abuses the limits that are internal to language. It defiles the very thing it claims mastery of.

If Socrates is right, one could see how to construct a similar argument to condemn intellectuals when they lie to serve a cause. The condemnation of them would not depend on standards external to intellectual activity. Nor would the obligation on them to be truthful be based on an historically contingent tradition, such as the one which imposes standards on academics. The requirement that they be strictly truthful would lie in something utterly basic to their activity. Orwell's belief that, when they lie, intellectuals do something worse and different from lying plumbers and politicians, would then be vindicated.

Sadly, I believe Socrates' argument fails, as do all arguments of that kind, such foundationalist arguments, as they are now called. He was right to think oratory parasitic on conversation. He may also have been right to believe (if he did) that conversation is essential to language. That is a more radical thesis, but it is hard to see how we would count something as language if conversations could not be conducted in it. If creatures, who are said to have a language, cannot seriously be imagined to take part in conversational gambits—Come now, you must be pulling my leg. Be serious. Think! and so on—then we may be right to suspect that they cannot do the *kind* of thing, even primitively, that we do when we talk to one another. All that, however, can be acknowledged by the orators, without it requiring them to decline to exploit language and conversation, including the trust necessary to them. One can acknowledge that trust is internal to conversation, yet exploit it in the pursuit of good or evil ends.

In order to see the abuse of trust as a corruption rather than as an opportunity to be exploited as the orator does, one must already see it from the perspective on truth and its value that the Socratic argument tries to show to be both right and necessary. From that perspective, truth, the respect for the other, the renunciation of power, and the critical vocabulary are interdependent, as Socrates believed. And yet, his foundationalist hopes were not be realised. That does not mean that the values he hoped to ground were just superimposed on the facts. The Socratic perspective integrates our understanding of language, truth, belief and the ethical in ways that deepen our sense of them all. But it will not enable one to challenge an intellectual who lies in politics with the question, Don't you understand what it means to be an intellectual? Which is not of course to say that there is no standpoint from which to condemn him and his lies. We are almost always—perhaps always—wronged by those who lie to us.

Goodness & Truth

Talk of commitment to truth, or of the love of truth, is talk that seems to be of truth with a capital T. For many people that is precisely the difficulty. They do not believe that such talk is anything more than rhetoric. They will say that there are merely truths—true statements, propositions, judgments, thoughts. These cannot be the object of fidelity or of love. Truths may serve things which may be the proper objects of love and fidelity. When someone speaks of defending truth, he or she means defending the possibility of telling certain kinds of truths because of their importance to other things we value. If truth were important in itself, then we could satisfy our need for it by counting the chairs in the room, the clouds in the sky or the hairs on our arms. Thus goes a natural and influential line of argument.

Is it just rhetoric, then, to speak, as I have often done, of the love of truth? I don't think we can answer that question unless we reflect on examples which can show why one might want to speak that way and what it can mean. Abstract investigations of the concepts of love and truth could not show why someone would speak seriously of the love of truth, rather than of a passion or enthusiasm for certain studies or inquiries. The inclination to speak that way must be awakened in us by something quite different. Often it will have been a fine teacher whose example revealed to us what a love of truth may be and what it may be to live a life in fidelity to it. This will be personal to each of us. But in our intellectual and spiritual tradition there are examples which are common to us. I shall give two. The first is Saint Augustine and the passage I shall quote is from his *Confessions*. It is from the section where he is thinking about time and has fallen into terrible metaphysical confusions:

> I confess to you, Lord, that I still do not know what time is. Yet I confess too that I do know that I am saying this in time, that I have been talking about time for a long time, and that this long time would not be a long time if it were not for the fact that time has been passing all the while. How can I know this, when I do not know what time is? Is it that I do know what time is, but do not know how to put what I know into words? I am in a sorry state, for I do not even know what I do not know!
>
> My God, I am in your presence. You see that I do not lie, for I say only what is in my heart. 'It is you, Lord, that keep the lamp of my hopes still burning; shine on the darkness about me.'

The passage and all that led up to it expresses a mind labouring in obedience to the claims of reason and of truth upon it. One could quote it wit h edifying effect against certain forms of irrationalism and against anyone who has forgotten the role of character in the development of the intellectual virtues. But one could not reveal the power and the beauty of the passage without referring to the love that is manifest so purely in it. One might, therefore, say that the passage is a fine expression of the discursive capacities of mind in service to a love of truth. That would not be wrong, but it could be misleading. Simone Weil indicated why when she said that it is misleading to speak of a love of truth. One should speak instead, she suggested, of the spirit of truth in love. This passage from the *Confessions* is an excellent one to quote in her support, for the spirit of truth in love is exactly what is expressed in it. That's what makes it so wonderful.

The love revealed in the passage informs our sense of Augustine's passion for lucidity and his despair of achieving it, yet I doubt that it would tempt someone to say that it is, therefore, an example of the extrinsic concern for truth. To put the point another way. Concepts of intrinsic and extrinsic value and their associated motivational concepts—doing something for its own sake or doing it for the sake of something else—can be the focus of complex and subtle elaborations which make it especially easy to miss the wood for the trees. An account of intrinsic value and of the motivation structured by it, which would count Augustine's concern as extrinsic because of its connection with his love of God, would have cut itself off from the kind of example which should be its source. Some students used to write *Ad maiorem Dei gloriam* (To the greater glory of God) at the head of each page of their exercise books. Some still do. One would seriously misunderstand what that can mean if one saw in it the deflection of intellectual endeavour from truth as its intrinsic object—even though it is an example of thought in service to a certain kind of love. The value of truth—what it may be to value truth 'for its own sake'—is revealed only in the ways it deepens the lives of people who care for it. Independently of that we can have no serious sense of it

In his essay, 'Is Goodness a Mystery?', the English philosopher R. F. Holland criticises functional accounts of why we value truthfulness. He says:

> All that is necessary for this is a modicum of truth or something that approaches it yet keeps its distance, a

conventional sort of standard truthfulness but anyway a
relative truthfulness...but anyhow my point is that alongside it there could co-exist for at least some people in the
society a concern with truth of an altogether different
character, in which *not to falsify* became a spiritual
demeanour. Where then could this spirit come from?

Holland's phrase 'a spiritual demeanour' expresses one kind of
value we accord to truthfulness. But, in the life of a person such as
Holland describes, truthfulness is not valued *for the sake of* spiritual
ends. One could not describe the actions that would express that
'spiritual demeanour' without referring to the person's concern
for truth—a concern which we would naturally describe as being
for truth 'for its own sake'. Such a person would, for example, be
concerned to know the truth about important events in her past.
That need for lucidity about her past would be connected with
her sense of the meaning of her life, with the kind of integrity it
may have. But she does not value truthfulness for the sake of any
of this. For, again, the nature and value of that kind of integrity
could not be appreciated apart from a person's concern for truth
for its own sake.

The confusion I have been trying to expose is evident in this
passage from Richard Rorty: 'The idea of Truth as something to
be pursued for its own sake, not because it will be good for one, or
for one's real or imaginary community, is the central theme of this
tradition.' The person in my example, however, for whom truthfulness about her past is fundamental to the integrity of her life, is
neither concerned with truth because it will be good for her, nor,
as Rorty intends it by way of contrast with that, with truth for its own
sake. The fact that we cannot give an account of the value of truth
for its own sake independently of the place a concern for truth
may have in our lives misleads some people into believing that we
delude ourselves when we think that truth has intrinsic value.
They would be right if the placing were of a kind that revealed

truth to be a means to something whose value we could characterise independently. But it is not so.

Love of truth—the love in which there is the spirit of truth—is evidently a spiritual love. Must it be religious as it is with Augustine? My second quotation shows that it need not be. It is from the autobiography of the great cellist Pablo Casals, and I have taken it from R. F. Holland's fine essay called 'Education and Value'.

> For the past 80 years I have started each day in the same manner. It is not a mechanical routine but something essential to my daily life. I go to the piano, and I play two preludes and fugues of Bach. I cannot think of doing otherwise. It is a sort of benediction on the house. But that is not its only meaning for me. It is a re-discovery of the world of which I have the joy of being a part. It fills me with awareness of the wonder of life, with a feeling of the incredible marvel of being a human being...
>
> I do not think a day has passed in my life in which I have failed to look with fresh amazement at the miracle of nature.
>
> If you continue to work and to absorb the beauty in the world about you, you find that age does not necessarily mean getting old.

Casals expresses a love as pure as does Augustine. The purity of Casals' relation to the music and to the world tells us that love is the name we must give to that relation. It is also evident that it is a spiritual love. In fact, this is the kind of example which could be used to teach the more profound meaning of that concept. Casals does not speak as he does because he experienced the joys of spring for each day of eighty years. Remarkable though that would be, it would still be the accidental repetition of a feeling which he may have had only once. Such repetitions and their frequency, however impressive, remain accidental and cannot be the occasion for speaking of life as a gift and of the love and the duties which go with it. Even eighty years of the daily repetition of feeling that it is good to be alive could not, of itself, lead someone to think of suicide or of living one's life as a lie, as a species of ingratitude. But unless one has a sense of those duties whose observance is an expression of gratitude and whose denial constitutes a species of ingratitude, there can be nothing substantial in one's talk of life as a gift. In this context, there is little difference between speaking of life as a gift, and speaking of a love of the beauty of the world.

In his essay Holland discussed the idea of the mastery of a subject—its connection with standards and with value. He wishes to speak of the deepest of the possibilities which it offered. This is what he says:

> In our officiation over the various levels of relative mastery, we are concerned as teachers with the conditions of a possibility which has still to be categorized in its deepest aspect. I shall now try to say what I most of all want to say about it.
>
> It is the possibility of coming into an inheritance. It has to do with no less a question than whether a man can be at home in the world—whether he can find it a good world despite the ill...by being brought into contact with forms of understanding and apprehension in which some good is to be encountered, some wonder to be seen, whether in nature or the work of human beings, a person might be helped to see the beauty of reality, helped to live more fully, helped to be glad he is alive. The expression knocking at my mind here is 'nourishment of the soul'.

The quotation from Casals is an inspired choice. It teaches us something important about the concepts of the psychological, the spiritual and the religious. People often identify the spiritual with the religious or with strange occurrences—ghosts, seances, paranormal phenomena—that is, with the shallow fascination for spiritualism characteristic of the nineteenth century. This leaves them with a barren conception of what is honestly available to someone who is not religious, by which I mean, to someone who cannot speak God's name in prayer or in worship.

In a discussion of what she calls 'forms of the implicit love of God', Simone Weil includes amongst them the love of the beauty of the world. She would say, I think, that the spirit in which Casals played expressed an implicit love of God. I don't say that she would be wrong to do so, but it seems to me that someone who speaks as Casals did need not agree. Such a person need not feel that what she says needs honest completion by a more explicitly religious statement or by metaphysical propositions of the kind which are often propounded by philosophers of religion. It is true that the spirit in which Casals plays the prelude and fugues and the spirit in which someone does his work *Ad maiorem Dei gloriam* are similar, but one should resist the temptation to think that the spiritual dimension of the former is only properly or completely expressed in the religious statements of the latter.

The acknowledgment of the similarity cuts both ways. To someone who would insist that something is lacking in speaking of life as a gift unless one speaks of it as God's gift, or that the grateful love of the beauty of the world of the kind expressed by Casals is a form of the implicit love of God, I would say that one does not—that certainly one need not—first come to see life as a gift and then, as a consequence of that, act and speak in accents of gratitude. On the contrary, a sense of life as a gift comes from speech and action which are in the key of a certain kind of gratitude. If someone were now to insist that the gratitude is the *kind* whose specification would take us into explicitly religious propositions, then I would say that it need not be so. It can be specified by its relation to the concepts 'goodness', 'love' and 'truth'.

In *Phaedo*, Socrates is asked why he is opposed to suicide. He replies, 'The allegory which the mystics tell us—that we men are in the world as a soldier is at his guard post, and that one must not release oneself or run away—seems to me a high doctrine with difficult implication.' I think that Socrates saw his philosophical life in the same way, as a requirement to be faithful to a love of the world sustained by a gratitude which was not conditional upon how things went for him. He saw suicide (he was, I think, discussing the kind of suicide which Kant characterised, in his *Lectures on Ethics*, as 'leaving the world as though it were a smoke-filled room') as both infidelity and ingratitude. I believe that he saw the life which did not struggle against illusion in much the same way. His passionate sense of an obligation to lucidity, which he expressed in his famous remark that an unexamined life is unworthy of a human being, was a form of fidelity and gratitude. It was fidelity to the love which revealed the world to him as his gift.

This shows where Richard Rorty goes most deeply wrong when he says that we have in the West substituted the idea of the love of truth for the idea of the love of God. Because he has no serious conception of a 'spirit of truth in love', informed by examples such as I have been giving, he can make no sense of the metaphors of submission and obedience which have been so fundamental to our characterisation of a concern for truth. Again these are most beautifully expressed by Simone Weil when she writes of her intellectual vocation:

> The degree of intellectual honesty which is obligatory for me, by reason of my particular vocation, demands that my thought should be indifferent to all ideas without exception...it must be equally welcoming and equally reserved with regard to every one of them. Water is indifferent in this way to the objects which fall into it. It does not weigh them; it is they which weigh themselves, after a certain time of oscillation.

Any attempt adequately to characterise what Casals describes must use the concepts of love and of the spiritual. It also requires the concept of goodness—the kind which invites a capital G. As with the concept of the spiritual, so with that way of speaking of goodness: its sense is shown in this kind of example. It is not straightforwardly moral goodness, but it is connected with it. Such love seems not to be compatible with evil.

The example of Casals is a musical one, but its similarities with the examples of Augustine and Socrates reveal how it is possible to extend its lesson to discursive inquiry. We may then see connections of the kind Plato stressed between goodness, truth and love. For Plato, the True and the Good (and, if we are guided by the *Symposium*, the Beautiful) are aspects of the one object of the same passion. It will, I know, strike many as obscurantist to speak of the True and the Good as aspects of the one object of the same passion. We can capture what is essential to it, however, by noting that the 'desire to see things as they are' may take the form of a spiritual love rather than merely a neutral passion which is sometimes in service to spiritual ends, and by thinking of the spiritual character of that intellectual love as conditioned by a certain kind of goodness—the kind which invites a capital G. If we keep our attention fixed on examples such as I have given, then we may see that it need not be empty rhetoric to speak of the unity of Goodness and Truth.

Only a very limited number of compositions, Bach's included, could substitute for the preludes and fugues in the passage which I quoted from Casals. Not everything of Bach's could be substituted for them. We may argue about which could, but we would have to exclude much of what should be studied in a university school of music. The point extends beyond music. There are works studied in other disciplines which may awaken in us the same love and the same sense of goodness and gratitude. They are few, and for any discipline they can probably be counted on the fingers of one hand. Quite obviously university studies must include much more. Nonetheless, there is a fundamental division to be drawn, here as in other realms of value, between things which may worthily inspire that love of the world which

Casals found and celebrated through his love of Bach, and things which, though they are splendid or even glorious achievements, cannot. Anyone sensitive to the tone of what I quoted from Casals and Augustine would not, I think, see in that division the contempt for ordinary people and ordinary life which some condemn when they speak of 'elitism'. In case I am wrong, I shall try to dispel doubt on this point by quoting from Simone Weil:

> A village idiot in the literal sense of the word, if he really loves truth, is infinitely superior to Aristotle in his thought, even though he never utters anything but inarticulate murmurs. He is infinitely closer to Plato than Aristotle ever was. He has genius, while only the word talent applies to Aristotle. If a fairy offered to change his destiny for one resembling Aristotle's he would be wise to refuse unhesitatingly. But he does not know this. And nobody tells him. Everybody tells him the contrary. But he must be told. Idiots, men without talent, men whose talent is average or only a little more, must be encouraged if they possess genius. We need not be afraid of making them proud, because love of truth is always accompanied by humility. Real genius is nothing else but the supernatural virtue of humility in the domain of thought.

I know that will strike many people as absurd. Lovers of Aristotle will be outraged. If one keeps in mind, however, the distinction between works that can inspire in us a worthy love and those which, glorious and dazzling though they may be, cannot, then I think we may be more open to Weil's point, even if we want to substitute other examples for Plato and Aristotle. Even more so, I believe, when one attends closely to her tone, which one may at first mistake as contemptuous of Aristotle. There is, I think, no contempt. Such works as she thinks lack genius may also be praised and treasured, companions in wonderful adventures of the mind and spirit. And they will be read in the spirit of seeking the truth in love, in love sometimes awakened by works of 'genius'.

Weil believed only a handful of the great works of Western civilisation speak truthfully of the human condition, to our vulnerability to affliction and our relations to good and evil. Apart from the Gospels, and some books of the Old Testament, she includes on her list only the plays of Aeschylus, some of Sophocles' plays, some dialogues of Plato, Shakespeare's *King Lear*, Racine's *Phaedra* and one or two others. The idea of such a list will not, I think, strike one as silly if one reflects on why Primo Levi would have added Dante to it. Nourished even in Auschwitz by the beauty of some passages in the *Canto of Ulysses,* Levi says, '[It is] as if I also was hearing it for the first time: like the blast of a trumpet, like the voice of God. For a moment I forget who I am and where I am.' Dismayed, almost desperate, when he forgets some lines, he writes that he 'would give today's soup' to remember them. Other people will compose different lists and each list will excite a degree of intractable disagreement. But can anyone seriously think that a list of what could be food for the soul, as Dante was for Levi, would be much longer than Weil's?

The distinction between the things that can and the things that cannot inspire a worthy love does not correspond to the distinction between high and low culture, nor to the distinction between things studied for their own sake and things studied for more practical reasons. Most of what is properly called high culture can, as I have already remarked, be admired, prized and gloried in, but it cannot be loved as Levi loved Dante or Casals loved Bach. Yet it is a relatively indiscriminate notion of high culture that sustains George Steiner's question—and it is a very real question—'After the Holocaust what can we honestly salvage of the great hopes for liberal studies, a hope whose classic expression is to be found in Matthew Arnold's *Culture and Anarchy*?' Steiner writes in *Language and Silence*:

> When barbarism came to twentieth-century Europe, the arts faculties in more than one university offered very little moral resistance, and this is not a trivial or local accident. In

a disturbing number of cases the literary imagination gave servile or ecstatic welcome to political bestiality... Knowledge of Goethe, a delight in the poetry of Rilke, seemed no bar to personal and institutionalized sadism. Literary values and the utmost of hideous inhumanity could coexist in the same community, in the same individual sensibility; and let us not take the easy way out and say 'the man who did these things in a concentration camp just said he was reading Rilke. He was not reading him well.' I am afraid that is an evasion. He may have been reading him very well indeed.

Steiner's tone has point against question-begging denials that anyone who served in the concentration camps or who knowingly supported the Nazi regime *could not* properly have appreciated the writings of Rilke or the music of Bach or of Mozart. If one puts that aside, however, then he is a little too quick and his tone a little bullying. There would be no interest in his question, in his intensity, if one did not seriously feel the pull of just such denials as he dismisses. One needs, therefore, to look more closely at what was supposed to be compatible with planning and executing the Final Solution. And one needs to be clearer than Steiner appears to be about exactly what the death camps challenge. Is it the hope that an education in the humanities will make a person morally better? Is it the hope that mass education in the liberal ideal will ensure humane government? Or is it the claim that there are forms of the pursuit of truth which are intimately related to goodness? I have said little in support of the first and nothing in support of the second. The last needs argument less than it needs examples to reveal it. I have given some. Argument will primarily have the modest function of removing obstacles to their appreciation. Having done that, it should step into the background.

We have no difficulty in believing that some Nazi doctors who experimented on living human beings were passionately interested in their work. It is true that we sometimes ask, how could they have done it? But the tone in which that question is asked rules out any answer to it. It certainly does not question that they may have done it out of sheer interest, rather than out of fear for their lives if they refused, or because of sadism or because of a desire to serve the Reich.

There is an inclination to think that what we call disinterested inquiry in the case of a scientist who would never dream of experimenting on a living human being and what we call disinterested inquiry in the example of the Nazi doctors amount to the same phenomenon if they are considered only as the expression of a natural disposition of the human mind. According to this conception, what makes it morally unthinkable for one and of no moral account for the other is quite external to that disposition. What else is the lesson of the Nazi doctors? That view of the matter is often expressed in contemporary discussions concerning the moral and social responsibility of scientists. Scientists, particularly those working in the more abstract regions of science, are often pictured as being in the grip of an essentially amoral thirst or drive for knowledge, to which morality is either irrelevant or opposed, and we look upon such passion with a mixture of awe and fear.

From such a perspective it may look as though our talk of the love of truth is a fictitious moralisation of the essentially amoral energies of the mind—a fiction invented to tame such potentially destructive energies. It may look as though we believe that we are hitting such people where it most hurts them if we say that they do not *really* love truth, rather as someone might suspect some Christians believe themselves to be doing when they say that a *real* man turns the other cheek. We therefore add culture, a bit of humane learning, to their scientific education. It is easy to see that this is superficial and one does not need to be reminded of the Nazi doctors to see that it would be foolish to hope for much from it. Yet it is, in essence, what Matthew Arnold calls 'culture' in *Culture and Anarchy.*

Arnold calls 'the sheer desire to see things as they are' the 'scientific passion', and if the word 'sheer' with which he qualifies the desire does any work then it presumably isolates the desire from any moral or spiritual context. Speaking of Socrates he says: 'Socrates has drunk his hemlock and is dead; but in his own breast does not every man carry about with him a possible Socrates, in that power of a disinterested play of consciousness upon his stock notions and habits, of which this wise and admirable man gave all through his lifetime the great example?' Should we take the 'disinterested play of consciousness upon his stock notions and habits' as an example of 'the sheer desire to see things as they are' applied, in the case of Socrates, to his own 'stock notions and habits'? I ask the question rhetorically because, although the reason is difficult to state, the answer must be that we cannot. Indeed, the fascination of Socrates lies in the necessity for that answer together with the difficulty of explaining it.

Socrates' example—as we have it in Plato's dialogues—should make us suspicious of the idea that he was 'wise and admirable' because he directed a morally and spiritually neutral disposition of his intelligence to worthy ends—the examination of his 'stock notions and habits'. Or, to put it another way: his example ought to make us suspect any conception of the 'sheer desire to see things as they are' which suggests that to the extent that the moral or the spiritual enter more intimately into the characterisation of a disposition of the intelligence than as objects upon which it may fasten, or as ends which it may serve, then that disposition is not, strictly speaking, of the intelligence. Socrates' passion to understand himself was both disinterested and essentially spiritual. If we place his passion for lucidity, to 'see things as they are', in a context which reveals its essentially spiritual character and value, we will not attenuate the sense in which it is a 'desire to see things as they are', a 'disinterested play of consciousness' or a love of truth.

When Arnold spoke of the 'scientific passion', the 'sheer desire to see things as they are', he went on to say:

But there is of culture another view, in which not solely the scientific passion, the sheer desire to see things as they are, natural and proper in an intelligent being, appears as the ground of it. There is a view in which all the love of our neighbour, the impulses towards action, help, and beneficence, the desire for removing human error, clearing human confusion, and diminishing human misery, the noble aspiration to leave the world better and happier than we found it—motives eminently such as are called social—come in as part of the grounds of culture, and the main and pre-eminent part. Culture is then properly described not as having its origin in curiosity, but as having its origin in the love of perfection; it is *a study of perfection*. It moves by the force, not merely or primarily of the scientific passion for pure knowledge, but also of the moral and social passion for doing good.

The 'scientific passion' and 'the moral and social passion for doing good' together combine to form what Arnold calls 'culture' but they combine as distinct passions. He tried to achieve a certain kind of intimacy between the pursuits of truth and of goodness by making them equally essential to what he called culture, but in his argument they remain externally related to one another.

Arnold wanted more from the concept of culture than it could possibly give him and was therefore left with a fiction. That fiction's primary purpose was to provide him with a way of appearing to give an account of how a concern for truth and a concern for goodness may be indivisible. He failed, but he felt compelled to give such an account because the requirement to do so has been, since Plato, an important part of our intellectual history. (As has the suspicion that it is a high-minded illusion.) When he described culture as 'sweetness and light' Arnold tried to speak, in his own way and for his own times, of what is fundamental in that tradition. But the difference between him and Plato is critical. For Arnold the intellectual and the moral remain distinct passions—contemplative and practical. For Plato, as we have already noted, the True and the Good are aspects of the one object of the same passion. Rather than calling the love of truth a contemplative rather than a practical passion, we should rethink that contrast if we are to be true to Plato's dramatisation of the life of Socrates.

It is quite contingent that part of our intellectual and cultural tradition should include such spiritual possibilities as are revealed in the examples I have given. Their capacity to awaken in people a sense of goodness of the kind that Arnold sought in high culture, and of the kind that drives Steiner's question, depends more often than not on the kinds of teacher we have. That in turn is crucially dependent on whether or not teachers can overcome the disabling consequences of the conceptual loss which makes it very difficult for them to characterise, let alone to rise to, the highest possibilities in their vocation.

Teachers are, in principle, dispensable—they are the contingent means of getting into the heads of students what we think should be there. Good teaching is a transferable skill or technique which may be enhanced in the best teachers by an inexplicable knack which facilitates the learning of things which students may have learnt for themselves. Many people now believe that. Teachers, they think, do for their students what autodidacts do for themselves.

Much educational theorising starts with the question, What do students need to know? and then focuses on what are the best means with which to get it into their heads. Natural though it is to think this way, it ignores a teacher's love of his or her subject and what the enactment of that love may teach students about the worth of what they—teacher and students—are doing together. Through a teacher's example one may begin to understand the intrinsic worth of the life of the mind which at its deepest is to understand it as something to which a life may be worthily devoted and sometimes, as the fate of Socrates reminds us, for which it may worthily be given. One cannot learn this from a machine or from a teacher who might as well be a machine. That is not because a machine cannot teach enthusiastically. It is because it makes no sense to speak of the place of the subject in the life of a machine, or of a machine's revelation of the worth of the life of the mind through the authoritative enactment of its vocation.

The deepest values of the life of the mind cannot be taught: they can only be shown, but, of course, only to those who have eyes to see. They may reveal themselves in a teacher's style of teaching when it is determined by her attentive obedience to the disciplines of her subject. She must make something inspirational of her subject but it cannot be her motive to inspire. Teachers who set out to inspire have their attention in the wrong place and are too distracted from their subject to be able to offer anything deep no matter how many hearts they set afire. False semblances of genuine goods abound here. Teachers can give passionate but corrupt inspiration. Just as genuine charity must be motivated by the needs of another rather than by the desire to do something charitable, so teachers inspire their students into a proper love of what they are doing by the manner of their attention to their subject rather than by setting out to inspire them.

A fine teacher, then, is made so by his or her love of the subject. In their teaching they will reveal the worth of the life they have given to teaching—the worth of their vocation. They cannot be taught how to do this because there is in no substantial sense a 'how' of the matter: there is nothing which could informatively be called the means or the method of it. That does not mean that they do it 'spontaneously' or that it 'comes naturally'. Sometimes people say that good teachers are born rather than made, or that teaching is an art rather than a science, and they usually have in mind a knack of passing things on. I hope that I have made it clear that I am not thinking of that when I speak of what a teacher's enacted love of his or her vocation can do. The power of fine teaching is delicately nuanced through its disciplined perception of its many possible corruptions. What teachers will understand to be corruptions will depend upon the concepts under which they understand what they are called upon to rise to. Those concepts are, like all concepts, public, but unlike some concepts, they both permit and require a depth of continuing reflection which is possible only because of the resonances and echoes they have acquired through the history of their use. A teacher's understanding of what she is doing is necessarily mediated by her rootedness in a particular culture which alone gives what she seeks to understand the kind of depth whose penetration we call wisdom.

A teacher's vocation, her privileged obligation, is, as Plato saw, to initiate her students into a worthy love. There is nothing finer that one human being can do for another. When teachers do it for their pupils, rare and wonderful though their example is, they have done no more than their vocation requires of them. Mostly teaching is less than this and there is nothing much to be done about it. But it remains the highest standard in the light of which teachers may describe and judge what they do and in whose light students may recognise the treasure which school and university studies may offer them.

It is a treasure whose recognition depends upon the concepts which identify it being available to us in our living speech. We therefore grievously wrong young people when we corrupt the ways of speaking which alone can name the most precious of the gifts we are able to give them. We do it when we speak of teaching and of learning in ways which make it difficult or even impossible to speak soberly of love—when, for example, we speak of teaching as a career rather than a vocation or when we displace a serious conception of a subject with the relatively shallow idea of the acquisition of skills.

Love is seldom spoken of seriously in discussion of education. We speak of it interchangeably with enthusiasm and, generally, to praise enthusiasms in teachers, because they are catching, because they are psychological aids to learning. Many of our enthusiasms, however, are worthless and banal. We can never say this of a real love. That is revealed in the different ways we apply the distinction between the real and the apparent to love and to enthusiasm. The criteria for whether an enthusiasm or passion is real centre on the concept of sincerity. The criteria for whether something is really love centre on a deeper set of critical concepts of which goodness, lucidity and purity are pre-eminent. Plato expressed this by saying that love is of the good and not of its appearances although he knew better than many of his critics that we are capable of any number of worthless passions which we mistake for love. That is why he thought that nothing went deep in education unless it was under the inspiration and discipline of a certain kind of love.

This shows, I think, the questions we should ask when we think about education. We ought not to ask, What is the essence of education or what is the essential function of schooling or university study? We should ask whether our tradition has revealed to us something which is not only worthy of interest, fascination, enthusiasm, enchantment or delight, but something actually worthy of our love. Are there treasures we are obliged to bequeath to future generations? If there are, can we find words that will name them and reveal their value? Which practices will nourish them? Which will undermine them? In all probability what we most value will have arisen quite contingently in the course of our history. That does not diminish it. What matters is not the essence of school or university. What matters are their treasures.

A subject cannot be loved for its extrinsic benefits, although a concern for some of them is far from philistine. But there are many ways of thinking of the intrinsic worth of a subject and some of them yield even less appropriate objects of serious love than do the extrinsic benefits. One may care for a subject 'for its own sake', for its 'intrinsic worth', in ways which leave a teacher accidental to the discovery of such worth, in ways which make it accidental that there are teachers at all. One may care for it as a 'higher pleasure', as a source of the natural pleasure which comes with the disciplined exercise of the powers of the mind. A stimulating intellectual agenda and a mind and character capable of enjoying its challenges are all one needs for this. If teachers are needed, the need for them will be explained by elaboration on a motivational theme, that, for example, enthusiasm is catching.

The pleasures we take in the exercise of the powers of the mind are a natural human good, as is the pleasure we take in the development of the powers of the body. But we need more than the idea of a natural human good to make sense of a life devoted to thought and to teaching as a worthily human life. It is, therefore, not surprising that those who are unable to think of an individual human being in ways that go deeper than is allowed by a spiritually reductive psychology of self-fulfilment should turn to a political conception of education to redeem their sense that something serious had been promised them in the edifying rhetoric of their graduation ceremonies. Such politicisation of education invariably obscures its deepest value, but those who have deplored it have often failed to see how far they are from any honest way of speaking of its value and that those who have sought it in politics have often done so in honest despair of finding it elsewhere. The reason for speaking more seriously than we do of the love of truth and of a teacher's love of his subject is to deepen our understanding of what it may mean to care for a subject 'for its own sake' or for its 'intrinsic worth'.

There are, therefore, deeper and shallower conceptions of the intrinsic value of education. The problem for us is not merely to sort them out, but to see how much of what is deep is accessible to us beyond its mere acknowledgment. Even if the value we acknowledge is of the highest kind, even if we think that finding a place for it in our lives would immeasurably deepen them, we may nonetheless be unable to find a place for it in our living speech. Why this should be so is one of the most difficult problems in the epistemology of value, but it is so and it marks one of the fundamental differences between judgments of value and our ordinary paradigms of true and false beliefs, according to which a truth acknowledged is a truth possessed. But an appreciation of the grammar and even of the beauty of a dead form of speech cannot make that speech living for us. The 'linguistic turn' of the latter half of this century, the emphasis on 'language games' and 'forms of discourse' and so on, has rightly made us aware of how vulnerable the concepts in our living possession are to changes in language, and how vulnerable language is to changes in our lives. When certain ways of speaking go dead on us, we cannot necessarily extract our old thoughts from those ways of speaking and express them in an idiom more congenial to the present. Our task therefore is to see how much of the intimation of depth in our rhetoric of the intrinsic value of the scholarly and intellectual life is honestly and lucidly accessible to us in living and authoritative speech.

Plato described philosophers—by which he merely meant lovers of wisdom—as clinging in recollection to wonders they had once seen. It is a beautiful image of the waxing and waning of the forms of spiritual understanding. The conceptual geography I have been attempting—marking the relations to one another of those concepts which enable us to speak soberly of a love of truth—is one, very modest, form of that recollection.

Truth As a Need
of the Soul

Could anyone not care whether she was really in love rather than merely infatuated? Could anyone not care whether her grief at the death of a loved one—a parent, a child, a lover—was genuine rather than self-indulgent? I don't ask these questions rhetorically. Even so, I think the answer is No. Or, at any rate, when it is Yes, then explanations are called for and I am sure they will show exceptions to be of a kind that proves the rule.

Many people prefer not to talk or think about what they really feel. Some think it suspect, even dangerous to do so. They may think it is precious, or navel-gazing, or destructive of the innocence of their feelings. But that does not show it does not really matter to them. For it not to matter would be like it not mattering whether what one thought was true or false.

This comparison with belief is more than an analogy. The distinction between the real and the counterfeit seems, as I have often noted, to be fundamental to the very nature of the states that make up our inner lives. We are reluctant to call something love if it does not admit of it. Generally the distinction gets no grip in the lives of animals. And when it applies to human beings, they must be capable of exploring the real and the counterfeit in their inner lives if they are to be seen as fully human. That was the lesson we learnt from reflecting on M.

Because animals cannot generally reflect on their feelings and responses, we can see why people have thought they do not have souls. There were, of course, other reasons, more metaphysical ones like those offered by Descartes who thought animals were machines. That division between the reasons for saying that animals do not have souls corresponds to metaphysical and other conceptions of the soul.

The metaphysical soul is an entity whose existence is often the subject of speculation. For the metaphysician it is not only an hypothesis whether animals have souls. It is also an hypothesis whether human beings do. If, however, one speaks more naturally of soul-destroying work or of suffering that lacerates the soul or, as Simone Weil remarked of the ancient Greeks, that a man loses half his soul the day he becomes a slave, or even of soul music, then the sense of this talk, the place it may have in one's life, does not depend on speculation about whether there exists an entity which work may destroy, or which may be divided in half, or which can best be expressed in a certain kind of music. The conception of the soul that is destroyed by certain kinds of work, that is lacerated by suffering, is not a speculative conception of it. The sense of such ways of speaking does not depend on the outcome of metaphysical speculation about the existence of immaterial entities. When someone speaks this way of the soul, one should not ask, so you believe in the existence of the soul?

Nor do such ways of speaking require religious support. If there is a connection to religion it is indirect and, I would say, it is the religious or metaphysical conception that depends on the conception expressed in the more natural ways of speaking mentioned earlier. It seems essential to the very idea of a religion that its adherents must claim that it deepens our understanding of what matters to us, especially of those big facts that define the human condition—our vulnerability to suffering, our mortality, our sexuality. They may be wrong, of course, but we cannot imagine (because it makes no sense) someone saying, 'I know it does the dirt on life, that it cheapens everything we hold dear, but there it is, it's my religion.' It is natural then—in fact it is probably inevitable—that religious people concern themselves with the inner life in its orientation to suffering.

Talk of the soul in this more natural way, the non-speculative way, is connected with suffering, and with the possibility of it going deep. That possibility is, as we saw when we discussed M, inter-dependent with a certain kind of reflection. Animals suffer, but they cannot reflect on their suffering, they cannot be driven to despair about it, not at any rate the kind that drives someone to curse the day he was born. 'Man that is born of a woman hath but a short time to live, and is full of misery.' Life conceived in those accents of sorrow and pity is the natural home for talk of the soul. Conceived this way, the soul is, non-accidentally, the mortal soul. In saying this, I do not wish to pre-empt any speculation about whatever might be meant by an immortal soul. I mean only that in its non-speculative sense, the soul is essentially the soul of a mortal creature, vulnerable to misfortune. To define the soul as the immortal soul is still to retain more than a verbal connection with mortality. Death where is thy sting? can only be a question for someone whose mortality gravely matters to her.

Why then use the word, if it is so likely to be misunderstood in times when the soul is almost universally identified with a non-material substance, the property of religion and spiritualism? Is it not bound to be assimilated to speculation about the existence of an immaterial entity, which might or might not survive the death of the body? A clue to an answer lies in the fact that it is so odd to substitute 'psyche' (which is often favoured amongst modern translators as the word to translate the ancient Greek word *psuchē*) for 'soul' in the expressions I mentioned earlier. In those expressions, 'psyche' is not a bad substitute for 'soul'. It is no substitute at all. Consider, for example: a man loses half his psyche the day he becomes a slave; or psyche-destroying work; or psyche music.

The inner life, the life of the soul, consists of our emotions—love, grief, joy and, of course, intellectual passion—whose very existence is partly constituted by reflection. We say that cats love their kittens or dogs their pups, but animals do not reflect on whether they love well or badly. That is not because they love either well or badly, nor because they lack the intellectual powers to discover which. It is because it makes no sense to apply the distinction to them. Animals do not feel the kinds of things we do, not even a primitive version of them, though it is almost certainly true that what we feel has its primitive origins in the kinds of feelings animals have.

Our sense of the difference in kind between human beings and animals is (as was M's sense of the difference between 'us' and the Vietnamese) partly as a function of our belief that to be 'one of us', to be fully human, one must be the kind of being whose reflection on the real and the counterfeit forms of the inner life can deepen without limit.

We are required to be lucid about our inner lives under pain of superficiality. It is of the nature of the states that compose the inner life that they profess their authenticity, that they profess to be truthful and true. To grieve is to take oneself to be properly related to the reality of someone's death; to be related, that is, in a way that makes grief true to ('correspond to', 'be in tune with') that reality. When it is pure, grief is a form of relatedness to reality whose cognitive character is marked by the critical vocabulary that distinguishes real from false forms of it. Sentimental grief falsely professes what pure grief achieves.

One can no more be indifferent to whether one's grief takes

one to or away from reality than one can be indifferent to whether one's beliefs are true or false. And to grieve is to take oneself to grieve authentically, that is, in accord with the reality whose nature—and whose status as a genuine form of reality—is revealed in the grammar of the critical concepts to which grief is answerable. Unlike factual beliefs, however, which may be false without the person who holds them being untruthful, the sentimental distortion of the meaning of death is always both false and untruthful. We record that in the ways we connect concepts of truth, truthfulness, authenticity and authority, as we might apply them, for example, in assessing whether we have been rightly moved by someone's words or example.

The requirement to distinguish between the real and the false forms of the inner life seems, therefore, to arise from its very nature. When we reflect on M and see how basic our inner life is to our sense of humanity, the observation that they are composed of states whose nature requires lucidity of us goes some way to supporting one version of the Socratic claim that an unreflective life is unworthy of a human being. And if we remember the natural connection between the concept of the inner life and the concept of the soul when it is not used speculatively, then we can see why it has so often been said that truth is a need of the soul.

Socrates made his famous remark at his trial. Addressing his judges, who he knew would condemn him to death, he said:

> Perhaps someone may say 'But surely Socrates, after you have left us you can spend the rest of your life in quietly minding your own business.' This is the hardest thing of all to make some of you understand. If I say that this would be disobedience to God, and that is why I cannot 'mind my own business', you will not believe that I am serious. If on the other hand I tell you that to let no day pass without discussing goodness and all the other subjects about which you hear me talking and examining both myself and others is really the very best thing that a man can do, and that life

without this sort of examination is not worth living, you will be even less inclined to believe me.

The question of whether one really loves or grieves is not far from the question of how one should live. Whether one really loves or grieves rarely has practical consequences, which is why it is easy to make such rhetoric about it, to call it navel-gazing, precious and so on. But if it is true that it would require some explaining why someone really was indifferent about whether he felt love or grief or one of their many egocentric counterfeits, then in their actual lives the most hard-headed people are not as far from this question as their rhetorical denunciations of its relevance might at first make one think. And one knows that when affliction strikes one really needs to be hard-headed and that that kind of 'realism' often evaporates. Then there is a revaluing of what matters. But if I am right, that is not such a conversion as it may at first seem. Such questions are always there for us, implicit in the very nature of our inner lives.

The questions people often ask when affliction strikes are about what things are really valuable, about how they should have lived, about what really matters. Do money, prestige, career, for example, matter as much as we thought they did? Then we often realise that, as Plato put it, we have mistaken the necessary for the good. We have mistaken as the source of value that which was merely necessary to us, without which our lives would have appeared senseless to us. Such questions are about life's meaning and they need not be metaphysical. One gets a better grip on them when one thinks of relatively ordinary things—about how terrible it is to live a lie, for example. Or when one remembers how important it can be to be truthful about the past though it has no prudential value, or, if it has, then the value of the truthfulness transcends it, can't be explained entirely by it. To discover that one's dead friend had betrayed one, or that one's wife, husband or lover was unfaithful. Most people acknowledge that in such cases truth is important in itself, irrespective of how it affects the future.

Socrates' concern to know how one should live is not narrowly moral. In fact, his question can be asked at a sufficient distance from morality to place it amongst other things that matter to us. But it could be asked in the same spirit in which Socrates asked it only by someone who took morality seriously, even if it did not override other values for him. It is hard to imagine why such a question would be so important to someone unless the pressing need to ask it connected with a sense of the integrity or the dignity of her life.

Questions about what attitude it is right to take to our mortality, to our vulnerability to suffering, to the fact that we may lose everything which gives sense to our lives, to the fact that other human beings matter to us in ways we cannot fathom and in ways which we sometimes fear and resent, these and like questions are questions which people often take to be about the meaning of life—not questions about the meaning of their lives but about the meaning of *life*. That does not mean, however, that when people ask such questions they are asking whether life has an external end or purpose. It is true that people often speak as though they believe that the question whether life has a meaning is the same as the question whether life has an external purpose, but I believe they often mistake what is really at issue for them. Primary amongst the many reasons for this confusion is a misunderstanding about what is implied by the concern for life as a whole, for its having a unity which is not given merely by its movement (conscious or uncon- scious) towards some end. Such a concern might show itself in (amongst other things) a need to be truthful about the past, even though it may make no difference to the future. It matters to many people that they should not live a lie and that they should not die in a way that makes a mockery of their past.

Others, of course, don't care. If the psychotherapist Viktor Frankl is to be believed, they are few. He tells us that many years as a practising therapist and reflecting about his experiences in a Nazi death camp taught him that people are more concerned with meaning than they are with happiness. Most people ask questions which are recognisably of the kind which explicitly or implicitly express a concern for the meaning of life. If they did not, human life would hardly be recognisable to us. But I do not believe that reflection on such questions as Socrates asked is natural to us as a biological species. The sciences which deepen our understanding of our nature as a species have little to tell us about these things— little to tell us about, for example, love, little even about erotic love. Biology will not teach us the difference between real and counterfeit love. We think of science as a cultural achievement which enables us to see things as they are more or less independently of that achievement—which enables us to penetrate the appearances of things in nature so that we can know what is of their essence and what are merely superficial appearances. But the inner life as I have been speaking of it—the inner life as we mean it when we say that some people have rich and others impoverished inner lives—is not a discovery which a sophisticated culture has made possible for us. Its very existence is a cultural achievement. It is constituted by our culturally mediated, reflective responses to the defining facts of the human condition. Indeed that expression 'the human condition' implies a sense of common humanity whose character—whose common-ness—is conditioned by our reflective responses to those facts of human life the importance of which is evident to everyone.

If the natural sciences will not deepen our understanding of the inner life, what will? Psychology? To answer that question I want to reflect on what might at first seem a narrow controversy within a narrow part of psychology, a controversy about reductionism in psychoanalysis. I hope it emerges quite soon that the discussion has very wide implications. Current hostility to Freud and psychoanalysis, some of which is justified, has obscured I think how deep and how pervasive his influence has been. He was at once wonderfully innovative and profoundly a child of his times. Whatever one makes of the details of his theory, I think it highly unlikely that we will abandon the general proposition that an adequate psychology of the human personality will need a substantial concept of the self, an account of the way it develops, or fails to, an account of the working of the unconscious and a theory of its interpretation.

The psychoanalyst Bruno Bettelheim wrote a controversial little book entitled *Freud and Man's Soul*. In it he argues that James Strachey, Freud's English translator, had systematically mistranslated key words in Freud's writings in an effort to make him scientifically respectable. Bettelheim claims that Strachey thereby misled generations of readers about what Freud believed to be the proper objects and methods of psychoanalytic inquiry and therapy. He gives many examples which together support his claim that Freud was indeed mistranslated in the service of a scientistic conception of the nature of psychoanalysis. Bettelheim is, however, too quick to conclude that the mistranslations are false to the main bent of Freud's spirit. Freud had a virulent reductive streak. Martin Buber said of him in *The Knowledge of Man*:

> Freud, a great, late-born apostle of the enlightenment, presented the naturalism of the enlightenment with a scientific system and thereby with a second flowering. As Freud himself recognized with complete clarity, the struggle against all metaphysical and religious teachings of the existence of an absolute and of the possibility of a relation of the human person to it had a great share in the development of psychoanalytical theory.

Buber was right, I think. Freud believed that he had discovered a new dimension of the mind and a new method of inquiry. But he also believed that he had arrived at a new and deepened understanding of the concept of the psychological which enabled him to subsume morality and religion into it. He appeared to believe that if our understanding of, for example, morality—of its nature and the kind of seriousness it has for us—could not be deepened by metaphysics, then it would be deepened by psychoanalysis.

Freud's followers have argued about the extent and depth of his reductive disposition. Some claim, plausibly, that it was most virulent in his more 'philosophical' works, but subdued and sometimes completely absent in the best of his clinical writings. Others claim that, though the reductionism was thoroughgoing, his key insights may be developed in a non-reductive direction. Bettelheim makes much of Freud's humane learning and of his love and knowledge of literature. He emphasises how Freud's writings are rich in parable, allusion, simile and metaphor. There can be no doubt that Freud was a great writer in the tradition of humane letters. But if he wrote with the sensibility of an artist, then that does not show that he did not wish and believe himself to be a scientist. Perhaps there is inconsistency not only between what Freud preached, but also between what he preached and his clinical and literary practice.

Bettelheim complains most about the fact that Strachey translated the German word '*Seele*' as 'psyche' or mind rather than as 'soul'. '*Seele*' may, in fact, be used in contexts where it does not carry the connotations that support the kind of humanistic case that Bettelheim makes on Freud's behalf. There are contexts, however, as we have seen, in which 'soul' discourages substitutions for it of 'mind' or 'psyche'. We hesitate to speak of a science of the soul and of experts of the soul, but not—at least not so instinctively—of a science of the mind. That gives some support to Bettelheim's polemic, albeit unwelcome, for it tends to undermine the claim that there can be knowledge of the soul and therapeutic expertise derived from it which could command the same kind of authority as does medicine. Viktor Frankl, another 'humanistic' analyst—the founder of 'logotherapy'—wrote a book in which he claimed that the need human beings have to find meaning in their lives was a fact of such importance that psychoanalytical theory and practice required considerable revision in order adequately to acknowledge it. He called his book *Doctor and the Soul*.

There is not much in clinical psychology that counts as knowledge of the kind that we judge to have a deserved place in text books and in encyclopaedias—the kind that has authority because it commands agreement between those whose competence to assess it and to adjudicate between competing claims to it can be characterised in ways that do not beg any questions in favour of those claims, and which can therefore sustain a substantial concept of expertise. In many of the most interesting parts of psychology which bear on clinical practice and on theories of the nature of personality and identity—those which may lay claim to be 'a study of the soul'—disagreement is radical, pervasive and sometimes transparently ideologically driven. This is not, I strongly suspect, just because psychology (in the broad sense which includes psychiatry and psychoanalysis) is a relatively new discipline. Nor is it just because the subject matter is too complex or of a kind that arouses deep passions and anxieties.

All that is, for the most part, true, but it does not take us to the heart of the matter. The deeper reason is that psychoanalysis, and all forms of psychology which study the inner life, have a subject matter whose understanding is distorted by the kind of impersonality that marks forms of inquiry that lead to what we (rightly) call knowledge, and which justify the claim that their subject matter is of a kind which would ideally command agreement amongst those who are competent and serious in their concern for truth. And if (as seems to be the case) our understanding of our inner life and its actuality are interdependent, if the concepts with which we identify and explore our inner life partly determine the character of that inner life, then a scientistic distortion of those concepts will not only distort our understanding: it will distort the inner life itself.

The dispute between analysts such as Bettelheim and their more scientifically minded colleagues is largely over how we should probe the appearances to seek a deepened understanding of the inner life. Disagreement over the place of art is central to that dispute, in particular over whether it is true, and if it is true what importance it has, that the cognitive content of most propositions which psychologists try to extract from art cannot be separated from their form.

Many psychologists (and philosophers) believe that art and life yield data upon which we can reflect and that the sciences, in friendship perhaps with a scientifically minded philosophy, approximate the perfect form of that reflection. The assumption that informs this way of thinking is that intellectual disciplines of the kind found in science and in scientific philosophy are needed to extract the properly cognitive content from the forms in which art and life present experiences to us. Hardly anyone will deny that it requires disciplines of mind and character to 'see things as they are' as opposed to how they appear to be and, especially in the case of psychological phenomena, how for many and subtle reasons we fantasise them to be. Nor are many people likely to deny that we must often distance ourselves from our subject so that our fears, fantasies and affections do not interfere with our sense of what is objectively the case.

But there is a wrong and tendentious way of taking those platitudes about objectivity, which urges us to seek, to the extent that is humanly possible, a language of critical appraisal only contingently vulnerable to our passions, our fantasies and our failings of character. According to this conception, affective states such as sentimentality or pity, or virtues such as justice, are causal conditions, which sometimes enhance and sometimes diminish our capacities for cognitive achievements whose nature makes no essential reference to the fact that we possess such affective and moral dispositions. Recall Iris Murdoch's marvellous insight that to see the reality of another person is a 'work of love, justice and pity'. She did not mean that love, justice and pity are the characteristic causal conditions which enable a distinct cognitive capacity to grasp the truth about another person. She means that these are *forms* of understanding rather than the enabling conditions of understanding, and that what is there to be understood cannot be characterised independently of that fact.

To see more clearly what is at issue here, consider the concept of sentimentality. Imagine a scientist—Konrad—whose colleagues say that his observations of the behaviour of animals are distorted by his sentimentality. One of his colleagues says something like this, to his research students: 'Konrad has published certain claims about the behaviour of dogs. They look to be false. Quite likely they are yet another expression of the old man's sentimentality. The language in which he presents his observations strongly suggests that. But that does not matter. I am not interested in whether he is sentimental. I am interested only in whether his claims are true or false. We can extract the cognitive substance of those claims from his emotive language and investigate them in a properly scientific manner. I would like you to do it.'

The distinction invoked here between sentimental, emotive form and cognitive content seems to make sense. Sentimentality is invoked as a causal explanation of why certain factual claims are likely to be false and why such claims are characteristically entered by this person. It functions in the same way as appeals to tiredness or drunkenness do, that is, as a cause external to the thought it distorts. This gives us one conception of how feeling can distort thought, of how it relates to form, of how it can threaten objectivity, of what it means to resist its distortions in order to see more clearly how things really are, as opposed to how one would wish them to be, and so on. Such a conception often gives rise to (or may be the expression of) the idealisation of a thinker who would be unaffected by these failings, who would free himself or herself as much as possible from the ways of being and living which generate such threats to the proper functioning of the mind.

That supposition finds expression in the idealisation of a being who occupies the Archimedean point, who sees the world as from no place within it, as God would see it. This being is, *ex hypothesi* one whose thought is not answerable to critical categories which are conditioned by the contingencies of particular ways of living and being. Such idealised knowers cannot be sentimental, not because they are so virtuous or so lucky that they have become invulnerable to sentimentality, but because it makes no sense to attribute to them either sentimentality or its absence. Whether one speaks here of the world as God would see it, or merely of the view from nowhere, the idea is the same. The thoughts of such idealised thinkers are expressions of thinking as it is in its essence for any thinking thing that thinks perfectly. It is evident that, insofar as this represents an idealisation of our cognitive and epistemic aspirations, it assumes that the content which is common to us and these idealised thinkers is one whose cognitive character can be extracted from those forms of expression that mark particular forms of life—in our case, the natural languages shaped by and which give shape to our lives as human beings. Such beings have no use for idioms in which form and content are inseparable.

Consider now a case which reveals a different way that 'sentimentality' functions as a critical concept. Suppose that someone is accused of being sentimental in her thoughts about what the death of a dog may mean. She believes that it is proper and (for her) obligatory to bury the dog in a dog cemetery, to erect a monument to it and each year to light a candle to its memory, and other things like that. She might try to support her beliefs by false empirical claims about the capacity of animals, claims which would stand in relation to her feelings in the same way that Konrad's claims stood in relation to his feelings. She might say, for example, that dogs can understand most of what she says to them in English, only they cannot reply. But she might not do anything like that. She might simply give poetic but sentimental accounts of what it means for human beings and dogs to be fellow creatures, sharing a common fate, destined to die, and so on.

Suppose that someone does judge her to be sentimental.

Could someone else who is unsure say, 'I don't care whether she is sentimental. I want to know whether her beliefs are true or false'? I think not. What could they be after, in insisting on that distinction? It made sense in the scientific case, and would make sense here if she entertained false empirical beliefs about dogs. But on the assumption that she does not, her sentimentality is not rightly thought of as a *cause* of her thought's failure on a dimension that could be specified independently of its vulnerability to sentimentality and similar afflictions. Its being sentimental is the primary *form* of its failure as thought.

Both examples are informed by a conception of how feeling can distort thought. But they are different. One way of expressing the difference would be to say that in the second case feeling cannot be separated from thought, nor form from content. Both are examples of the bad effects of sentimentality on thought, but that similarity accommodates a difference whose importance is of the first order. The difference is between occasions when concepts like sentimentality are critical concepts marking cognitive failures in their own right, and occasions when they mark only emotional conditions external to thought, which sometimes hamper it and which sometimes facilitate it, but which are not themselves forms of it. Sentimentality is, in the second case, a form of the false, a way that belief can be false, rather than the cause of it.

None of this gives us reasons to doubt that a substantial conception of truth applies to thought about our inner lives. We can say much the same about the concept of truth as it applies to our efforts to understand our inner lives as we say of it elsewhere—it is interdependent with the concepts that mark what it is to think well or badly. At a general level those concepts appear to be the same whether we are thinking about physics or about poetry. In all inquiries we try to see things as they are rather than how they appear to us, to strive for reality rather than illusion, to try to think clearly and relevantly rather than in ways that are muddled and distracted, and so on.

It is a fact of great importance that these general truisms about truth and objectivity obtain across all forms of intellectual life. But it is equally important to note that such generalities may disguise differences of the first importance. In physics and in reflection about poetry we try to 'see things as they are' rather than how we would like them to be, or how they appear from distorting perspectives. We try to resist distorting forms of subjectivity. But what it is to do this will differ from one to the other. The effort to resist sentimentality, jadedness, bathos and cliché is intrinsic to the very nature of reflection on poetry as, of course, it is to poetry itself. Those critical concepts play little part in most of the natural sciences, and when they do, they function as terms which mark external obstacles to thought—obstacles like hastiness, the desire to protect a pet theory, tiredness or drunkenness—rather than as ailments to which thought is intrinsically vulnerable.

What is true of the woman thinking about her dog is true of virtually all our reflections on the inner life. We cannot resist the distorting effects which our fantasies and projections have on our thought about other human beings by hoping to refine a method of inquiry which would enable us to speak in ways which are only contingently vulnerable to sentimentality, rhetoric and so on. Or, more precisely: if we do, we will limit ourselves to kinds of descriptions which, whatever their other virtues, cannot lay claim to represent things as they 'really' are in connection with the kinds of issues I have been discussing. Such descriptions do not allow us to speak of love, justice and pity as forms of understanding. They require us to say that they may be the *causes* of certain truths or certain errors which are marked as such by more fundamental (and neutral) criteria of appraisal, of which the factually true or false would be an example.

The moral to be drawn is that if we fear that our thought has been distorted because we have been sentimentally moved, then instead of striving not to be moved we should strive to avoid being sentimentally moved. That means that our thoughts must remain within a conceptual space which is conditioned by a natural language, rich in phrases and descriptions which come to us from, and which resonate against, that in our history—most notably our art—whose content cannot be separated from its style. Sentimentality may be the contingent cause of certain kinds of errors in, for example, the scientific observations of animals. It is not contingent to what we may learn from art that it is in an idiom vulnerable to sentimentality.

Freud did not believe this; at least not officially. It is true that he believed that one needed to be in a certain psychological condition whose true nature was discovered and described by psychoanalysis in order even to understand psychoanalysis at any depth. This arouses understandable indignation amongst scientifically-minded psychologists. And not only amongst them. Freud's defenders may say that doesn't matter; that they do not aspire to be scientists. Despite Freud's often repeated claim to be a scientist they are right to disclaim such aspirations, but I think that the disclaimer will not take them far.

Freud was attracted to scientism, but that was because he was attracted to something deeper that often lies behind it. Scientism is sometimes a function of people's vulnerability to the prestige of natural science, but in Freud it rested on a more general vulnerability to a certain (enlightenment) rhetoric about the nature of reason—a rhetoric whose edifying attractions appear again and again in his pages. He believed, I think, that those psychological states, which enable one to understand and those which hinder understanding of the discoveries of psychoanalysis, function as they do because of the kind of inquirers we (human beings) *happen* to be, and that this shows nothing interesting about the conceptual character of psychoanalytical propositions. Those propositions could, in principle, be understood by rational inquirers who possessed none of our non-cognitive psychological attributes. That is why Buber was right to call him essentially a child of the enlightenment. And why the Canadian philosopher

Charles Taylor was right to say, 'Freud was a prototypical example of the believer in disengaged objectification, one who sees the mastery of reason as a kind of rational control over the emotions, attained through the distance of scientific scrutiny.'

For that reason Freud's official attitude to literature and more generally to art is at odds with the claims made by Bettelheim for the actual role that Freud's literary sensibility played in the development of psychoanalytical theory. Freud's official attitude is in substance little different from the attitude of those who openly condescend to poets and novelists, and who call them insightful amateurs in an enterprise whose cognitive nature has only recently (in our scientific age) properly been appreciated and which has, accordingly, developed appropriate methods of inquiry that will yield the impersonally corroborated kind of knowledge I spoke of earlier and, with it, legitimate claims to expertise in its practical applications. They acknowledge, of course, that the enterprise is in its early stages and that for that reason insightful amateurs may, even in their ill disciplined writings, provide fertile hypotheses to be framed and tested in proper scientific style. Ideally, however (the thought continues), we would—and perhaps eventually actually will—need them only for entertainment and edification.

I have already suggested that the fact that Freud was wrong about the scientific character of psychoanalysis is less interesting than is the fact that he was wrong about the kind of impersonality required in psychoanalytical understanding. In a moment I shall try to explain this more clearly and justify it. First, however, it is important to note that this is a point that bears importantly on our understanding of the sense in which psychoanalysis is an *empirical* theory. In some sense of that difficult word, it clearly is, for the clinical material is indispensable to it. But the concept of an empirical discipline is essentially the concept of a discipline whose theories are formed by and tested against experience. The concept of experience, however, is a complex one.

Psychoanalysis is often taken to be empirical in the sense that the cognitive character of its propositions would ideally be confirmed by experiment. Or, to put the point more precisely, confirmed by evidence of a kind which is secured by methods whose prototype is controlled experimentation. Many psychoanalysts believe that and Freud himself, in many moods, believed it too. To be sure, many of the same psychoanalysts believe that experimentation is impossible for a variety of reasons, but they believe that is regrettable. They believe that the cognitive character of psychoanalytical propositions is of a kind that makes such regret intelligible and appropriate.

There are then at least two different things which may be meant when it is said that psychoanalysis is not and can never be a science. The first is that the cognitive character of psychoanalytical propositions is such that, ideally, they would be experimentally vindicated by clinical (and other) material, but that for a variety of (contingent) reasons they cannot be. The second is that the cognitive character of psychoanalytical propositions is such that they could not be experimentally verified even in an ideal world. It has been my argument that if one conceives of psychoanalytical claims as only contingently incapable of experimental verification, then one will distort their relation to the clinical experience from which they arise and in which they are—in ways appropriate to them—tested and modified. One will also distort the concept of experience as it matters in this context, and with it the kind of understanding that issues from and is brought to bear upon it.

If I am right about this, then the second (and correct) account of why psychoanalysis will never be a science will bring with it a different understanding than does the first, of how the distinctions between appearance and reality and depth and surface function in the exploration of the kind of subject matter that psychoanalysis concerns itself with. A different account, also, of what, in such contexts, it means for something to be an appearance, of what it means for something to count as going below the appearances and of what depth and shallowness amount to. Freud's misunderstanding of this informed his reductionism, including his hostility to the idea that morality is *sui generis*.

To take stock. Our understanding of the inner life is liable to distortion by a reductive psychology. The impulse to reductionism is a conception of psychological phenomena as intrinsically suited to forms of inquiry which separate cognitive from emotive content. That impulse is often called scientistic. It can be that. But even when it is, scientism is the expression of a more general disposition which goes very deep in philosophy and more generally in our culture. It is the disposition to see thought about the inner life as answerable to an idealisation of thinking that treats sentimentality, pathos etc as merely the contingently disabling conditions of a cognitive function whose character can be specified independently of our vulnerability to them.

Someone who strives to avoid sentimentality when thinking about what her life means is someone who aims to think what is true and who necessarily aims to think truthfully—necessarily, because as well as being a form of falsehood, sentimentality is a form of untruthfulness. Truth and truthfulness are inseparable in the conceptual structure of sentimentality, as they are in the structure of most of the critical concepts with which we assess our thought about the states of the inner life. This shows itself in the way authenticity and integrity are often invoked as concepts which partly characterise the forms of thinking well rather than as the names of virtues which help us to think well. Clearly this is not so for all forms of thinking. It seems not to be in physics. Truthfulness is important there, of course, but as a means to securing and protecting truth. It is not intrinsic to the conception of truth that is sought and protected.

Rising to the requirement to be lucid about one's inner life is an effort to be objective whose success depends upon the realisation of a distinctive individuality. It is the kind of individuality we refer to when we say that each human being is a unique perspective on the world. Though it might seem paradoxical at first, all efforts to see our inner lives 'as they are', rather than as we would wish them to be, or as they appear from a limited or distorted perspective, require thought to be disciplined by critical concepts that individualise the thinker. That lies behind our meaning when we say that someone has 'something to say' (and we don't mean that they have a new theory to propound or new facts to report), that they have 'found their voice', that they speak from an authority that is inseparable from the fact that they have lived their own life and no one else's.

Putting the thought the other way about should diminish the sense of paradox. If we ask what it means to be someone who has something to say, who speaks with an authority that depends on authenticity, then the answer is that the thought of such people is disciplined by concepts which reveal, for this kind of thinking, what it is to strive to see things as they are rather than as one would wish them to be, or how they appear from this or that perspective.

The air of paradox in the claim that objective thought about the inner life is essentially personal is generated by the common and natural assumption that truth and thought which aims at it are essentially impersonal. Simone Weil expresses that assumption in her essay 'Human Personality':

> What is sacred in science is truth; what is sacred in art is beauty. Truth and Beauty are impersonal. All this is too obvious.
> If a child is doing a sum and does it wrong, the mistake bears the stamp of his personality. If he does the sum exactly right, his personality does not enter into it at all.
> Perfection is impersonal.

Weil's point is characteristically forceful, but the notion of the impersonal is, as I hope I have shown, more complex in relation to truth than she allows. There is point in saying that even reflection on ethics and on what our lives may mean is impersonal, for here too—here especially!—one must resist the blandishments of what Iris Murdoch calls the 'fat relentless ego' and struggle to see things as they are. But there is also point in saying that when truth and truthfulness are inseparable—when we are thinking about the human spirit—thought is essentially personal. Perhaps that is what Kierkegaard had in mind when he said, misleadingly, that truth is subjectivity. It is best, however, to resist saying flatly that thought about value is personal or impersonal. Attention to the critical vocabulary that tells in its various applications what thinking well or badly come to will in some contexts incline us to emphasise the way thought is personal and in others to emphasise the way it is impersonal.

Much of what is called postmodernism recognises that truth but often distorts it. It distorts it because it oscillates between treating the ideal of an Archimedean point—of 'seeing the world as from no place within it'—as incoherent, and treating it as merely unachievable. Only the latter thought—that we are contingently unable to attain the Archimedean perspective—gives sense to postmodernism's debunking rhetoric and its rhetoric of heroic resignation. That rhetoric relies on a conception of truth and objectivity that assumes the coherence of the Archimedean perspective, deplores our incapacity to reach it and ridicules those who do not see this. But if the perspective is incoherent, and if, as I am sure is the case, our ordinary conceptions of truth and objectivity do not assume it, then Wittgenstein was right to believe that a critical philosophy of truth will leave things more or less as they are.

A Common Humanity

Recall that M could not imagine having serious conversations with Vietnamese women about motherhood, about what it means for one's child to die, about sexuality, about death, indeed about anything that mattered to her. She could imagine well enough that warm companionship could exist between her and them—the same kind that existed between white slave-owners and their black slaves, particularly between white women and children and black nannies. Friendship, however, with its requirement of equality, would be impossible. Recognising all that, we see that M cannot conceive that the Vietnamese could be wronged, by us or by themselves, in the way 'we' can be.

Yet—and this is startling—M unhesitatingly attributes to the Vietnamese all that makes up the raw material for philosophical accounts of morality, of its content, and, more interestingly, of its nature and authority. She knows that the Vietnamese are persons according to most accounts of that concept. No doubt crosses her mind that they are self-conscious, rational, with thoughts and feelings, and are able to reflect critically on their desires, thoughts and feelings. She therefore attributes to them all that is usually attributed to rational contractors in a state of nature deliberating about how most fairly to reconcile their interests; all that utilitarians assume when they develop their theories, and all, I think, that Kantian moral theorists require to construct the categorical imperative, the Moral Law with its awesome authority, governing autonomous rational beings in a Kingdom of Ends.

Without needing at all to alter her sense of the difference between them and us and all that it implies, M could note, if her mind were disposed that way, that philosophers amongst the Vietnamese could construct theories of exactly the same kind as we have done. If that is true, then it shows what we take for granted when we accept such theories as serious candidates for an account of the moral life. It seems that we do not notice what sets the stage for their acceptance. To put it another way, we fail to notice how little those theories achieve. If rational negotiators, deploying the spartan rationality and the kind of raw materials that M can attribute to the Vietnamese, devise rules more or less like our moral rules, covering the same range and kinds of conduct, they would not thereby capture what it means to wrong someone. Whatever reasons we may have to assent to such rules, therefore, they are not the reasons why we accept morality's authority over us.

The fact that we can straightaway see that M could not find it intelligible that the Vietnamese could be wronged as 'we' can provides strong evidence for the claim that morality and our inner lives, the meaning we attach to things, form a seamless web. Some people think that needs no support, but, as we saw, philosophers as great as Kant have denied it explicitly and ferociously. Some of the appeal of Kant's distinction between categorical imperatives and hypothetical imperatives resting on 'inclination' (roughly, the distinction between imperatives which do and imperatives which do not appeal to our interests and desires) relies on it. Recall the rhetorical importance of his appeal to the person whose inner life was poisoned by grief and bitterness, but whose capacity to perform deeds, motivated by the categorical imperative—deeds which would 'shine like a jewel'—was in no way diminished. If all of what Kant called 'inclination' were states and dispositions no different from those M could recognise in the Vietnamese, it would not affect his account of the nature of morality.

It is a powerful image, this one of a person broken and embittered but doing his duty. To the extent that it works for us, it does so only because we take it for granted that he is 'one of us'. We take it for granted that he could rise to the call to see things differently. He therefore belongs with us in that conceptual space from which M excluded the Vietnamese. The point is formally analogous to the one I made against Kant when I agreed that we have obligations to those whom we do not love, but argued that that does not show that we could make sense of those obligations if we did not see those people as the intelligible object of someone else's love—real love, that is, not 'love'. Analogically, I shall grant for the sake of the argument that we could perform all our duties to others while being embittered and twisted. That does not mean, however, that we would find intelligible an idea of duty that broke all conceptual ties with an inner life of the kind M unhesitatingly attributes to us and which gives life and power to the language with which we explore what things mean to us.

Another reason why we fail to see what sets the stage for our understanding of what it means to wrong someone when we theorise about morality is that we are often tempted to think a sense of a common humanity rests on an acknowledgment of the basic things that all human beings have in common. At bottom we are all the same, we think, and that if we could realise how unimportant our differences really are, then those differences could not fuel our hatreds. Is that not the lesson of stories like Orwell's, or the scene from Costa-Gavras' film?

To this I want to answer Yes and No. Yes, because the appeal to nakedness and vulnerability is, of course, an appeal to something basic. But reading that passage from Orwell we see the man's vulnerability—as he runs along the top of the parapet holding up his trousers—in the light of the assumption that he is one of us in the way that M denied the Vietnamese to be, or a white slave-owner denied a slave to be. It never occurs to us that a slave-owning Confederate soldier could respond in the same way to a former black slave fighting with the Yankees. Yet it is so. Or, to take an even more telling example: it never occurs to us when we read the parable of the good Samaritan, that it could be the story of a slave-owner responding to a black slave. Were we to read it that way, only the words identifying the characters in the parable need be changed. The slave-owning soldier, could say, 'I could not shoot. A man holding up his trousers is a fellow human being.' And the slave-owning 'Samaritan' could say, 'I could not walk past. He is a human being.'

Does that show how useless it is to speak of seeing someone as a fellow human being? At this stage it might seem that perhaps the answer doesn't matter. Does it really matter what *kind* of thing a thing is so long as we respond appropriately to its morally relevant features? Have I not emphasised that M's attitude to the Vietnamese is a function of her failure to see that they have inner lives of any depth? Whether or not one goes on to say that therefore she sees them as less than fully human may be unimportant. If something has the features that make a full moral response to it appropriate, then perhaps it is irrelevant whether it is a person, a human being, a member of some other species, or even a machine.

Undeniably, that view has its attractions because it does seem irrational to place much weight on a general term such as 'human being' or 'person' when it appears that only the features possessed by the being to whom we are responding should matter. Such a view lies behind the claim that it is speciesist to respond to human beings differently from other species merely because we are human beings. Racism, sexism and speciesism (this thought continues) treat as morally relevant features of a person things that are irrelevant—race or skin colour, gender and species membership.

If 'human being' meant only *homo sapiens*, then the term could play no interesting moral role. And if, beyond identifying a species, it were merely a way of recording a moral opinion—as in 'What a human being!'—then it would play no interesting role either. But we have already noted our sense of the importance of our humanity to our ways of thinking and feeling that seem to serve neither biological classification nor moral expostulation. The insistence that it is the scientific concept *homo sapiens* that carries the cognitive weight, the rest being rhetoric, fails to notice how many, how varied and how basic some ways of speaking of our common humanity are. The matter is so important that I must ask for the reader's patience to follow a discussion that might at first seem like a digression.

In a marvellous passage in *Philosophical Investigations* Wittgenstein writes:

> But isn't it absurd to say of a *body* that it has pain?—And why does one feel an absurdity in that? In what sense is it true that my hand does not feel pain, but I in my hand?
>
> What sort of issue is: Is it the *body* that feels pain?—How is it to be decided? What makes it plausible to say that it is *not* the body?—Well, something like this: if someone has a pain in his hand, then the hand does not say so (unless it writes it) and one does not comfort the hand, but the sufferer: one looks into his face.
>
> How am I filled with pity *for this man*? How does it come out what the object of my pity is? (Pity, one might say, is a form of conviction that someone else is in pain.)

Earlier Wittgenstein had asked, 'What gives us so much as the idea that living beings, things, can feel?' The radical import of that question comes from the classical formulation of scepticism about 'other minds'. It presupposes an observer wondering what justification he has for believing that there are other people with thoughts and feelings as he has. The problem arises for such an observer of the human scene when he notices that he has direct (perceptual) contact only with the bodies of other people, never with their thoughts and feelings. From his perspective the answer to Wittgenstein's question would be, 'It is their behaviour that gives me so much as the idea.' Once he has the idea, he must determine how much more he has than that. Does he have knowledge, or must he settle for a reasonable hypothesis?

The trouble with this classical picture of the problem and what might count as its solution is that the behaviour which is supposed to give me the idea that others have thoughts and feelings like mine is behaviour like mine. When I am in pain, for example, I might groan or wince. When I am pleased, I might smile. Others seem often to do the same. But groans and smiles are already saturated with the mental. If I stand on your toe I may not know whether your groan is one of pain or embarrassment, but if I take it as a groan then I can be in no doubt that you are a being with sensations, thoughts and feelings. If scepticism is to get a foothold, therefore, the spectator must take behaviour as less than expressive, as colourless bodily movement as the behaviourist psychologist C. L. Hull thought it would appear to us if we achieved scientific objectivity.

Now, I think, one can see the radical import of Wittgenstein's question. If behaviour ceases to be seen as expressive, then it ceases to be behaviour like mine, and the basis for mooting the idea that others have thoughts and feelings like I do—the basis for the famous 'argument from analogy'—looks to have vanished. The point is not that I am now less secure in my conjecture that there are other people. It is that I have no basis even for the conjecture. Colourless bodily movements cannot give me so much as the idea. I may as well assume that stones flee from me when I kick them.

Wittgenstein diagnosed the trouble to lie at the beginning, with the assumption of the spectator's stance. When we take it, we naturally assume the behaviour of others yields evidence, weak or strong, for the supposition that they have thoughts and feelings. We assume that if a person's behaviour together with the circumstances in which it occurs provides good grounds for me to believe that she is in pain rather than embarrassed, then it provides good grounds for me to believe that she is a conscious being. But, of course, what provides the evidence is not a colourless bodily movement or a meaningless sound, but her grimace and her groan, and I take these for what they are only because it never occurs to me to question that she is a sentient being.

In one of the most radical passages in the history of philosophy, Wittgenstein reflects:

> 'I believe that he is suffering.'—Do I also *believe* that he isn't an automaton? It would go against the grain to use the word in both connexions. (Or is it like this: I believe that he is suffering, but am certain that he is not an automaton? Nonsense!)...
>
> 'I believe that he is not an automaton,' just like that, so far makes no sense.
>
> My attitude towards him is an attitude towards a soul. I am not of the *opinion* that he has a soul.

Nothing should be read into Wittgenstein's use of the word 'soul' (*Seele*). This is an example that goes counter to Bettelheim's polemic. Wittgenstein means nothing more than a being with thoughts and feelings. He means an inner life, to be sure, but not as we mean it when we speak of an inner life with deeper and shallower possibilities. His point is that generally I cannot doubt that others are sentient beings, but that is not because I *know* they are. It is not because of anything the classical spectator is after to assure himself that there are other minds. Behaviour (together with the circumstances of its occurrence) *counts as evidence* for the existence of a person's psychological states only against the background that (in normal circumstances) no one could seriously doubt that she is a human being with thoughts and feelings.

One must be careful not to treat this unhesitating acknowledgment of others as based on an *assumption* that they have minds. Assumptions invite questions about whether they are justified. The trouble with this is not that under sceptical probing they might prove not to be. Even if we answer confidently and with justification that the assumption is correct, in doing so we stand on common ground with the sceptic in thinking that our unhesitating certainty is the kind of cognitive achievement that he is looking for but suspects cannot be given. In doing that, in thinking we can stand on the same ground and refute the sceptic—and there is no other ground on which something will count as a refutation—we distort the role that our behaviour plays in our understanding of ourselves and other people. 'What gives us so much as the idea that living beings, things, can feel?' The answer Wittgenstein gives is that nothing gives us so much as the idea, for it is not a matter of having an idea. It is not an assumption, a conjecture, or a belief, or even knowledge.

Following Wittgenstein, Peter Winch calls many of the forms of an attitude towards a soul 'primitive reactions'. In his essay 'Eine Einstellung zur Seele' (An Attitude Towards a Soul) he argues that they are a condition rather than a consequence of ascribing states of consciousness to others. Such reactions—a variety of interacting responses to the demeanours of the human form—are partly constitutive of those concepts with which we describe the forms of bodily expressiveness—groans, smiles, grimaces, tension, relaxation and so on. They are the concepts with which we describe what we ordinarily call 'behaviour', all the subtle inflexions we bring under the notion of 'body language', and which distinguish behaviour from 'colourless bodily movement'. Binding a person's wound while looking into his face is an example of an attitude towards a soul.

Wittgenstein's radical remark turns on its head the almost irresistibly natural thought that we react to others as to persons—as to 'other minds'—because we know, believe, or conjecture that they have psychological states more or less as we do. The fact that it is, in general, natural for us to look into a person's face while binding his wounds, and other facts like that, conditions our concept of pain, and inseparably from that, our sense of the object of our pity—a-human-being-in-pain. I intend by this lapse into nominalisation to signal the interdependence of our concept of pain, what it means to be in pain, the kind of beings to whom we may intelligibly attribute such suffering, and those interacting responses which are 'attitudes towards a soul'. We cannot, Wittgenstein argues, radically detach our expressions of sympathy from our understanding of their objects. We cannot detach our sense of what it is for someone to be in pain—ourselves included—from our ways of living with the language of sensation, without detaching ourselves from what makes our concept of pain what it is (from its 'grammar', as Wittgenstein would have said).

Which does not mean that whenever we know that someone is in pain we must respond with compassion or in any way at all. We may be quite indifferent. Wittgenstein's point is only that it is not generally so with us, and the fact that it is not partly conditions our understanding of pain. It also explains why we distinguish indifference to a person's pain from indifference to facts like the distance between Sydney and Melbourne. To the latter someone can say, 'What is that to me?' But someone who says, 'What is that to me?' in the face of another person's suffering will have their indifference described as callousness. Pity is normative for our descriptions of the forms of our indifference to suffering, not because of moral beliefs we hold about how we should respond, but because pity is partly constitutive of our understanding of what it means to suffer. 'Pity,' one might say, 'is a form of conviction that someone is in pain.'

Wittgenstein seems to believe that our interactions with one another which are of the kind he calls 'an attitude towards a soul' form rather than depend upon our sense of being of a common (human) kind, and form also that humanly centred sense of what we find *intelligible* to say of creatures who are in some respects like, but in others quite unlike, ourselves—other animals for example. Without hesitation we acknowledge that dogs feel pain; but we are not sure about fleas. That is because dogs have faces and eyes and fleas do not—not the kind one can look into when tending their wounds. ' "But doesn't what you say come to this:" ' Wittgenstein imagines an objector who has misunderstood him to say, ' "that there is no pain, for example, without pain-*behaviour*?"—It comes to this: only of a living human being and what resembles (behaves like) a living human being can one say: it has sensations; it sees; is blind; hears; is deaf; is conscious or unconscious.'

Wittgenstein does not mean *homo sapiens* when he speaks of human beings in that passage, nor does he think the extension of those terms would necessarily be the same. The scientific definition of *homo sapiens*, which determines its extension, treats as *superficial* properties of the species, those things which make attitudes 'to a soul' what they are, which enable them to play the role they do in the constitution of our concepts—faces, for example, and the fact that we are of flesh and blood. Obviously there must be faces if there are to be lookings into them, but if there were not such responses as looking into a face, then, Wittgenstein would say, we would not have the concept of sensation that we do. Indeed, the constituency I just appealed to, when I said that *we* would not have the concept of sensation that we do, would not exist.

Attitudes towards a soul mark out a kind in a way that superficially appears like the biological classification *homo sapiens* because it distinguishes us from other animals on the basis of physical and behavioural features characteristic of the species. The scientific notion, however, prides itself on its detachment from the forms of our responses to the human form and to one another. The essence of the kind *homo sapiens* is a genetic code. Anything that has that code is a human being, no matter what it looks like. Anything which doesn't have that code is not a human being no matter what it looks like. But the conception of humankind that is built out of our responses—and which is interdependent with concepts as basic as sensation—takes little notice of the scientific criterion for *homo sapiens*. It is not a rival species classification.

The responses that form and are formed by our sense of belonging to a common kind cannot be elicited by beings that do not look and behave like us. This is not because we find it psychologically impossible to ignore appearances even though we should in the interests of objectivity. It is because those responses are built into the concepts with which we identify what could be the appropriate objects for our responses. This is a circle—a non-vicious one—from which we cannot escape without losing the relevant concepts—in the case under discussion, the concept of pain. For the same reason we cannot—necessarily we cannot—tell in advance all that we will count as looking and behaving like us. We have to see how we respond. And reflect on our responses of course. But such reflection cannot escape the circle made by the interdependence of our responses and the concepts with which we identify their appropriate objects. (That is why I said that M's sense of who she will count as belonging to 'us' is necessarily indeterminate.)

Our concepts which mark the states of the inner life—in the thin sense that refers merely to states of consciousness and the richer sense which enables M to distinguish 'us' from 'them'—are therefore profoundly anthropocentric. I hope that my discussion has shown that that need not be a bad thing. It can be consistent with a disinterested love of the natural world and also with regarding species other than human beings as morally our equals. It is consistent with all that is edifying in the ringing rebuke by Enlightenment thinkers against the arrogance of supposing that we human beings are at the centre the universe. It is consistent in other words with anything that is properly found edifying in attacks on 'speciesism'.

It is not, however, consistent with the aspiration to see things 'from the point of view of the universe', as Peter Singer puts it. But that is no cause for lament. To try to use concepts while withdrawing from the conditions of their application, from what conditions their sense, is to saw away the branch on which one is sitting. There is no such thing as objectivity-in-general, and the forms of objectivity consistent with the acknowledgment of the circle between response and object are substantial, and, as always, revealed only in the critical vocabulary that tells us what it means for this or that inquiry to strive to see things as they are, rather than as they might appear, distorted, from this or that perspective.

And therein lies one of the deepest of Wittgenstein's lessons—his exposure of the confused aspiration to transcendence represented in the idealisation of the thinker situated at the Archimedean point. Wittgenstein reclaimed the living human body—and so a non-reductionist sense of our creatureliness—from much of traditional philosophy. Classically the mind–body problem has for all intents and purposes always been the mind–matter problem. The living body was of no account. Descartes thought it to be a machine. Anti-Cartesians, especially modern day materialists, tend to think that there is no reason in principle why we could not be made of the same materials as computers. The significance of human behaviour to the philosophy of the mind has largely been as evidence for the existence of mental states which cause it. Whistles, bangs and flashing lights might have done as well if they were consistently caused by those states. Theories that claim we know the mental states of others by intuition often showed even greater disregard of the body. It is not hard to see in all this a disdain for the human body and the conditions of human living.

It is pervasive in our culture, this difficulty in seeing when 'mere surfaces' go deep. People routinely give credence to the idea that machines might be made which will think and feel and converse with us. They find nothing absurd in the idea that we might place a little box at the table with which we converse over dinner. If it acts strangely, a repair kit in the bathroom next to the medicine cabinet will probably enable us to fix it. What after all is the difference in principle, they ask, between using a screwdriver to help keep one guest's conversation up to the mark, and giving another an aspirin when her headache interferes with the quality of her thought? If you insist, they say, we will paint a face on the box. But why be so vulgar as to need it?

None of this is a parody. If it seems that way it is because, despite ourselves, we cannot seriously entertain the idea that we could interact with a machine in ways we think are sometimes necessary to conversation. 'Come now, are you serious? Stop thinking in clichés. Speak for yourself. Can I take *you* seriously? *Think* about what you are saying!' and so on. It is difficult to imagine that we would seriously attribute the kind of understanding necessary to conversation unless it were to a subject to whom we may intelligibly respond in such ways. As things stand with us, it is equally difficult to imagine the mutually constitutive sense of self and other without conversation.

Martin Buber wrote:

> Every attempt to understand monologue as fully valid conversation, which leaves unclear whether it or dialogue is the more original, must run aground on the fact that the ontological basic presupposition of conversation is missing from it, the otherness, or more concretely, the moment of surprise. The human person is not in his own mind unpredictable to himself as he is to any one of his partners: therefore, he cannot be a genuine partner to himself, he can be no real questioner and no real answerer.

The interest in whether we can build a machine which would be both rational and unpredictable to its makers is, I believe, the shadow cast by this more substantial conception of the surprise which is both promised and threatened by conversation. It has little to do with novelty that is conditional upon routine or upon ignorance. It is astonishment at alterity, at otherness, at how other than *and other to* oneself another human being can be.

In her extraordinary essay 'The *Iliad*, Poem of Might', Simone Weil writes:

> The human beings around us exert just by their presence a power which belongs uniquely to themselves to stop, to diminish, or modify, each movement which our bodies design. A person who crosses our path does not turn aside our steps in the same manner as a street sign, no one stands up, or moves about, or sits down again in quite the same fashion when he is alone in a room as when he has a visitor.

This, as Peter Winch brings out, is also an example of 'an attitude towards a soul', and of how human beings present to us under concepts structured by such and other responses—an example, wonderful for its simplicity, of the origins of our sense of alterity. Weil was, amongst other things, concerned to reveal how human beings may become 'things' to other human beings, no longer constituting a distinctive limit to their will, no longer having the power 'to stop, to diminish, or modify, each movement which our bodies design'. Immediately before the passage I have just quoted, commenting on a passage in which Achilles thrusts Priam aside, Weil writes, 'It is not for want of sensibility that Achilles had, by a sudden gesture, pushed the old man glued against his knees to the ground. Priam's words, evoking his old father, had moved him to tears. Quite simply he had found himself to be as free in his attitudes, in his movements, as if in place of a suppliant an inert object were there touching his knees.'

To call such reactions 'primitive' can suggest that they are animal-like, perhaps pre-linguistic. One might think of dogs responding to other dogs as to creatures of a common kind. Orwell's response to the sight of the enemy soldier losing his trousers, however, is also an example of spontaneously responding to a human being as to something different from anything else in nature. My hypothetical slave-owners, one saying that he cannot shoot his black slave, the other saying he cannot walk past his injured slave, also respond as though the presence of another human being constitutes for them a distinctive limit to their will. But these examples are very different from one another and only confusion could result from calling them all examples of 'primitive reactions'. Nonetheless they have something important in common. They are all examples of responses which in their generality are constitutive of the concepts with which we identify their objects, but taken individually they are forms of the recognition of those objects, of what they are responses to.

The general fact that we do not move around in the same way when someone is in the room as when we are alone is part of what conditions our sense of others as a distinctive limit to our will of the kind we express in modalities of moral necessity and impossibility. In any individual case, however, such modifications in our behaviour caused by others are forms of the recognition of their presence, which is why when our behaviour is quite unaffected by them, when we treat their presence merely as we would a natural obstacle, we say quite naturally that we are oblivious to their humanity. (I am of course speaking generally. There are circumstances in which that would not be so.) And, again quite naturally, we describe as dehumanising the social and natural conditions which cause the extinction or radical attenuation of such responses.

It is important, therefore, always to remember how conceptually complex is that little word 'because' when we say that the good Samaritan behaved as he did because he saw the humanity of the man on the roadside. One might equally say that to respond as the Samaritan did is in itself to recognise the other's humanity. But to emphasise one way of putting it over the other is to lose sight of the interdependence of object and response. The structure of that interdependence is relatively simple when we are dealing with what are rightly called 'primitive reactions', binding the wound and looking into the face, for example. But when we ask what makes that face appear as the face of 'one of us', what conditions our sense of the kind of suffering attributable to 'one of us', then the matter becomes immeasurably more complex because of the parts played by culture and language, especially, of course, by the languages of love.

Moral contexts furnish the most dramatic examples of modalities that express the ways human beings constitute distinctive limits to our will. But morality does not have an exclusive claim to them. It is a facet of the seamless connections between morality and meaning that these modalities should occur both in moral and non-moral contexts. Again M is an instructive example.

As we noted, she thinks the Vietnamese can 'just have more' children and that she cannot. We know that she is not confessing to a physical or psychological incapacity which might incline us to ask whether she had tried. If someone does what he has claimed to be physically or psychologically impossible for him, we can say that he was mistaken, it was possible after all. But if someone says that morally he cannot do something and then does it, it would be cruelly insensitive to say, 'I see that you could, after all.' It would also be cruel to say such a thing to M were she to do what she says she—'we'—cannot do.

Would it simplify matters if we said that M means that, although she literally can have more children because there is no physical or psychological obstacle to her doing so, she believes that she *ought not* to? It would not, I think. The thought that she can, just as they can, but that she ought not to under pain of superficiality will not do justice to the way her belief that she cannot determines the character of her inner life and with it, her identity insofar as that is formed by the way she distinguishes 'us' from 'them'. One would separate her sense of morality from her inner life and both together from her identity in a way that is inconsistent with her sense of what constitutes 'us'.

To explain this I must again come back to the fact that the way we distinguish the real from the counterfeit forms of our response to the big facts of life is internal to the nature of the conceptual space from which M excludes the Vietnamese when she finds it unintelligible that she could have serious conversations with them about, for example, what it means 'just to have more'. If one *really* grieves, if one's grief is fully informed by an understanding of what it means to lose a child, then one 'cannot just have more', in a sense of 'cannot' that implies that one will not. This would not be true if we substituted 'ought not' for 'cannot'. If the impossibility she expresses were fully to determine the disposition of her will then that would mark the purification of her grief and her full understanding of what it means to have a child.

The concepts that mark the inner life in which morality is embedded, therefore, have modal features similar to those that are usually reserved for morality. Yet, whatever their relation may be to morality, love, grief and joy are not themselves moral states. Nor are they 'merely psychological' states, 'merely inclinations'. That denigratory 'merely' depends either upon a sense of the inner life as adequately characterisable without reference to the kind of impossibility M expressed when she said 'we cannot have more', or on a belief that the strictly moral modalities are independent from it and from the inner life as structured by it. I think that Kant and most philosophers who operate with a sharp distinction between the psychological and the moral believe the first. Someone who acknowledges the way that the inner life is conditioned by such modalities is unlikely to find the second plausible.

The point can be put more strongly. The modality that prevented M from having more children, that prevented Orwell from shooting a man holding up his trousers, that prevents the slave-owning 'Samaritan' from walking past the injured slave on the roadside—these are I think the same. When they operate directly on the will—when someone says in reply to a question about why she helped an injured person 'What else could I do?'—

then action is pure. Echoing Simone Weil, Iris Murdoch said in *The Sovereignty of Good* that in the movement towards perfection the world becomes ever more compulsively present to the will. The reason why perfection and purity are both connected here with necessity is, I think, because, in circumstances such as I have described, action that has become necessary—'I must help, I can't walk past'—is the expression of full responsiveness to the reality of another human being in need. That reality—a human being in need, become compulsively present to the will—is expressed in those modalities of necessity. Generally perception is not so clear and full and action not so pure. A sense of obligation steps into the breach.

An important qualification, however, needs to be entered. The slave-owning Samaritan may say, 'I cannot leave him here,' and that too may be a recognition of the slave's need, one that is rightly expressed when he goes on to say, 'He's a human being.' I do not think that undermines my claim concerning the connection between the acknowledgment of necessity and the recognition of the full reality of those to whose need one is responding. There are acknowledgments of human fellowship which are not, at the same time, acknowledgments of a person's full humanity. The slave-owner's pity can be a form of the conviction that a slave is in pain. The acknowledgment that he cannot walk past is the form his pity takes on that occasion. His pity is, as Wittgenstein remarks, not for the man's body; it is for the man, but a man whose humanity is not fully visible to him. That does not mean he is fully aware of the need, or the pain, but not fully aware of the man. Because he is not fully aware of the man, he is not fully aware of what *that pain* means. Such partial blindness no more undermines the connections between necessity, purity and the full awareness of another, however, than error undermines the connection between knowledge and truth.

Philosophers have been suspicious of expressions of this kind of necessity because they are not impersonal in the way they think morality should be. Expressions of physical and psychological incapacity are generally personal—'I can't pluck a chicken, but perhaps you can.' Expressions of necessity of the kind I have been elaborating, in the kinds of examples I have chosen, are also personal. 'I can't leave him bleeding on the side of the road' is not better expressed by saying 'One ought not to leave him bleeding by the side of the road.' And can one imagine Luther saying, 'Here one stands. One can do no other.'?

Weil says that purity of thought and action requires the destruction of the self. When I commented on her remarks about the impersonality of truth, I said one shouldn't flatly endorse them. I would say the same now. One gets a sense of what is at issue when one remembers that for Murdoch, who was profoundly influenced by Weil, the destruction of the self is the destruction of the 'fat, relentless ego'. Finding one's own voice is not an expression of that ego. And the spiritual desire to destroy the self is, of course, quite different from the aspiration merely to be a rational agent who sees things from the Archimedean point. Both express the desire to see things as they are, but when that is achieved after a victory over the ego of the kind envisaged by Murdoch, by attention to things which are pure and good, then the achievement is, as she says, a work of love, justice and pity.

The reality which is disclosed only in works of love, justice and pity, is, as R. F. Holland noted, the reality of meaning, not of fact. Lucidity about meaning—understanding what it means to grieve truly, what it means to do evil, what it means that this person is hungry—is personal in the way I have indicated even when it is achieved unreflectively. We must do justice both to Socrates and to the virtuous peasant, said Iris Murdoch, and I believe she is right. The way to do justice to Socrates is to point out that the need to be lucid about what it means to live a human life appears to arise from the very nature of our inner life, and appears, therefore, as he insisted, to be intrinsic to our humanity. We do justice to the virtuous peasant when we acknowledge such lucidity need not come through reflection, certainly not through the kind of self-examination of himself and others that Socrates refused to abandon even under the threat of death. In a fine culture it can be achieved through unreflective, disciplined absorption of the culture, and the modes of discriminations implicit in it. The difference between absorption that undermines lucidity—parroting what one has picked up, for example—and the kind that does not, need not depend on whether the latter can give an account of itself, as Socrates insisted it must. Thoughtfulness, lucidity and wisdom need not be reflective or articulate. They count as thoughtfulness, wisdom and lucidity, however, only because they are answerable to a range of critical concepts, even when they have not actually been made to answer to them under the pressure of reflective questioning. Those critical concepts demand the kind of individuality that a peasant in an unreflective, stable culture achieves in her lucidity.

Even in an unreflective, homogenous culture, untroubled by plural and incommensurable values, moral advice will sometimes be sought, and even in such a culture lucidity and wisdom will be distinguished from expertise. The personal character of thought about morality, about the inner life and about life's meaning, is reflected in the fact that there can be no expertise about them. If we are accused of being sentimental in our grief, and if we are unsure whether the accusation is justified, we cannot delegate thought about it to an expert, asking her to deliver a conclusion, or even the main options, no later than Monday morning. We can no more do this than we can delegate thought about our moral dilemmas to an expert ethicist, with the same request, that she have a range of options, no later than first thing Monday morning. These scenarios are parodies of what it is seriously to think about such matters.

The point, however, is not that we must *decide* these matters for ourselves. That is true of all practical matters, but it is not true of all practical matters that we cannot delegate thinking about them to experts. On the contrary we can and do, and when we do it legitimately, we *can* say that we want solutions or a range of options by Monday morning. We must, of course, decide whether to accept the recommendations. And it is a truism that no one can make our decisions for us. But the lesson of my parodies is not that practical problems are personal because decisions are necessarily personal. It is that we must think those problems through for ourselves, and that means more than reviewing for ourselves the deliberations of the experts and deciding amongst them. The personal shows itself in the thinking, not just in the deciding, and it shows itself differently and more fully than is implied in the truism that in all matters we must think for ourselves rather than just parrot what others have said. That is true of mathematics as much as it is true of morality.

None of this means that we cannot seek advice, and that we cannot rightly judge some advice to be wise and some to be foolish, true or false. It means only that wisdom and foolishness are quite different from expertise and inexpertise, competence and incompetence, and that is reflected in the grammar of 'true' and 'false' as they apply in these different cognitive domains. When Kierkegaard said (misleadingly) that, for the 'ethical thinker', 'truth is subjectivity', I suspect this is at least part of what he meant.

Kierkegaard was mistaken, however, in thinking that an acknowledgment of the personal nature of thought about morality and life's meaning should lead to an idealisation of the solitary thinker. In fact, such idealisation distorts the personal character of such thought. It also distorts our understanding of one of the most important facts about its epistemic character, namely that we often learn by being moved by what others say and do.

We learn from what moves us because its epistemic authority is inseparable from the fact that it moves us. We cannot always extract the cognitive content of what moves us from its form. Reflection on the authority of what moves us reveals, as we have noted, the dependence of our sense of that authority on concepts like authenticity, integrity and sincerity, as they apply to those who move us and to ourselves as critically responsive to them. That same reflection tells us that we cannot assess whether we have been rightly moved by appeal to a conception of reason whose constitutive categories can be specified independently of our vulnerability to being wrongly moved (because we are sentimental, or tone deaf to banality and so on).

In order to be critically true to what moves us we must be properly responsive to the disciplined individuality of the other as she is present in the speech or actions that move us. To speak here of the other, as present to us in ways that are internal to the authoritative force of what she has said or done, is to say that necessarily the authority and our critical acceptance of it are personal. The truism that something moves us, to the extent that it 'speaks to us', is an expression of it. Something speaks to us insofar as we hear in it the disciplined individuality of its speaker. But, of course, in rising to that, in responding to what moves me, I must acknowledge and submit to the same individualising disciplines which made the other authoritatively present in her words or deeds and which gave her a distinctive voice.

There is only one way to do that. It is by submitting to the disciplines demanded by the critical categories that both tell us and determine what it is to be rightly moved. This is true whether we think in the presence of what moves us or in remembrance of it. If I am right, then the public character of that thought is best conceived as a dialogical engagement between the first and second person, rather than between the first and third. To put the point in the idiom of Martin Buber, the philosopher who was one of the first to see this and who has been much misunderstood: in responding properly to what moves me, I must make myself I to someone's Thou. That is an essential part of what determines the commonness of the conceptual space from which M excluded the Vietnamese. It is essential to what we mean by 'experience', when we say that wisdom comes only with experience.

Why is it essential? Because the commonness of that space is nurtured by language, which can go dead on us. Necessarily, that language is vulnerable to our laziness, our sentimentality, our banality and our weariness of spirit. Our sense of what it means to wrong someone, to ignore someone's suffering, is always in danger of becoming weak and sometimes of dying, and, if it is dead, then the modality of moral necessity which most purely expresses moral response has nothing to nourish it. Kant nobly wished that we could retain a moral sensibility enlivened only by the thin vocabulary of rational agency even if we are dead to all forms of feeling and their vital expression in a natural language. If the arguments of this book are sound, he was profoundly wrong.

Simone Weil said that if we see someone as fully another perspective on the world we could not treat them unjustly. By 'a perspective on the world' she did not mean merely a centre of consciousness.

For Weil's remark to be plausible, the idea of a unique perspective on the world must imply the concept of individuality which I have elaborated in this book. Our possession of that notion of individuality is partly a function of our attachments—that we cannot fathom the loss of another, that death strikes us as deeply mysterious, and many others. And indeed those attachments are what they are—love rather than 'love', for example—because we and those to whom we are attached can be called upon to be lucid about the reality of our inner lives.

M could accept Weil's remark and, without inconsistency, think it inapplicable to the Vietnamese. In her eyes the Vietnamese are not unique perspectives on the world as we are, because they are not subject to the individualising requirement to speak for themselves, for each to find her own voice—a requirement that is internal to the serious acceptance of the discipline of those critical concepts. Yet it is that individualising requirement which determines the nature of the conceptual space within which she can affirm with others a sense of common humanity that is also the expression of full moral fellowship. To make the point by drawing on my previous discussion: the existence and character of that space is interdependent with the possibility that she can be, and with the requirement that sometimes she must be, a respondent to another's call to seriousness, I to someone's Thou. Only within that space can there exist the kind of common understanding which aspires to the hope that, were it to be realised amongst all the peoples of the earth, we would live in a just world.

My story from Orwell allows us to observe how natural it is to speak of the *dehumanising* power of stereotypes which often make others only partially visible to our moral faculties. And to note that the sense of vulnerability, so powerfully conveyed by the image of an enemy soldier holding up his trousers, would not have found suitable words if Orwell had written, 'a man holding up his trousers is visibly a *person*'. Or, worse: a man holding up his trousers is visibly a rational agent, a rational being, someone with a rational life plan. I am parodying, of course, but I hope not unfairly. Why do these parodies work? Why do the words which are intended to reveal the nature of morality to a mind undisturbed by rhetoric fail so abjectly to do so? The general answer, I think, is that, preoccupied with the task of justifying moral rules, the philosophers who gave us these words fail to see how inadequate they are to the kind of seriousness that is intrinsic to morality.

Why is this so? After all, they are rules intended to ameliorate the harshness of the human condition. In these accounts, I think, the morally salient facts of human life are *too external* to our sense of morality's seriousness. Kant again provides a dramatic illustration. For him morality exists essentially between rational agents. The circumstances of their lives—in our case, the circumstances of human life—merely furnish the content of the morality. Other rational creatures who are perhaps not vulnerable in the way we are, or who are not mortal, would have a morality with a different content. As rational creatures, however, their sense of its authority over them, their sense of what it means to wrong someone, would be the same as it is for us.

When I spoke previously of the non-speculative conception of the soul, I noted its defining connection with suffering—a connection that is well established in expressions like 'soul music', 'soul-destroying work' and many others. Human beings were sometimes defined by their possession of a soul. It was natural to speak of them *as* souls. Signs outside villages, for example, told one how many souls lived in them, a way of referring to people that brings out the tender, compassionate resonances of the word. In a similar tone, the ancient Greeks called human beings 'the mortals', treating the universality of death as our common destiny rather than merely an (exceptionless) empirical generalisation. The same accents of sorrow and pity are heard in the beautiful words of the prayer for the dead in *The Book of Common Prayer*: 'Man that is born of a woman hath but a short time to live, and is full of misery. He cometh up, and is cut down, like a flower; he fleeth as it were a shadow, and never continueth in one stay.' The phrase 'the human condition', when it marks a difference from 'human nature', carries similar resonances.

In these examples, our mortality, our vulnerability to misfortune, our sexuality are not merely matters upon which we exercise our sensibility. They define its forms. We see the world as mortal, vulnerable, sexual beings. To adapt lines of Wallace Stevens: Our humanity passes through us like a thread through a needle. Everything we do is stitched with its colour.

It is therefore deeply right that the forms of reflection and inquiry in which that sensibility finds its natural expression should be called 'the humanities'. Within the humanities, however, there are disciplines which look to science for a prototype of the kind of inquiry that will reveal things as they really are, and there are disciplines which look more to art for a model for it. I have expressed and defended my sympathies for the pre-eminence of the latter kind of inquiry because, generally, reflection on the human condition must respect the inseparability of form and content if it is to avoid reductionism. Reflection that aspires always to separate cognitive content from form that it takes to be rhetorical and emotive, and reflection that respects the inseparability of form from cognitive content both seek to be universal, but differently. The former will try to purify thought of everything that it takes to be local, which will, of course, be almost everything that resonates in a natural language.

If my argument has been sound, the aspiration to that kind of universality will lead to the construction of theories that constantly fail to notice what they take for granted. Inevitably, I think, and without noticing it, they will describe our lives more or less as M sees the lives of the Vietnamese, because to capture and do justice to what distinguishes us from people seen that way, one needs a richer set of critical concepts than is available to those theories. My argument gives reasons for believing that, had philosophy been more attentive to the understanding of life offered by literature rather than by science or metaphysics (of a kind that also aspires to separate form from content), then we would be better able to cope with the tensions generated by the acknowledgment that thought about life and morality is inescapably *in medias res*, and the aspiration to a universal ethic based on a sense of the commonness of human experience. That misunderstanding has generated the wrong kinds of tensions between the full acknowledgment of the plurality of peoples and their cultures and the legitimate hopes for a universal ethics, and, connected with that, between ethical truth and the cultural determination of ethical value.

The sense we make of ourselves and the world is in crucial part determined by the art and culture of peoples—by art and culture which is steeped in, even when it is not expressed in, a natural language, rich in historical resonance, shaped by and shaping the life of a people. This shows itself in the universality we attribute to great literature, which, we often say, speaks to experiences that all human beings share in virtue of their common humanity. Great literature often speaks to peoples of all kinds, at all times and in all parts of the earth, but only as translated from one natural language into another. That is not because we have been unable to develop a single universal language, as some hoped to do with Esperanto. It is because that is the kind of universality that is appropriate to the content of great literature—content which often cannot be separated from its form and whose form cannot be separated from the contingencies that have nourished particular cultures, particular forms of living and particular natural languages.

Select Bibliography

Arendt, Hannah, *Eichmann in Jerusalem: A Report on the Banality of Evil*, Viking Press, New York, 1964.

Arendt, Hannah, *Men in Dark Times*, Harcourt Brace & Co, New York, 1968.

Arendt, Hannah, *On Revolution*, Viking Press, New York, 1963.

Arnold, Matthew, *Culture and Anarchy*, Cambridge University Press, Cambridge, 1963.

Bettelheim, Bruno, *Freud and Man's Soul*, Vintage, New York, 1984.

Bringing Them Home: Report of the National Inquiry into the Separation of Aboriginal and Torres Strait Islander Children from Their Families, Human Rights and Equal Opportunity Commission, Sydney, 1997.

Buber, Martin, *I and Thou*, trans. Walter Kaufmann, Scribner, New York, 1970.

Buber Martin, *The Knowledge of Man*, George Allen and Unwin, London, 1965. See especially 'The Word That Is Spoken'.

Cavell, Stanley, *The Claim of Reason*, Clarendon Press, Oxford, 1979.

Chesterton, G. K., *Orthodoxy*, Doubleday, New York, 1959.

Clendinnen, Inga, *Reading the Holocaust*, Text Publishing, Melbourne, 1998.

Connolly, Peter and S. E. K. Hulme, *The High Court of Australia in Mabo*, Association of Mining and Exploration Companies, Leederville, 1993.

Descartes, René, *The Philosophical Works of Descartes,* vol. 1, trans. Elizabeth S. Haldane and G. R. T. Ross, Cambridge University Press, Cambridge, 1931.

Diamond, Cora, *The Realistic Spirit*, MIT Press, Massachusetts,

1991. See especially 'Eating Meat and Eating People' and 'Having a Rough Story about What Moral Philosophy Is'.

Donagan, Alan, *The Theory of Morality*, Chicago University Press, Chicago, 1977. An interesting attempt to give a Kantian account of what Donagan calls 'traditional morality'.

Frankl, Viktor, *The Doctor and the Soul*, Souvenir Press, London, 1969.

Fuller, Timothy (ed.), *Voices of Liberal Learning*, Yale University Press, New Haven, 1989.

Gaita, Raimond, *Good and Evil: An Absolute Conception*, Macmillan, London, 1991.

Gaita, Raimond, 'Language and Conversation: Wittgenstein's Builders' in *Wittgenstein Centenary Essays*, A. Phillips Griffiths (ed.), Cambridge University Press, Cambridge, 1991.

Gilbert, Martin, *The Holocaust: The Jewish Tragedy*, Collins, London, 1986.

Goldhagen, Daniel Jonah, *Hitler's Willing Executioners*, Little, Brown and Co, London, 1996.

Gray, John, *Beyond the New Right*, Routledge, London, 1994.

Holland, R. F., *Against Empiricism*, Basil Blackwell, Oxford, 1980. See especially 'Education and Value' and 'Is Goodness a Mystery?'.

Kant, Immanuel, *Groundwork of the Metaphysics of Morals*, trans. H. J. Paton, Hutchinson, London, 1969.

Kierkegaard, Søren, *Concluding Unscientific Postscript*, trans. David Swenson, Princeton University Press, Princeton, 1968.

Korsgaard, Christine M., *The Sources of Normativity*, Cambridge University Press, Cambridge, 1996. A powerful defence of Kant's approach to ethics.

Krygier, Martin, *Between Fear and Hope*, ABC Books, Sydney, 1997.

Levi, Primo, *If This Is a Man* and *The Truce*, Abacus, London, 1987.

Lipstadt, Deborah, *Denying the Holocaust: The Growing Assault on Truth and Memory*, Plumstock, New York, 1994.

Manne, Robert, *The Culture of Forgetting*, Text Publishing, Melbourne, 1996.

Manne, Robert, *The Way We Live Now*, Text Publishing, Melbourne, 1998. See especially 'The Stolen Generations'.

Margalit, Avishai, *The Decent Society*, Cambridge, Massachusetts, 1996.

Mill, John Stuart, *On Liberty and Other Essays*, John Gray (ed.), Oxford University Press, Oxford, 1991.

Moore, G. E., *Philosophical Papers*, George Allen and Unwin, London, 1959. See especially 'A Defence of Common Sense' and 'Proof of an External World'.

Morrison, Blake, *As If*, Granta Books, London, 1997.

Nietzsche, Friedrich, *Beyond Good and Evil*, trans. Walter Kaufmann, Vintage, New York, 1966.

Nietzsche, Friedrich, *The Genealogy of Morals*, trans. Walter Kaufmann and R. J. Hollingdale, Vintage, New York, 1967.

Oakeshott, Michael, *Rationalism in Politics and Other Essays*, Methuen, London, 1977. See especially 'The Voice of Poetry in the Conversation of Mankind'.

Orwell, George, *Collected Essays, Journalism and Letters*, vol. 2, Penguin, Harmondsworth, 1970. See especially 'Looking Back on the Spanish War'.

Phillips, D. Z., *Interventions in Ethics*, Macmillan, Basingstoke, 1992. A vigorous attack on the idea that there can be a 'theory of morality and that morality serves a purpose which can be specified independently of it'.

Plato, *Gorgias*, trans. Terence Irwin, Clarendon Press, Oxford, 1979.

Plato, *Republic*, trans. Desmond Lee, Penguin, Harmondsworth, 1987.

Reynolds, Henry, *Aboriginal Sovereignty*, Allen and Unwin, Sydney, 1996.

Sereny, Gitta, *Cries Unheard: The Story of Mary Bell*, Macmillan, London, 1999.

Sharp, Nonie, *No Ordinary Judgment*, Aboriginal Studies Press, Canberra, 1996.

Singer, Peter, *Practical Ethics*, Cambridge University Press, Cambridge, 1979.

Tatz, Colin, *Genocide in Australia*, Aboriginal Studies Press, Canberra, 1999.

Weil, Simone, *The Simone Weil Reader*, George A. Panichas (ed.), David McKay, New York, 1977. See especially 'The *Iliad*. Poem of Might' and 'Human Personality'. These essays are also in *Simone Weil: An Anthology*, Sian Miles (ed.), Virago, London, 1986.

Weil, Simone, *Waiting on God*, Collins, Glasgow, 1977. See especially the section 'Love of Our Neighbour' in the essay 'Forms of the Implicit Love of God'.

Williams, Bernard, *Ethics and the Limits of Philosophy*, Fontana, London, 1978.

Winch, Peter, *Trying to Make Sense*, Blackwell, Oxford, 1987. See especially 'Eine Einstellung zür Seele' and 'Who Is My Neighbour?'

Wittgenstein, Ludwig, *Culture and Value*, G. H. von Wright (ed.), trans. Peter Winch, Blackwell, Oxford, 1998.

Wittgenstein, Ludwig, *On Certainty*, G. E. M. Anscombe and G. H. von Wright (eds), Blackwell, Oxford, 1959.

Wittgenstein, Ludwig, *Philosophical Investigations*, trans. G. E. M. Anscombe, Blackwell, Oxford, 1963.

Index